Eric Thomas Chester was born in New York City in 1943 and raised in Detroit, Michigan. After graduating from the University of Michigan, he taught economics at the University of Massachusetts-Boston. More recently, Chester lived for twelve years in Glasgow, Scotland. He moved to Chapel Hill, North Carolina, in 2021.

Chester was the 1996 vice-presidential candidate of the Socialist Party, USA; he remains a member.

He is the author of several books including *The Wobblies in Their Heyday: The Rise and Destruction of the Industrial Workers of the World during World War I* (Praeger, 2014) and *Free Speech and the Suppression of Dissent during World War I* (Monthly Review Press, 2020).

Silencing "Fighting Bob"

The Attack on Antiwar Progressives during the First World War

by ERIC T. CHESTER

MONTHLY REVIEW PRESS
New York

Library of Congress Cataloging-in-Publication data
available from the publisher.

ISBN 978-168590-126-4 paper
ISBN 978-168590-127-1 cloth

Typeset in Minion Pro

MONTHLY REVIEW PRESS | NEW YORK
www.monthlyreview.org

5 4 3 2 1

Contents

TO SUSAN

Acknowledgments

MOST OF THE RESEARCH for this book was done at the National Archives in College Park, Maryland. The National Archives holds a vast number of archival documents, and I would like to thank the archivists in College Park for their help in locating relevant documents.

The Library of Congress Manuscript Room holds many important collections, and I used some of them while researching this book. I would like to thank the archivists at the Library of Congress for their help.

Thanks to Michael Yates and Martin Paddio of Monthly Review Press, and to George De Stefano for helping me through the process of moving from a first draft to a finished published work.

Introduction

THE FIRST WORLD WAR was a watershed moment in world history. This was the first time a European conflict expanded from a regional conflict to a global war. The events that arose from the war and its immediate aftermath would set the course of world history for the next seventy-five years.

The toll of the war was truly horrific. In the end, twenty million people died as a direct result of the conflict, and another twenty million were seriously injured.[1] These huge losses would have an enormous impact on personal relationships as a generation of young men were either missing or maimed. At the same time, many women entered the workforce for the first time as the entire economy was mobilized for the war effort. In this new context, the demands of women to be recognized as active and equal participants in society could no longer be denied.

Governments toppled and insurgent movements flourished. The czarist regime of the Romanovs, who had ruled the Russian Empire for more than three hundred years, collapsed and was soon replaced by the Bolsheviks. The Cold War hostilities between the Soviet Union and the United States had their roots in the First World War.

In Germany, the imperial regime of the Hohenzollern family was totally defeated, and an onerous peace was imposed on its successor, the Weimar Republic. The crushing defeat of Germany in the First World War and the Treaty of Versailles, which ended it, set the stage for the rise of the Nazis and the Second World War.

Still, the most important outcome of the war was far less dramatic, and yet it continues to shape world developments. Before the war, Britain, with its vast empire, acted as the dominant global power. The First World War brought an end to British hegemony. Instead, power shifted toward the United States. New York became the financial capital of the world's economy, replacing London.

Nevertheless, the First World War was extremely unpopular in the United States. Most of those who immigrated to this country came from Europe. They saw this country as a haven from the endless wars and rampant militarism of Europe. When the war began in August 1914, most Americans enthusiastically supported the decision to remain neutral in the conflict. In spite of disastrous events such as the sinking of the *Lusitania*, a British passenger liner, by a German submarine in May 1915, popular opinion remained adamantly opposed to direct intervention in the war.

The administration was well aware of the widespread opposition to entering the war. Nevertheless, Woodrow Wilson chose to bring the United States into the war in the spring of 1917. The president understood that antiwar sentiment had to be quashed if the effort to conscript a huge army and to mobilize the economy were to succeed.

Throughout U.S. history, the enforcement of laws had rested with the authorities at the state and local levels. Intelligence agencies within the federal government were small and narrowly focused in their jurisdiction. The First World War dramatically changed this. Wilson was determined to crush any opposition to the war.

During the First World War, the Department of Justice was given the authority to prosecute hundreds of antiwar dissidents under the Espionage Act. The Justice Department relied on the Bureau of Investigation for evidence to support these prosecutions. The army's Military Investigation Division also monitored the activities of those opposing the war. These were the intelligence agencies that were most involved in suppressing dissent. The intelligence community also included the Treasury Department's Secret Service and the Office of Naval Intelligence. After an initial period of discord, the various agencies within the intelligence community began coordinating their operations and focusing on certain key targets.

Intelligence agencies grew rapidly during the war as they engaged in a wide range of covert operations. The information needed to track the activities of the Left was gained through intensive surveillance of activists. Some of the surveillance methods were legal, but others were flagrantly illegal. The White House was kept well informed of the operations of the intelligence community. In some cases, the president directly participated in the creation and implementation of covert measures.

This book probes the open and covert operations directed at suppressing progressives and the social democratic left. The federal government relied on a variety of methods to silence those who criticized the war effort. These ranged from open propaganda and the prosecution of dissenters in the federal courts to secret operations aimed at key individuals and organizations.

At first, the federal government focused on crushing the radical left and, in particular, on the Industrial Workers of the World. Soon, the scope of repression widened to include progressives and social democrats.

The Socialist Party of America (SP) had become a significant factor in U.S. politics in the years immediately before the war. In addition to its electoral successes, the party gained a solid working-class base. Several unions affiliated with the American Federation of Labor were closely aligned with it. The SP encompassed a wide spectrum of political perspectives, but most of its leaders came from its more moderate, social democratic wing. They were not eager to confront the federal government and yet they hoped to mobilize popular opposition to the war to pressure the administration into entering peace talks with Germany.

At the same time, progressives working within the two-party system had consolidated a considerable base of support before 1914. Although progressives were divided in their response to the decision to enter the war, most disagreed with the government's policy. Those who opposed the president's war policies sought to persuade the government to negotiate a rapid end to the conflict.

Social democrats and dissident progressives quickly discovered that their views on the conflict were very similar. A coalition of these two political tendencies had the potential to create a viable opposition to the war. The president understood this potential threat, so the intelligence community was authorized to disrupt the progressive opposition.

This book examines three cases in which the federal government utilized an array of methods to undermine the activities of progressives who opposed the war. A fourth case looks at a popular insurgency, the Nonpartisan League (NPL), which was targeted for repression by state agencies. The federal government was wary of the league but did not become directly involved.

The first chapter looks at the efforts made by the federal government to quash antiwar activity in the Jewish community of the Lower East Side of Manhattan. The Committee on Public Information (CPI) was central to this operation. Created by a presidential proclamation in April 1917, the Committee was specifically intended as the government's propaganda agency. It produced reams of literature zealously promoting the war effort. The Committee also engaged in covert operations aimed at disrupting and demoralizing the antiwar opposition. The CPI viewed countering the antiwar opposition of the Lower East Side as a priority.

George Creel served as the chair of the Committee. A muckraking journalist, Creel was an avid defender of the administration and the war effort. He was particularly incensed by *Forverts*, the *Jewish Daily Forward*, which was closely aligned with the Socialist Party. The Post Office succeeded in silencing *Forverts* by threatening to curtail its circulation through the mail. At the same time, the leadership of the American Federation of Labor cooperated with the Committee on Public Information in flooding the Lower East Side with pro-war propaganda. The CPI also aided in the takeover of a Yiddish-language newspaper that could counter *Forverts* with a pro-war perspective.

The second chapter examines the government's campaign to disrupt the People's Council of America for Democracy and the Terms of Peace (PCA). A loose coalition of the Socialist Party and progressives, the PCA grew rapidly in the summer of 1917. The Committee on Public Information, working with the leadership of the American Federation of Labor and pro-war social democrats, created a front organization, the American Alliance for Labor and Democracy (AALD). When the People's Council decided to hold its founding conference in Minneapolis in September 1917, the AALD scheduled a rally for the same time and place. The governor of Minnesota, Joseph Burnquist, banned the PCA meeting, but the AALD meeting was allowed to proceed without hindrance. The PCA's failure to convene a founding conference initiated a downward slide into disintegration. Still, the government continued to target the PCA. One of its leaders, Scott Nearing, was tried for violating the Espionage Act. PCA literature was also barred from the mails.

The third chapter focuses on Senator Robert La Follette. In the months following the entry of the United States into the war, La Follette became the leading spokesperson for the antiwar opposition. The president came to regard him as a dangerous threat, so La Follette became a priority target of government repression. A variety of tactics were used to discredit him. The Committee on Public Information worked covertly with the American Defense Society in implementing a campaign of vilification through the press. La Follette was also threatened with expulsion from the Senate. The constant bombardment of hostility and abuse took its toll. La Follette was silenced.

The fourth chapter focuses on a somewhat different situation. The Nonpartisan League (NPL) was an insurgent movement of small farmers. It urged its members to support candidates in both mainstream parties that were pledged to a program of farmer-friendly reforms. The NPL began in North Dakota but soon spread to Minnesota and other nearby states. Minnesota's authorities were intent on crushing the league. They worked closely with a small, secretive group of corporate executives. A variety of methods were used, ranging from vigilante violence to prosecutions under the state's sedition law that relied on perjured testimony. The league tried to deflect these attacks by adopting a pro-war program and by cooperating with the CPI. Still, Woodrow Wilson opted to have the federal government avoid becoming directly involved in the acrimonious battle in Minnesota. At the same time, the Justice Department remained suspicious of the Nonpartisan League and its Bureau of Investigation closely monitored the league's activities.

A great deal of effort went into the suppression of the antiwar opposition. Much of this campaign of repression was done through covert operations, without any public scrutiny. The progressive opponents of the war were not prepared to counter the relentless attacks of the federal government. As a result, the progressive opposition to the war was silenced. This enabled Woodrow Wilson to continue the war until the bitter end, the unconditional surrender of Germany, and the imposition of the Treaty of Versailles.

CHAPTER 1

Targeting the Jewish Community of the Lower East Side of New York City

NEW YORK CITY WAS the largest metropolis in the United States during the First World War, with 5 percent of the country's total population. It was the financial center, the primary media nexus, a key port, and a major industrial center. A city of immigrants from many countries, New York contained a sizable community of recent Irish immigrants. Irish Americans were critical of the war, viewing the U.S. support of the Allies as a bulwark to British imperialism. Still, it was the Jewish community on the Lower East Side of Manhattan that most concerned Washington decision-makers. The largest ethnic community in the city, Jews constituted nearly 30 percent of New York City's population during the First World War. Popular opinion within the Jewish community overwhelmingly opposed the war effort.[1]

The Socialist Party (SP) had built a solid base of support in the Lower East Side. Indeed, despite the blatant efforts of the Democratic Party's Tammany Hall to rig elections, the SP succeeded in electing a Jewish attorney, Meyer London, to the U.S. House of Representatives.[2]

Forverts, the *Jewish Daily Forward,* the Yiddish language newspaper aligned with the Socialist Party, wielded enormous influence within the Jewish community. Its editor, Abraham Cahan, was widely respected. Thus, the coverage of the antiwar movement in *Forverts* greatly increased its visibility and credibility.

Woodrow Wilson understood that the decision to enter the war was deeply unpopular. He, therefore, created the Committee on Public Information (CPI) in April 1917 to promote support for the war effort and to counter the antiwar opposition. The president nominated George Creel to chair the committee. Creel was a muckraking journalist who had worked for Wilson's reelection in 1916. Creel worked closely with the president, who closely supervised the activities of the CPI.[3]

Creel set the suppression of the antiwar movement on the Lower East Side as an urgent priority. Working with Samuel Gompers and the American Federation of Labor, the Committee on Public Information distributed vast quantities of pro-war propaganda on the Lower East Side. Creel was especially incensed by *Forverts,* so silencing the newspaper and creating a pro-war alternative became a key goal of the Committee on Public Information.

Gompers and the Ladies' Garment Workers' Union

As president of the American Federation of Labor (AFL), Samuel Gompers played a crucial role in maintaining organized labor as uncritical defenders of the war effort. An ardent supporter of Woodrow Wilson's decision to take the United States into the First World War, he bitterly condemned those who organized for an immediate peace. Crushing the antiwar opposition in the Jewish community of New York became a critical priority for Gompers.

Gompers was particularly dismayed that unions within the AFL, especially the International Ladies Garment Workers'

Union (ILGWU), wavered in their zeal for the war. Its leaders were closely aligned with the Socialist Party of America, which opposed the war, but union leaders were anxious to avoid a direct confrontation with the federal government. Still, rank-and-file activists within the ILGWU sought to bring the union into active participation in the antiwar opposition.

Gompers was convinced that AFL unions should be at the forefront of "patriotic" campaigns to stir up sentiment for the war. Therefore, he worked closely with George Creel and the Committee on Public Information to develop a propaganda campaign directed at the Lower East Side. They were spurred into action by the success of the Socialist Party in catalyzing a broad coalition of progressives in opposition to the war. At the end of May 1917, this coalition held a conference followed by a mass rally in Madison Square Garden. The conference provided the springboard for the creation of a new organization, the People's Council of America (PCA).[4]

The ILGWU, as well as other predominately Jewish unions in New York City, endorsed the People's Council and formed the Workmen's Council as a PCA affiliate for union members. Although the People's Council organized locals around the country, its strongest base of support remained in the New York City area.

These events occurred while the Industrial Workers of the World (IWW) was growing rapidly in the Western states. IWW affiliates in the copper mining and timber industries called effective, militant strikes that halted the production of these vital wartime commodities.[5] The federal government and the AFL hierarchy were determined that the militant radicalism of Western workers be counterbalanced by a quiescent working class in the urban centers of the East.

Launching the American Alliance for Labor and Democracy

In early June 1917, the Central Federated Unions of Greater

New York (CFU) asked Gompers to speak on the issues arising from the war. Gompers denounced the People's Council, urging the New York City Council of AFL unions to formulate a program that could counter the success of the Workmen's Council. The CFU then voted to establish a five-person committee to take charge of this program. At its next meeting, the Central Federated Unions approved a resolution agreeing to "cooperate" with Gompers by initiating "activities to Americanize the labor movement in Greater New York." Furthermore, the CFU acted to "condemn" the People's Council and insisted that it did "not represent the American labor movement."[6]

The threat posed by the People's Council on the Lower East Side was viewed as so serious by the AFL leadership that they turned to the government for help. On June 28, 1917, Gompers and other top AFL officials secretly met with James Graham Phelps Stokes, who would play a crucial role in ensuing developments. The group agreed to form a new committee, with Gompers as its chair, that would act as a counterforce to the People's Council.

Stokes was a captain in the Army's Military Intelligence Division. He also had excellent contacts with the left, having been a prominent member of the Socialist Party before the war.

Stokes had been mandated to act as the MID's agent in covert operations involving those with close ties to the left. Gompers could return to the Central Federated Unions with the assurance that government funds would be forthcoming to finance the intensive propaganda campaign that New York City union officials viewed as essential in countering the increasing influence of the People's Council.[7]

The five-person committee from the CFU then began meeting with a committee of AFL officials selected by Gompers. On July 21, 1917, two top officials of the AFL, Frank Morrison, its secretary-treasurer, and Hugh Frayne, the head of the AFL's New York office, conferred with Robert Maisel and Chester Wright to formulate a propaganda campaign specifically aimed at the Lower East Side ghetto. The planning group was convinced of the urgent need for "sufficient counter-publicity to offset the surge of so-called pacifist propaganda."[8]

Maisel and Wright would become the central figures in the American Alliance for Labor and Democracy. Maisel had worked as a journalist for the *New York Call*, an English-language newspaper closely aligned to the Socialist Party of New York, before resigning from the party to support the war.[9]

Wright was a journalist and a veteran member of the social democratic wing of the Socialist Party. He had worked for several socialist newspapers before becoming an editor of the *New York Call*. Although Wright quit the *Call* in March 1917, he did not officially resign from the party until that August. Wright had initially opposed U.S. participation in the First World War. Indeed, in April 1915, he had written that "Labor loses by war—profiteers win." It followed that labor had "had enough of war."[10] Nevertheless, once the United States entered the war as a combatant nation in April 1917, Wright became a zealous proponent of the war effort.

Gompers had the power to push a resolution through the AFL executive council fervently supporting the war. Nevertheless, there was little enthusiasm for the war effort, even among the AFL's leaders, and even less for using union funds to distribute pro-war propaganda. The organization that was being hatched in confidential meetings could only become a reality with government funding.

On July 25, 1917, Gompers met with Creel to discuss the difficult situation in New York. Creel had recently discussed the state of popular opinion on the Lower East Side with Louis Miller, leaving Creel "profoundly disturbed." Miller had been one of the seminal figures during the early years of the socialist movement in New York City in the 1880s. By 1917, he was an ardent proponent of the war. Miller was certain that none of the Jewish newspapers would "dare to aid" the government, given the overwhelming opposition to the war on the Lower East Side.[11]

In this context, Creel was "ready to get behind" the AFL's efforts "to Americanize the labor movement." Creel looked forward to "a speaking campaign" that would "cover the entire East Side," as well as to literature and posters reinforcing a pro-war message. In other words, the government would fund an intensive propaganda blitz targeting the socialist stronghold of the Lower East Side.[12]

Creel insisted that this entire effort "must be open and above board," and that the "entire movement [must] be governed and directed by organized labor." This was typical propagandistic rhetoric, pretentious platitudes without any substance. In fact, almost all the project's funds came from secret disbursements by the Committee on Public Information. Furthermore, Creel supervised every activity, determining the strategy of the organization and the political thrust of its propaganda.

The propaganda project targeting the Lower East Side would soon be subsumed into a broader covert operation aimed at promoting the war effort at the national level. Thus, the propaganda campaign focused on the Jewish community of New York City would be implemented within the organizational structure of the American Alliance for Labor and Democracy.

Propagandizing the Lower East Side

The American Alliance for Labor and Democracy (AALD) brought together AFL officials and pro-war intellectuals who had recently resigned from the Socialist Party. The organization was funded and controlled by Creel and the Committee on Public Information. Its founding conference was convened on July 28, 1917, at the Hotel Continental in New York City.

From the start, the American Alliance for Labor and Democracy focused much of its resources on the Jewish community of New York City. Days after the founding conference, Maisel sent a memorandum with a tentative budget, including funds to open an office on the Lower East Side. Gompers took the budget proposal to Creel, who agreed to fund it. Gompers understood very well that the AALD was a clandestine project of the Committee on Public Information. He informed Maisel that he had gone "over the matter again with Mr. George Creel under whose supervision and direction the entire project" was "to be carried into effect." Supervision was so detailed that Creel forwarded the AALD pamphlets written by CPI staff and then specified which should be translated into Yiddish. Four million pamphlets in Yiddish and English were printed and distributed, with the Lower East Side a prime target. This huge volume of propaganda was "paid for by the government of the United States." Gompers also notified Maisel that the AALD staff, including Maisel, would receive their salaries "directly from the disbursing offices of the Committee on Public Information."[13]

In August 1917, the AALD began producing and distributing propaganda aimed at the Lower East Side. Articles ardently supporting the war were placed in Yiddish-language newspapers. With the aid of Jewish charities, the AALD created a mailing list of 15,000 names so that pro-war leaflets could be sent directly to the residents of the Lower East Side. The AALD hosted a conference specifically aimed at the Jewish community. In addition to the top executives of major Jewish charities, many of them wealthy businesspeople, the conference included those officials from Jewish unions who were willing to publicly promote the war.

A press release following the conference insisted that it was "high time to stop the movement which misleads the Jewish workers of the country." It warned, "Suspicious persons are telling the Jewish workers that the war which the U.S. declared against Germany is a war of capital." Indeed, "We have very strong suspicions that German money is being spent right and left for peace propaganda purposes."[14]

In fact, the People's Council of America relied on the small donations of thousands of its enthusiastic supporters. Furthermore, intelligence agencies were well aware of this.

On the other hand, the AALD, which was spreading libelous charges against the proponents of peace, was the recipient of lavish covert funding from the U.S. government through the Committee on Public Information. The irony of this situation must have been apparent to all of those involved.

Stalking Forverts

Despite this government funded propaganda blitz, the Jewish community of the Lower East Side remained steadfastly opposed to the war. Creel was furious, convinced that the Socialist Party and its supporters were behind this mass resistance to his propaganda. Within the Lower East Side, *Forverts* continued to dominate the public discourse. Although its chief editor, Abraham Cahan, ensured that the paper did not promote the antiwar opposition, the government still viewed *Forverts* as a significant threat.

At the suggestion of William English Walling, a former Socialist Party member with close contacts with top government officials, Henry Slobodin wrote a lengthy memorandum in August 1917 to Frank Polk, counselor to Secretary of State Robert Lansing. The memorandum outlined a coordinated effort to pressure Cahan, as well as other leading New York City Jewish socialists, into accepting an openly pro-war stance.

Slobodin was writing as an insider. Having fled to the United States from czarist Russia in 1890 at twenty-four, he quickly gravitated to the emerging socialist movement on the Lower East Side. In 1899, Slobodin joined Morris Hillquit in leading a split from the Socialist Labor Party. Two years later, this splinter joined another small group to form the Socialist Party of America. Slobodin was a prominent figure in the socialist milieu of the Lower East Side, serving as the chair of the New York State Socialist Party for fifteen years.[15]

When the United States declared war on Germany in April 1917, Slobodin broke sharply with the great majority of socialists in the Jewish community. Slobodin was a vocal and enthusiastic supporter of the war effort. Although he was convinced that the Allied Powers were fighting a "war for liberty," he conceded that "the United States was confronted with an active and widespread opposition." Much of this opposition came from recent immigrants who were not native English speakers. Instead of relying entirely on force, the government also had to persuade these ethnic groups that it stood for a just peace.[16] Of course, Wilson created the Committee on Public Information for precisely this purpose.

Slobodin focused his memorandum on the Jewish community. It was essential that the federal government counter the influence of the Socialist Party, which continued "to pursue a pacifist policy" that was "playing directly into the hands of German militarism." Socialists had created a solid base of support on the Lower East Side with an interconnected network of organizations buttressing the Party. With a daily circulation of 300,000, *Forverts* was essential to the continued success of the SP in the Jewish community.

Slobodin began with an acute analysis of the New York Jewish left: "The labor movement and the socialist movement of the [Lower] East Side is almost in the control of the wealthy German Jews of the Jacob A. Schiff variety." The wealthy Jewish elite of New York City was a closed, tightly interconnected group, almost all of whom had either been born in Germany or whose parents had been born there. At the center of this tight network stood Jacob Schiff, the head of Kuhn, Loeb, one of Wall Street's most powerful investment banks. In general, Schiff worked behind the scenes, but he held enormous power. Indeed, Kuhn and Loeb challenged the efforts of J. P. Morgan and Co. to control much of U.S. industry.

Coming from Slobodin, who had been a prominent member of the socialist movement of the Lower East Side, this represented a devastating critique. Socialists defending the interests of the working class came into diametric conflict with Schiff and the other investment bankers. Still, Slobodin correctly understood that beneath the surface, the socialist and trade union leaders of the Jewish community believed that there was a community of interests between them and Schiff, and that arrangements could be made that were mutually beneficial.

Slobodin did not disagree in principle with such cozy arrangements between socialists and capitalists. The problem arose because Schiff had resisted the push to bring the United States into the war as a combatant nation. Indeed, he had given quiet support to liberal pacifists such as Lillian Wald and Jane Addams in their effort to block the president's preparedness program. After April 1917 and the declaration of war on Germany, Schiff distanced himself from those who continued to question the government's war policies, and yet he still did not enthusiastically support the war effort.

Recognizing the problem, Slobodin proposed a complex set of measures to counter the antiwar sentiment within the Jewish community. Cahan, as chief editor of *Forverts,* was the primary target. Slobodin recognized Cahan as "an old-time socialist and certainly a man of honor." As such, he could not "be gotten by a direct bribe". Instead, Slobodin proposed a more subtle "policy of penetration." In part, this would entail financial pressure on *Forverts* by restricting its circulation and advertising revenues. Still, Slobodin understood that threats would not suffice.

According to Slobodin, Cahan had a major "weakness," his desire for social recognition. Most Jews on the Lower East Side came from shtetls, small towns in czarist Russia. In Cahan's case, he had arrived in the United States from a village in Lithuania, then a part of the Russian Empire. Assimilation for shtetl Jews involved an enormous cultural shift. The wealthy elite came instead from families in Germany who had assimilated into Germany. For them, the United States was a backwater, not a land of marvelous opportunity.

Slobodin proposed that the federal government make use of this impulse for recognition. Cahan liked "to be received with his wife socially by cultured and wealthy ladies." Instead of Schiff, Slobodin suggested that "American ladies of equal intelligence and social standing show him like patriotism."

Slobodin's memorandum was referred to the intelligence bureau of the State Department. The head of the bureau, Leland Harrison, was impressed by Slobodin's suggestions. Harrison realized that the Committee on Public Information had been authorized to deal with such issues, although he worried that Creel was "ill-fitted to handle" the situation. Nevertheless, Harrison advised Secretary of State Robert Lansing that a "loyal Socialist and $100,000 would go far to improve the situation."[17]

Lansing then sent a note to President Wilson stating that he had read Slobodin's memorandum "with very great interest" and that the situation had been "given too little attention."[18] Creel almost certainly saw the memorandum, and he relied on Slobodin as his liaison to the Social Democratic League. In any case, the CPI conducted a "policy of penetration" that successfully pressured Cahan into implementing an editorial policy for *Forverts* that placed the war effort in a more favorable light.

Hillquit's Campaign for Mayor

The widespread popular opposition to the war within the Jewish community became an even more critical issue in the fall of 1917. Morris Hillquit, a central figure in the Socialist Party national leadership, ran for mayor of New York City. Beginning with a solid base on the Lower East Side, Hillquit made significant inroads in other communities, convincing Irish Americans and middle-class progressives that his election would be both a blow to Tammany Hall corruption and a signal to the president that he needed to open negotiations with Germany in order to reach a speedy peace settlement.

Hillquit's success spurred AALD to intensify its propaganda efforts on the Lower East Side. In October 1917, the CPI sponsored a new organization, the Jewish Socialist League of America, with Slobodin as a member of its executive committee. At its public debut, the new organization held a tumultuous mass meeting on the Upper East Side, a wealthy neighborhood several miles away from the Jewish ghetto on the Lower East Side. Nevertheless, the event drew two thousand people to the meeting hall, who heard the keynote speaker denounce Hillquit and Victor Berger as "the two greatest traitors to the Socialist Party." The *New York Times*, very much a pro-war newspaper, reported that half of the audience loudly heckled the speakers, interrupting the proceedings several times for five-minute rounds of booing and jeering.[19]

Undaunted, and with the resources of the federal government behind them, the Jewish Socialist League issued a proclamation through the AALD claiming that the "majority of Jews" remained "loyal" to the war effort in the belief that the United States was "upholding democracy and liberty." Still, even this propaganda front group had to admit that "a large number" of those in the Jewish community continued to oppose the war. To counter this resistance, the AALD deployed a hundred speakers to attack Hillquit and promote the war throughout the Lower East Side.[20]

Forverts *Muzzled*

In spite of the government's campaign of propaganda and coercion, Hillquit's campaign continued to gain momentum. This led to a further ratcheting up of pressure on *Forverts*. Although Jacob Schiff was considered unreliable, there were members of the Jewish elite who were viewed as trustworthy allies by the government. Two senior partners in an influential corporate law firm closely tied to Schiff, Louis Marshall and Samuel Untermeyer, became involved in the effort to pressure Cahan.

In early October 1917, Cahan and the editors of *Forverts* received a notice from the U.S. Post Office of a hearing to be held on October 12, 1917. The hearing would lead to a determination by the Post Office as to whether the newspaper was printing seditious articles, and therefore, would have its second-class permit revoked. Newspapers and journals were permitted to send copies through the mail at a greatly reduced rate. Sending this material at first-class postage rates was prohibitively expensive, so almost all subscribers relying on the mail would cancel if second-class privileges were revoked. Although most *Forverts* readers lived in New York City, the paper had a national base of subscribers, and a significant number of them received their copies through the mail. Furthermore, the Post Office's threat to cancel *Forverts's* second-class permit did not rely on a provision of the Espionage Act, a wartime statute. It thus could remain in force even after the war had ended.[21]

Cahan issued a defensive statement to the mainstream press insisting that *Forverts* was "not pro-German." Indeed, it had been "absolutely loyal" since the United States entered the war. According to Cahan, the Post Office used the wartime crisis to strike at *Forverts* because it was a "Socialist paper."[22]

Marshall and Cahan met before the hearing before the Post Office's censors to discuss the problem. Cahan made it plain that he was eager to avoid any conflict with the administration. *Forverts* was willing to print articles urging its readers to buy war bonds. In covering Hillquit's campaign, articles would focus on local issues rather than Hillquit's call for a negotiated end to the war. On October 8, 1917, Marshall wrote to Cahan that he would vouch for *Forverts,* if Cahan wrote a letter pledging to abide by all wartime laws.[23]

Cahan understood that the threat to *Forverts* was real, so he immediately responded with a confidential letter to Marshall pledging that the newspaper would "unreservedly" abide by "any and every law." Nothing would be printed in *Forverts* that "could be interpreted" as encouraging readers to violate any law or that "might be regarded as inimical" to the government. Cahan also emphasized that a revocation of its second-class permit "would seriously cripple" *Forverts.*[24]

Marshall then arranged a meeting with the two key decision-makers in the Post Office, Albert Burleson, the Postmaster General, and William Lamar, the department's solicitor. Marshall brought along Lessing Rosenwald as further support for his position. This was a powerful duo acting to defend *Forverts*.[25]

Rosenwald was one of the richest individuals in the United States. In addition to being the president of Sears Roebuck, he was also a philanthropist and an influential figure in the Jewish community. Rosenwald and Marshall had both served on the board of the American Jewish Committee, where they had developed a strong working relationship.

It seems curious that an influential corporate attorney and a wealthy capitalist would be willing to act as the defenders of a Yiddish newspaper aimed at working-class readers that printed articles with a social democratic message. Still, it makes a certain sense. *Forverts* was the voice of New York City's Jewish community. Marshall and Rosenwald were eager to negotiate an agreement with the government that would permit *Forverts* to continue publishing without becoming a government repression target. Marshall was worried that an attack by the federal government on *Forverts* would fuel anti-Semitism by reinforcing the belief that American Jews were not patriotic and were, indeed, sympathetic to the German cause in the war. Even after the war ended, Marshall wrote that Jews should be "extremely cautious" in their public statements to avoid being discredited "with the taint of Germanism."[26]

Marshall presented Burleson and Lamar with the letter from Cahan, and yet this was not a sufficient guarantee. Marshall promised the postal authorities he would "act as a private censor." This meant that he would carefully monitor each issue of *Forverts* and would meet with Cahan to ensure that his pledge to the government was being fulfilled.[27]

These were major concessions, and Cahan seems to have followed them. On October 31, 1917, Marshall informed another member of the Jewish elite, Judge Julian Mack, that Cahan had "been behaving very well." Thus, nothing had been "published during the past three weeks that could be criticized." In its reporting of the last weeks of the mayoralty campaign, *Forverts* had "acted with the greatest discretion."[28]

Nevertheless, the administration still viewed the newspaper with considerable suspicion. When Marshall notified Cahan of this, Cahan defended his record, insisting that he had not "shirked" his duty, while denying that he had "failed to live up" to his promises. Rallies promoting Liberty Loan war bonds had been featured on the first page of *Forverts.* Furthermore, Cahan had come to believe that every member of the Jewish community, "irrespective of party or social creed," should demonstrate "their devotion to the country" by buying war bonds.[29]

In a later review of the situation, Marshall defended Cahan's record in a lengthy letter to Lamar. He was convinced that Cahan had "studiously observed" the pledge he had given to the Post Office. Not only had the newspaper printed articles urging readers to purchase war bonds, but its editors had agreed to buy $20,000 in bonds out of the paper's profits. Marshall had "been in frequent conference" with Cahan to further this outcome.[30]

Despite Cahan's frantic efforts to mollify the government, Creel was not satisfied. *Forverts* could not uncritically extol the war effort or urge young men to join the army and still hope to retain its mass base of readers. Furthermore, the newspaper refused to print most of the propaganda bulletins produced by the Committee on Public Information. Cahan tried to make Marshall understand "the peculiar circumstances" in which he was operating, but his explanation failed to persuade the administration's decision-makers.[31]

At the end of October 1917, Creel told President Wilson that *Forverts* was "absolutely responsible for the demoralization of the East Side." Indeed, it continued to be "the most dangerous influence" the Committee on Public Information had "to combat." The president replied that the issue of "disloyal newspapers" was "a thorny business," but he was "in close touch" with Burleson, and the issue was "being worked out."

Purchasing an Alternative

In spite of the intense pressure, *Forverts* could not be coerced into uncritical support for the war effort. In August 1917, Maisel reluctantly reported to Gompers that "no Jewish papers" had "the backbone to stand up and fight the *Forward*, and its anti-Americanism." The only "way to break through" was "ownership of a Jewish paper." Fortunately, Maisel concluded, the *Jewish Daily News* was available for $130,000, with 40 percent due as a down payment.[32] (This upfront installment of $50,000, a substantial sum in 1917, would now be worth more than $1 million, allowing for inflation.) The fact that Maisel was willing to endorse such an expenditure indicates the importance the Committee on Public Information placed on molding popular opinion on the Lower East Side.

Creel hoped to avoid a direct expenditure of CPI funds to purchase a Jewish newspaper, but rather to "appeal to a number of rich Jews and get them to start a daily that will serve our purpose." Unable to suppress *Forverts,* Creel moved ahead with the alternative of creating a newspaper that could directly counter it. A Bureau of Intelligence (BI) agent who surveyed the Yiddish press in New York City in late September 1917 categorized virtually every newspaper in this group, including *Forverts*, as seditious, "in the danger class." There was one exception to this rule: the *Jewish Morning Journal*. Until September 1, this newspaper had wavered in its support for the war effort but recently the *Morning Journal* had "completely changed its attitude," much to the pleasure of the BI agent. Through "private sources," the agent had learned that this rapid conversion was due to the influence of Samuel Untermeyer, Marshall's law partner.[33]

Forverts and the Intelligence Community

Despite the efforts of the CPI to flood the Lower East Side with pro-war propaganda, *Forverts* remained the overwhelming choice of most of its residents. Cahan was very careful to avoid printing articles that could be viewed as critical of the government or its war policies. Nevertheless, the intelligence community closely monitored *Forverts* to ensure that its editors fully complied with the agreement that permitted its continued publication. In particular, Creel and the CPI were still convinced that the government should take even more drastic actions.

The immediate point of contention arose when Gompers traveled to Europe in the fall of 1918. Gompers went at President Wilson's express request to convince British and European social democratic leaders to block any attempts at a negotiated peace settlement. His visit was covertly funded by the U.S. government.[34]

A few days after he departed, the AFL issued an official statement that Gompers had left on a trip to Europe to "cooperate with President Wilson" in insisting on "an overwhelming victory" against Germany "instead of a compromise peace at any price proposition."[35]

This description of the aims of Gompers's trip was truthful, but indiscreet. In the midst of a total war, and with German submarines sinking ships heading toward Britain, a voyage to Europe was not undertaken lightly. Popular opinion in Western Europe was eager to see a rapid end to the war with a peace treaty that did not impose a humiliating defeat on Germany and its allies. Woodrow Wilson was vehemently opposed to such a negotiated settlement, so Gompers was sent in an effort to block it.

The official announcement of the trip issued by the AFL was not favorably received on the Lower East Side, where opposition to the war was widespread and growing. It only reinforced the belief that Gompers did not represent the members of AFL-affiliated unions, but rather that he took his orders from the president.

Thus, when Gompers arrived in Britain on August 28, 1917, Maisel issued a statement for the AALD that obfuscated the issue rather than clarifying it. According to Maisel, Gompers had gone to Europe to meet with labor leaders and social democratic politicians in Britain, France, and Italy to explain to them the "aims and principles" underlying American labor's support for "the prosecution of the war."[36]

In its report on Gompers's trip, *Forverts* stated that he had left for Europe to "prevent any peace by compromise." The article attributed this explanation to the AALD. In fact, *Forverts* was paraphrasing the statement issued by the AFL.[37]

Maisel was furious at what he believed was a deliberate attempt by the paper to undermine the administration and Gompers by providing a report on the trip that would be bound to trigger an antagonistic response from its readers. In a letter to a contact in the Army's Military Intelligence Division, Maisel complained that the "Jewish press" was "controlled by one paper practically" and that newspaper, *Forverts*, was "not even 25% loyal."[38]

Clearly, Maisel and the Committee on Public Information were trying to involve the Military Intelligence Division in a further push to silence *Forverts*. When the CPI's propaganda efforts failed to quash a dissident voice, the MID could deploy its resources in the effort to suppress anyone who challenged the government and its war policies.

Creel was also angered by the coverage given by *Forverts* to Gompers's trip, so he sought the aid of the Post Office. To Creel, the article on the trip was a definite indication that Cahan and the newspaper's editorial staff were still not fully supporting the war effort. Creel, therefore, wrote Lamar of his belief that the time had "come when something should be done to this paper."[39]

By September 1918, the war was drawing to a close, and the administration was not willing to further antagonize progressives by silencing *Forverts* as punishment for accurately describing the purpose of Gompers's trip to Europe. The newspaper was permitted to continue publishing until the end of the war in November 1918, but only under the careful monitoring of Marshall and the Post Office. Nevertheless, these incidents indicate how careful *Forverts* had to be in vetting its articles in order to comply with the guidelines set by the government.

In the end, the government muzzled *Forverts*. The garment workers' unions that had initially endorsed the effort to establish an antiwar opposition soon opted to cooperate with the government.[40] The Lower East Side could not be cajoled into supporting the war, but it could be silenced.

CHAPTER 2

Quashing the People's Council of America

THE PEOPLE'S COUNCIL OF AMERICA for Democracy and the Terms of Peace (PCA) brought together a broad coalition of progressives and social democrats. By the summer of 1917, it had become the primary organizational vehicle for the antiwar opposition. Although the Socialist Party of America (SP) furnished many of its leaders and rank-and-file activists, the PCA was not a front organization. Influential liberals joined the organization and took an active part in determining its strategy and tactics.

Woodrow Wilson came to view the People's Council as a significant threat to his administration. This was not just because the People's Council could provide leadership for those who opposed the war, but because it had the potential to become an important component of a new third party. These fears were greatly heightened by the organization's close ties to Wisconsin's senator Robert La Follette.

Disrupting the PCA became an important priority for the Wilson administration. Still, the president did not want to be seen utilizing the government's repressive apparatus to quash the People's Council. After all, the organization included prominent progressives, and Wilson liked to view himself as a progressive reformer.

Instead, the government initially relied on covert operations to hamper and harass the PCA. The Committee on Public Information and its front group, the American Alliance for Labor and Democracy, played a key role in countering the People's Council. As the war ground on, the administration turned to harsher measures to complement those of the CPI.

Unfortunately, this coordinated assault prevailed. The People's Council could not withstand the government's repressive measures and spiralled downward until its dissolution.

Forming the People's Council

The People's Council of America emerged from an earlier organization, the Emergency Peace Federation (EPF). Formed as a loose national network in February 1915, the EPF sought to counter the slide leading toward the United States entering the war. The organization became dormant in the fall of 1915 as its leading members became involved with Henry Ford's Peace Ship effort. In February 1917, the EPF was revived to lead a last-effort push to block a declaration of war.[1]

On April 6, 1917, as Congress convened to vote on a declaration of war on Germany, the Emergency Peace Federation organized mass meetings in Washington, hoping to block the declaration. A delegation met with several sympathetic members of Congress. At one of these informal meetings, Senator La Follette suggested that a new, more inclusive organization should be created to press for a negotiated peace.[2]

La Follette's proposal was enthusiastically accepted, so on May 2, 1917, forty delegates representing a wide array of organizations met in New York City to create an organizing committee to lay the foundations for future action. Morris Hillquit was elected as chair, and Louis Lochner as secretary.[3]

From this meeting came a call for a mass rally in Madison

recently quit the Socialist Party in order to gain support for the administration's war policies.

John Spargo had been a leading member of the Socialist Party before the U.S. decision to enter the war. Indeed, he had been elected to its five-person National Executive Committee in 1909. At the April 1917 emergency conference of the SP, Spargo presented a minority resolution that urged the party to avoid taking any action to resist the war or the draft.[11]

When a huge majority in a membership referendum upheld the militant antiwar resolution approved in St. Louis, Spargo resigned from the Socialist Party. The *New York Times* printed his public statement of resignation as front-page news. According to Spargo, the Socialist Party was "committed to a program essentially unneutral, un-American and pro-German." Spargo was a true believer, convinced that the global war was simply "a conflict between militant democracy and autocracy." In this context, SP leaders had "been, with notable uniformity, on the German side."[12]

This vitriolic, public denunciation by one of its most prominent leaders was a damaging blow to the Socialist Party. Needless to say, the Committee on Public Information hoped to utilize Spargo's reputation and talents in its covert projects. In early July 1917, Chester Wright wrote to Spargo, querying his interest in participating in the CPI's propaganda project aimed at the Lower East Side. Spargo responded by confirming his support for the AFL's uncritical support for the war, but he avoided any commitment to the propaganda project.[13]

Instead, Spargo met personally with Woodrow Wilson in the latter part of July 1917. The president was very disturbed by the depth of the antiwar sentiment and was eager to counteract it. Spargo and Wilson agreed on the need to create a new organization covertly funded by the Committee on Public Information. The new organization would combine the organizational weight of the American Federation of Labor (AFL) with the propagandistic talents of the pro-war intellectuals who had recently quit the Socialist Party. Its scope would go well beyond the Lower East Side. Indeed, the intention was to challenge the People's Council, both by organizing at the local level and by presenting an alternative ideological perspective.[14]

This was a far more ambitious project than the one originally envisioned by Gompers and the AFL and never fully implemented. Nevertheless, the White House meeting between Spargo and the president set the guidelines for what would become the American Alliance for Labor and Democracy (AALD).

On July 29, 1917, the American Alliance for Democracy held its founding conference at the Hotel Continental in New York City. Four distinct circles were represented. At the core was a group of AFL officials, including Gompers. In addition, several editors and publishers were invited, including those from the pro-war Yiddish press of New York City. A third group of pro-war intellectuals, most of whom had recently resigned from the Socialist Party, was added to these two distinct groupings. As well as Spargo, this group included James Graham Phelps Stokes and his wife, Rose Pastor Stokes. Finally, Maisel and Wright were there as the staff members of the Committee on Public Information who would implement the plans being formulated at the conference.[15]

Shortly after this founding conference, Gompers wrote to Maisel, making it clear that the AALD would be directly controlled by the Committee on Public Information and its chair, George Creel. Gompers informed Maisel that it would be Creel "under whose supervision and direction the entire project is to be carried into effect."[16]

Creel had ambitious plans for the AALD. Its purpose was not merely to neutralize the People's Council and to silence any form of antiwar opposition. Creel and the CPI hoped to launch a propaganda drive to engender fervent enthusiasm for the war effort. In line with this goal, the founding conference approved a resolution holding that it was "the duty of all the people of the

United States, without regard to class" to "faithfully and loyally support the Government of the United States in carrying the present war for justice, freedom and democracy to a triumphant conclusion."[17]

A later press release by the AALD declared that the "forces of disloyalty" were "actively at work." Furthermore, "their organizers" were "spreading treason from state to state."[18] The release suggested that countering these allegedly nefarious activities would be the primary purpose of the AALD. Although the People's Council and its union-based affiliate, the Workmen's Council, were not specifically mentioned in the press release, the reference was clear.

Shortly after this founding conference, Spargo wrote to Gompers more fully, developing his plans for the new organization. He had originated the concept of an "Alliance for Labor and Democracy" in the belief that it was not enough to merely counteract the People's Council, but rather that the AFL would have to sponsor and lead an organization for those "fundamentally loyal to American democracy" that could also carry the struggle to defeat "aggressive reactionary tendencies," while defending against "assaults" on "the democratic rights and initiatives of the people." As the PCA called for rallies around the country, the AFL, through the AALD, could stage "counter-demonstrations" to effectively undercut the opposition while promoting the war effort.[19] This idea was intriguing, albeit implausible, but it would have set the AFL and the AALD on a collision course with the Wilson administration. Of course, Gompers and Creel had no intention of actually criticizing the administration for its harsh repressive measures aimed at antiwar dissidents.

To put this program into practice, Spargo urged the AFL "to enlist" the aid of a "large number of writers and speakers" from the ranks of pro-war intellectuals. In particular, Spargo was eager to see well-known writers and journalists such as Upton Sinclair become active participants in the AALD. (Sinclair had recently resigned from the Socialist Party to support the war.)[20] Nevertheless, Spargo believed that the AFL, and Gompers, should set the policy guidelines for the new organization, with the pro-war intellectuals, such as himself, assuming a subordinate role. In fact, Creel and the Committee on Public Information called the shots, since the federal government paid the bills.[21]

Spargo was being carried away by wishful thinking. The AFL bureaucracy was unable to recruit large numbers of its own members into the American Alliance for Labor and Democracy since most workers, even those in the skilled crafts, opposed the war and hoped it would end quickly. Nevertheless, the AALD did succeed in making an impact.

The People's Council and the Terms of Peace

The People's Council soon developed friendly relations with progressives in Congress. In the summer of 1917, the organization became involved in a drive to convince Congress to set the terms of a peace treaty. The issue was a controversial one. Throughout the first years of the war, the UK government had consistently refused to publicly present its terms for a peace settlement. Instead, the United Kingdom negotiated secret treaties with its allies, providing detailed descriptions of the terms to be imposed upon Germany and the Central Powers once they were totally defeated.[22]

Popular opposition grew as the war dragged on. The United Kingdom and its allies came under increasing pressure to formulate their terms for peace. In March 1917, the Russian czar was overthrown in a peaceful revolution. The Soviet Council of Workers and Soldiers then became the dominant force in Russia. In May 1917, under intense pressure from a politicized populace, the Soviet Council issued a call for a rapid end to the war. An equitable peace treaty should be based on "the formula of peace without annexations and indemnities."[23]

The first Russian Revolution inspired the left in the United States and greatly influenced the program presented by antiwar progressives. Thus, the People's Council statement of principles drew heavily from the Russian Soviet's proposal for the terms of peace. Indeed, a press release issued in June 1917 declared that the PCA had been organized "upon lines similar" to the Soviet Workers and Soldiers Council in Russia.[24]

When the United States entered the war in April 1917, Woodrow Wilson refused to declare the terms upon which peace could be negotiated.[25] Furthermore, his supporters in Congress insisted that the president had the sole authority to negotiate an end to the war. This was the context in which the People's Council joined with congressional progressives in an effort to overcome the resistance of the president and his supporters.

An informal hearing in the Capital was arranged as the first public gathering to boost this campaign. The plan was to bring together leading members of the People's Council with those members of Congress who took a "favorable" view of the work of the peace movement. The organizing committee of the PCA decided to send a large delegation to Washington to participate in the informal meeting.[26]

Isaac McBride, acting as the Washington representative of the PCA, arranged the logistics of the meeting. A member of the Socialist Party, McBride had come to Washington as the private secretary of Oregon's Senator Harry Lane, a progressive Democrat who opposed the decision to enter the war. (McBride was also Lane's son-in-law.) When Lane died in May 1917, McBride joined the staff of the People's Council as a congressional lobbyist.[27]

McBride asked Senator George Chamberlain, a mainstream Democrat from Oregon, if the room in the Capital controlled by the Senate Military Affairs Committee could be used as a place where "some friends" could "meet some congressmen". As chair of that committee, Chamberlain agreed to McBride's request, since such informal receptions were commonplace. A fervent supporter of the war, Chamberlain was dismayed when he later discovered that the People's Council had held a meeting in the committee room.[28]

On the evening of August 9, 1917, several legislators attended a public gathering in the Capitol. Lochner chaired the meeting, and several speakers spoke to the need for Congress to set peace terms. The press generally ignored the event, and the articles that did appear were hostile.

Nevertheless, the event did demonstrate the ties between the People's Council and progressive, antiwar members of Congress. Two days after the gathering, La Follette introduced a resolution in Congress calling for it to set peace terms along the lines set in the Russian Soviet's proposal. Although La Follette insisted he was acting on his own, and not in tandem with the PCA, the two calls for peace were very similar. Furthermore, the People's Council distributed La Follette's resolution to its members and the public.[29]

Monitoring the People's Council

The emerging alliance between the People's Council and sympathetic members of Congress had demonstrated the ability to seriously embarrass the president. In response, the Wilson administration prioritized countering the PCA, both by producing propaganda promoting the war that could appeal to those on the left and by acting to disrupt its activities.

Covert funding from the president's secret National Security and Defense Fund enabled the AALD to produce literature on a vast scale. More than 300,000 copies of three pamphlets written by Professor John Commons of the University of Wisconsin were printed and distributed.[30]

In one of these pamphlets, titled *Why Workingmen Support the War*, Commons wrote that "never before" had "democracy for wage-earning made the progress" that had been made "in the nine months of the war." Because of this, the American Federation of Labor supported the war "almost unanimously and stands for fighting it out to the limit." Furthermore, those socialists who "belittle" the war effort were "playing the game of the German Socialists" who had "sold themselves to the Germans."[31] Commons and the Committee on Public Information not only defended the president's decision to lead the United States into the conflict as a direct participant, they went further and extolled the war as a golden opportunity for progressive reform.

As the American Alliance for Labor and Democracy printed vast quantities of propaganda denouncing the People's Council and its proposals for an immediate peace, it went further to actively disrupt its activities. The Committee's contacts were used to maintain covert surveillance of an organization peacefully protesting the war. In mid-August 1917, Maisel assured Gompers that he "could get all inside information about the People's Council at a very nominal sum." Two "trustworthy" informants were ready to provide the federal government with detailed reports on the inner workings of the PCA. In their initial reports, these informants reported that the People's Council had hired "nine organizers scattered through the country" at $50 a week, equivalent to the amount Maisel and Wright were receiving from the CPI.[32]

The confidential reports indicated that the People's Council was "pretty strong," and, indeed, "much more than" Maisel had expected. Even more disturbing, the PCA was closely linked to the Socialist Party, and there was a considerable overlap in the leadership of both organizations. Reports from informants indicated that Morris Hillquit was "the man who pulls the strings" and that informal meetings of the Council's leadership were "being held in his office" when he was in town.[33]

Maisel's letters to Gompers indicate how far the Committee on Public Information had moved beyond its stated mission of distributing propaganda boosting the war effort. The American

Alliance for Labor and Democracy, and thus the CPI, was orchestrating a sensitive clandestine operation targeting a dissident organization by soliciting confidential information from informants holding responsible positions within the People's Council.

Maisel did not name the two informants in his letter to Gompers, but a letter from a later date includes the information needed to identify one of them. Most of the PCA's funding came from small donations from its members, but it had two contributors who had given sizable sums. A wealthy Baltimore entrepreneur, William F. Cochran, told Maisel that he had changed his attitude toward the war and would soon resign from that organization. Cochran assured Maisel that he would no longer finance the People's Council or any other group critical of the war effort.[34]

The Minneapolis Conference

At a meeting on June 28, 1917, the organizing committee of the People's Council decided to hold its founding conference in early fall in a place yet to be determined. The conference would formally launch the organization and elect a leadership body with representation from local affiliates throughout the United States.[35]

Soon after the People's Council announcement of its plan for a founding conference, Phelps Stokes met with Maisel and Wright. Phelps Stokes proposed that the AALD hold its own event at the same time and place as the PCA conference. The event would be a mass rally where speakers would combine fervent support for the war with a vision of progressive change once the war ended. Phelps Stokes informed the others that the concept was not his, although he was unclear who had originated the plan. Since Phelps Stokes was serving as an officer in the Military Intelligence Division, it seems probable that the idea for a counter-conference came from within that intelligence agency. Wright was convinced and eager to see that the AALD rally took place. He, therefore, wrote to Gompers to get his support.[36]

On August 13, 1917, the People's Council announced that its founding conference would be held in Minneapolis, Minnesota, during the first week of September. The mayor of Minneapolis, Thomas Van Lear, a member of the Socialist Party, publicly stated that the conference would be protected from disruption. Van Lear even agreed to provide a welcoming speech.[37]

Once this decision was announced, the leaders of the AALD were ready to put into motion their own plan. Another small, secretive meeting was held, this time with Gompers, Phelps Stokes, Maisel, and Spargo attending. The four confirmed the plan to hold a counter-rally in Minneapolis in early September in direct opposition to the PCA's conference. Those persuaded to attend this conference would be urged to book reservations well in advance, thereby "making it impossible for the People's Council to find accommodations for their disloyal convention."[38] Thus, the leaders of the AALD were not only intent on providing a propaganda event to detract from the PCA's convention, but they were also intent on disrupting it as well.

The decision to include Phelps Stokes in this small, closed meeting was critically important. An officer in the Army's Military Intelligence Division who also served as the treasurer of the AALD, he provided a smooth link for the covert funding coming from the CPI. Phelps Stokes later wrote that he acted as the "Disbursing Agent for the Executive Department of the Government of the United States." Money to finance the AALD came directly from the president's secret National Security and Defense Fund, as well as through the CPI, which, in turn, received most of its funds from the same source.[39]

The decision of the People's Council to hold its conference in Minneapolis drew the administration's attention at its highest levels. When a friend of the president wrote a lengthy letter to the editor of the *New York Times* attacking the People's Council,

Wilson complimented him on his effort. Indeed, the PCA was "a bad and mischievous lot."[40]

At a Cabinet meeting held on August 17, 1917, the Postmaster General, Albert Burleson, warned of the "great danger" posed by the People's Council and called for "drastic action" to prevent the organization from holding its conference. Such an action would have required the deployment of federal troops and, perhaps, martial law if the delegates were to be indefinitely detained. The Justice Department had already been advised that the conditions required for the calling of martial law were not in place. In any case, Wilson did not want to be seen directly employing the federal government's powers to suppress the PCA. He therefore opted for a plan of action that would "show their impotence."[41]

The federal government initially relied on covert measures to disrupt the People's Council. Chester Wright of the CPI was assigned to organize the alternative conference in Minneapolis. The AALD would present a pro-war message as a counterpoint to the PCA's calls for a speedy end to the war through a negotiated settlement. According to Wright, the People's Council was "disloyal to America" since it engaged in "spreading propaganda that exactly meets the present needs of the German autocracy."[42]

Blocking the People's Council's Conference

The Committee on Public Information was not the only government agency targeting the PCA. A few days before the scheduled convening of the Minneapolis conference, the chief agent of the Bureau of Investigation in Minnesota, Thomas Campbell, reported that he had recruited a covert agent to "get some inside information" on the People's Council. Claude Swanson was a young journalist on the staff of a small-town newspaper, the *Fairmont Sentinel,* who had been assigned to cover the People's Council conference.[43]

Swanson agreed to act as a paid informant. He then met with the U.S. attorney for Minnesota, Alfred Jaques, who agreed that Swanson would be a "good man" for the job. Swanson proved to be a good choice, as he soon gained the "confidence of leaders" in the PCA. During the following days, he filed frequent confidential reports as the People's Council floundered in the face of government repression.[44]

The PCA conference was planned for several days, September 1 through September 7, permitting activists from around the country to meet and organize future actions. In contrast, the AALD projected a shorter conference, from September 5 through September 7, filled with speeches from notable dignitaries. This was not an organizing conference but rather an extended pep rally.

Suppressing the People's Council became a crusade for Gompers, who issued a series of statements denouncing it under the aegis of the AALD. Both the PCA and its union affiliate, the Workmen's Council, were "anti-American and pro-German." Nevertheless, Gompers found little enthusiasm for his crusade or the AALD counter-conference within the ranks of the AFL. As the date approached and the lack of grassroots interest became apparent, Gompers ordered union organizers to "devote" their "entire efforts" to persuading AFL locals to send delegates to Minneapolis.[45]

In the end, the People's Council was unable to convene its founding conference. On August 28, 1917, four days before the conference was scheduled to open, Governor Joseph Burnquist issued a proclamation prohibiting the PCA from meeting anywhere in Minnesota. Burnquist noted that Sheriff Otto Langum of Hennepin County had warned that the conference "would result in bloodshed, rioting and loss of life." (Minneapolis is located in Hennepin County.) Furthermore, he added that permitting the People's Council to hold a conference could "have no other effect than aiding and abetting the enemies of this country."[46]

Gompers issued a carefully worded statement declaring that the authorities should "permit" the PCA to hold its founding conference, despite the "menace of this organization." Minnesota should allow the constitutionally required exercise of free speech, "at least until their utterances actually become treasonable."[47]

After the People's Council was prevented from holding its conference in Minneapolis, a rump meeting was convened in Chicago. It was only able to meet for a few hours, with Judah Magnes giving the main speech. The People's Council's founding conference was then dispersed by 250 soldiers of the Illinois militia.[48]

While this fiasco played out, the American Alliance for Labor and Democracy proceeded with its conference, which, of course, had the full support and protection of the state of Minnesota and the federal government. Two hundred delegates listened to pro-war speeches from Governor Burnquist, Spargo and Rose Pastor Stokes. (Woodrow Wilson declined an invitation to speak, although he sent greetings.) Gompers regretted that the People's Council had been prevented from meeting in Minneapolis since the two conferences would have contrasted "loyalty against disloyalty." Still, he castigated those who called for an immediate start of peace negotiations as the "conscious or unconscious tools of Germany."[49]

In his initial plan for the AALD, Spargo had envisioned an organization that combined uncritical support for the war effort with a vocal defense of democratic rights against the arbitrary and unnecessary repression of government officials. His plan failed to be implemented at the Minneapolis conference. Instead, the delegates adopted a statement of principles uncritically supporting the president in his call for a total victory over Germany, while also condemning opponents of the war for acting to "abuse the rights of free speech" by "steadfastly attempting to incite sedition."[50]

Tracking Scott Nearing

Shortly after the disruption of the Minneapolis conference, Hillquit resigned from active participation in the People's Council to focus on his campaign for mayor of New York City. Scott Nearing then replaced Hillquit as chair of the organization's executive committee.[51]

Nearing had taught economics at the Wharton School of the University of Pennsylvania. An increasingly radical critic of capitalism, Nearing was fired in June 1915 after nine years of service. By now a well-known figure, he was hired by the University of Toledo in January 1916. When Nearing spoke out against the war, he was fired for a second time for his views in April 1917.[52]

Nearing was active in the People's Council from its inception. He joined the Socialist Party in July 1917 and began teaching full-time at the Rand School, an educational institute in New York City that was closely aligned to the Socialist Party.[53] Nearing was a logical choice to succeed Hillquit. Both Lochner and Nearing were young and energetic, but neither held Hillquit's standing within the left.[54]

As Nearing began holding a more influential position within the People's Council, the Bureau of Investigation began to take a greater interest in his activities. On September 12, 1917, a warrant was issued authorizing a search of Nearing's residence in Toledo, Ohio. In expectation of such a search, Nearing had moved some sensitive documents to another location.[55]

Although the BI agents were generally looking for lists of radicals, they were particularly interested in linking Nearing, and thus the People's Council, to the Industrial Workers of the World. The government was convinced that the People's Council was closely linked to the IWW. In fact, the Council's leadership had sought to bring the union into its loose network of organizations based on a common support for the right to dissent during wartime. (The IWW remained on the periphery of the PCA, primarily focusing on defending itself from a coordinated assault launched by the federal government.) In any case, the search of Nearing's house failed to discover any correspondence between him and the Wobbly leadership. Nevertheless, the agents carried away a great many documents, some of which were only returned two months later, in November.[56]

The Bureau of Investigation closely monitored Nearing's activities as he toured the country, giving speeches to local PCA groups and pacifist organizations. Since Nearing realized he was under surveillance, he was careful to phrase his comments to avoid prosecution. In his standard speech, Nearing avoided any discussion of peace or the draft and, instead, he focused on the need to tax the excess profits received by the wealthy few. Nearing also promised that the People's Council would defend free speech and civil liberties as it lobbied Congress.[57]

The Bureau of Investigation intensified its surveillance of Nearing after a pamphlet he wrote titled *The Great Madness* was published. The pamphlet was written in the summer of 1917 and was distributed by the Rand School that September. Nearing's pamphlet was intended as a piece of popular education, examining the war from a socialist perspective.

In *The Great Madness*, Nearing argued that the U.S. decision to enter the war provided the "greatest victory" for the rich and powerful since the 1898 war against Spain. This was because the "plutocracy wanted a free hand" to deal with radical trade unionists and socialists.[58]

Nearing went on to analyze the reasons behind the U.S. entry into the war. In his view, the war was being fought to protect U.S. arms exports to the Allies, a trade that generated huge profits. Contrary to the president's claim, the goal was not to extend democracy. Indeed, "American plutocracy was no more interested in establishing democracy in Germany than they were in establishing democracy in the United States."[59]

Nearing was scathing in his denunciation of the war and

the corporate interests profiting from it. Still, in his conclusion, he merely urged his readers to read critically and to speak with others who might oppose the war. He neither raised any demands calling for an immediate end to the war nor did he propose any form of collective resistance. Nevertheless, *The Great Madness* contested the administration's version of events and thus spurred the government into suppressing its circulation.

As the pamphlet circulated around the country, BI agents sent reports to headquarters calling on the Justice Department to prosecute Nearing. In November 1917, Bielaski wrote to John Lord O'Brian, the director of the War Emergency Division, asking if Nearing could be indicted for writing *The Great Madness*.[60] His query went unanswered at the time. The Justice Department had still not decided on its stance toward the People's Council.

Although the Justice Department was ready to authorize the close surveillance of Scott Nearing in the fall of 1917, it was not prepared to initiate his arrest and prosecution. The administration was prepared to harass and disrupt the PCA, but it was not yet prepared to directly suppress it by jailing its leadership. This policy guideline changed when the administration opted to target the Socialist Party's leaders for prosecution under the Espionage Act.

Suppressing the Socialist Party

The leadership of the Socialist Party hoped to continue their opposition to the war while remaining within the limits set by the Justice Department. Party literature generally avoided any hint of militant resistance to the war or the draft. Instead, the SP frequently reiterated its belief that the war arose out of imperialist rivalries, and that the only way to bring about a permanent peace was to establish a socialist society.

In the months immediately following the U.S. entry into the

war, the Justice Department focused on the Industrial Workers of the World. The SP was generally permitted to put forward its critique of the war. This tacit tolerance dissipated in the late summer and early fall of 1917 as U.S. attorneys sought indictments of Socialist Party members.

One of the first cases arose in Albany, New York, when the SP local decided to circulate a pamphlet produced at the party's central office. The pamphlet's author, Irwin St. John Tucker, was an Episcopalian minister and an influential figure in the Socialist Party. His pamphlet, *The Price We Pay*, condemned conscription, although it avoided any suggestion of draft resistance. Tucker also emphasized commercial rivalries as the basis for the war and pointed to the large holdings of British bonds held by J. P. Morgan and Co.[61]

In August 1917, Clinton Pierce, the chair of the Socialist Party's Albany local, and three other members of the local were arrested for distributing Tucker's pamphlet. A federal grand jury then indicted them for allegedly violating the Espionage Act. One count in the indictment charged that by criticizing the draft, the defendants were guilty of obstructing the recruitment of soldiers, a charge that had been levied against others who protested the war. Another count brought a new twist by claiming that the four socialists were distributing false reports by insisting that the war was not being fought to bring democracy to Germany. The defendants were convicted and sentenced to serve twelve to thirty months in a federal prison.[62] The case, *Pierce v. US*, would move through the appellate courts until it reached the U.S. Supreme Court to become a key moment in the history of civil liberties law.

The Albany prosecution was initiated before the War Emergency Division was created in October 1917, when decisions on who to prosecute were still being made at the local level. After then, the War Emergency Division determined which cases under the Espionage Act would be brought before a grand jury. John Lord O'Brian, the director of the division, delegated the day-to-day decisions to his deputy, Alfred Bettman.[63]

In November 1917, Bettman wrote to O'Brian on the need to clarify the question of what constituted a false report. The Espionage Act of June 1917 made it illegal to circulate "false reports" with the "intent to interfere" with the success of U.S. military operations. This section of the statute was borrowed from the British government. Regulation 27 of the Defence of the Realm regulations, issued in November 1916, made it illegal to "spread false reports" that were "likely to cause disaffection" among the populace.[64]

The Justice Department had to decide whether a clause in the statute designed to stop those who maliciously spread rumors of food shortages or huge battlefield casualties could be stretched to cover those who argued that the war was being fought to maximize profits. Bettman hoped to get a clearer view of whether statements attributing the U.S. entry into the war to the defense of J. P. Morgan and Co.'s purchase of British bonds constituted a "false report" as listed in the Espionage Act. He thought it would be "useful" to collect a "correct statement" on the causes underlying the war along with "proof" to substantiate this argument. The relevant evidence "ought to be furnished" to the Justice Department by the State Department and the Committee on Public Information.[65]

In fact, no credible evidence substantiated the argument that the war was not being fought for profit and imperial gain. On the contrary, there was reason to believe that these were some of the factors in a complex mix that had led to the start of the First World War. There is no evidence in the record that Bettman was provided with documents buttressing the argument that profit was not a key motive behind the war. In spite of this, the Justice Department upheld the decision in the Albany case as it went through the appellate courts.

In March 1920, the U.S. Supreme Court affirmed the verdict by a vote of seven to two. Justice Mahlon Pitney, writing for the majority, held that Tucker's pamphlet constituted a "false report" within the meaning of the Espionage Act. As evidence in support of this assertion, Pitney pointed to "common knowledge" and the president's speech to Congress on April 2, 1917, urging a declaration of war against Germany. In that speech, Wilson insisted that the United States was entering the war because the "world must be made safe for democracy." This noble goal motivated the United States, not the desire to bolster this country as a global power. Indeed, he argued, "We desire no conquest and no dominion."[66]

The Supreme Court thus validated the administration's position that those who voiced their disagreement with the president's justification for entering the war could be jailed for violating the Espionage Act's prohibition of false reports.

In a landmark dissent, Justice Louis Brandeis held that the "causes of a war are not single," but rather there were "many cooperating causes." Indeed, "historians differ necessarily in their judgments." The statements in Tucker's pamphlet were "matters of opinion and judgment, not matters of fact." Even Wilson's speech to Congress was not sufficient to prove that the war was being fought on "high moral grounds."[67]

Brandeis's dissent remains an important guideline. Its basic message remains all too pertinent to this day. Nevertheless, his dissent went unheeded, and the Albany defendants, who had been released on bail, had to serve their prison sentences for expressing their dissent from the official doctrine.

Although a local U.S. attorney initially decided to seek indictments in the Albany case, the decision would soon be made at the national level to set the Socialist Party as a priority target for prosecution. This was a significant policy decision, and it was made at the highest level. Attorney General Thomas Gregory directly participated in determining this policy, and the president must have also been consulted.

In December 1917, the U.S. attorney for northern Illinois, Charles Clyne, presented the case to a federal grand jury, since the headquarters of the SP was in Chicago. Gregory wrote to O'Brian asking him to review this decision before a final decision was made since the indictment would name the "high-up people in the Socialist Party." It was therefore necessary that "the policy in regard to prosecuting them should receive very careful consideration."[68]

The question was a sensitive one, but the Justice Department still proceeded to move forward. By the end of January 1918, the grand jury was prepared to issue the indictment. Gregory then warned Clyne that a public statement should not be immediately released. These were "matters of great international importance"; thus, a public statement should only be released upon approval by the Justice Department and "those still higher in authority."[69] Woodrow Wilson was the only person with greater power to determine the enforcement of federal statutes than the attorney general.

Once the final decision was made, the Justice Department pursued the case with all its resources. The grand jury indicted five Socialist Party leaders on February 2, 1918, and a public announcement was released on March 9, 1918. In addition to Tucker, Victor Berger, who had been elected to the U.S. House of Representatives, and Adolph Germer, the party's national secretary, were charged in the indictment, along with two other prominent socialists. The trial began in December 1918 and lasted five weeks. All five defendants were found guilty. On February 20, 1919, Judge Kenesaw Mountain Landis sentenced each to the maximum term of twenty years in prison. The U.S Supreme Court reversed the convictions in January 1921, citing Landis's public expressions of hostility toward those who questioned the government's war policies.[70]

Targeting Scott Nearing

The decision to target the Socialist Party provided the legal and political context in which the Justice Department decided whether to prosecute the leaders of the People's Council. In the period following the dispersed founding conference, the People's Council at the national level consisted primarily of two people, Lochner and Nearing, both of whom were aligned with the Socialist Party. Nearing had joined the Socialist Party in the summer of 1917. Furthermore, both Nearing and Lochner taught at the Rand School of Social Science, which was closely tied to the Socialist Party.[71]

In its drive to quash the Socialist Party, the federal government increased the pressure on the People's Council. Nearing was a more visible public figure than Lochner and was, therefore, the logical target. In early February 1918, William Offley, the agent in charge of the New York office of the Bureau of Investigation, met with James McElhone, the director of the Bureau of Investigation of the American Defense Society. McElhone suggested to Offley that the BI should institute a "surveillance of Nearing's personal conduct and habits." Investigating his personal life would be "likely to make him amenable to the criminal law without regard to his disloyal activities." In particular, McElhone believed that Nearing had been dismissed from the faculty of the University of Pennsylvania for his personal conduct and not for his political views.[72]

Based on a report of this conversation from Offley, Bielaski authorized Frank Garbarino, the agent in charge of the Philadelphia office, to investigate Nearing's dismissal from Wharton. Bielaski ordered Garbarino to "give the matter special attention." Garbarino pointed out that the case had been fully covered in the local press and that there was no doubt that Nearing had lost his job because of "his attitude on Socialistic and Economical problems."[73]

Nevertheless, Bielaski was not convinced. He informed Garbarino that he had received information that "the real reason" for the dismissal was that Nearing "was guilty of degraded sexual practices." A BI agent was then dispatched to interview the provost of the University of Pennsylvania. Professor Edgar

Fahs Smith vouched that Nearing "was absolutely clean." His appointment to the faculty had been terminated in June 1915 because his speeches off campus had "become so wild" that "the college authorities were compelled to dismiss him."[74]

It is doubtful that the Bureau of Investigation hoped to prosecute Nearing for aspects of his personal life. Far more likely, the BI was fishing for something that could embarrass him as a public figure and academic. Nearing could then be blackmailed into cooperating with the government as an informant, or should he refuse, the gossipy information could be leaked to the press.

In any case, the report from the American Defense Society proved to be false. The wording of Bielaski's messages suggests that the ADS was claiming that Nearing was homosexual. This was a serious charge a century ago that could have major implications for one's career and public standing. Nearing was married with two children. At the time, his marriage to Nellie Marguerite Seeds seems to have been harmonious. In the 1920s, the Nearings grew apart and finally separated in 1928. Soon afterward, Nearing began living with another woman, Helen Knothe, although the two did not marry until twenty years later. This would have been a point of leverage for the government in 1918, but by 1932, Nearing and his partner were living on a farm in Vermont.[75]

Since the lead given by the ADS had turned out to be a dead end, the government returned to the issue of the publication of *The Great Madness*. Shortly after Offley met with McElhone, the issue of whether to prosecute Nearing under the Espionage Act became a matter of public controversy. On February 11, 1918, the *New York Tribune* printed a front-page story quoting the most inflammatory sections of the pamphlet.

The article also included comments from Henry Wood denouncing Nearing's pamphlet as seditious. Wood owned a lucrative firm that produced machinery for newspapers. A conservative Republican, he had been active in the preparedness campaign in 1915 pushing for a rapid build-up in the U.S. military. Wood urged the government to prosecute Nearing for treason. In his view, *The Great Madness* "incites pacifists and fanatics to burn factories." (Of course, pacifists oppose all forms of violence, from sabotage to war.) According to Wood, the failure to prosecute Nearing demonstrated that the attorney general was not "willing to suppress German activities in this country."[76]

The *Tribune*'s front-page article was not an effort to provide the newspaper's readers with the news of current events. Instead, it was a blatant effort to pressure the administration into initiating a prosecution. The *Tribune* followed the article with an editorial on the next day. Nearing was "preaching the same sort of sedition" that had led to the editors of several left-wing newspapers being prosecuted under the Espionage Act. The editorial concluded with the query: "What is the Department of Justice doing to enforce the law against Nearing?"[77]

It is doubtful that the *New York Tribune* articles had a significant impact on the Justice Department's decision on the case. The Bureau of Investigation had already begun to assemble the evidence needed to obtain Nearing's indictment. Indeed, the ADS and BI agents were discussing ways to ensure Nearing's prosecution before the articles appeared.

Still, the *Tribune* pieces had made Nearing a visible symbol of antiwar resistance. A few days after their appearance, Bettman wrote Bielaski that he had concluded that the publication of *The Great Madness* was "clearly a violation of the Espionage Act." Two days later, O'Brian wrote Bielaski to report that Attorney General Gregory was "personally interested in the matter." Nevertheless, O'Brian also informed Bielaski that the U.S. attorney for New York City, Francis Caffey, was "in doubt" that the circulation of the pamphlet constituted "a violation of the Statute."[78]

Despite his doubts, Caffey presented the case to the New York City grand jury investigating radical activities. On March

21, 1918, the grand jury indicted Nearing and the American Socialist Society, the organizational sponsor of the Rand School, on two counts of violating the Espionage Act. The indictment alleged that in circulating *The Great Madness* Nearing and the Rand School had sought to obstruct the draft and the war effort.[79]

The People's Council Unravels

The failure to hold its founding conference in September 1917 represented a major blow to the People's Council, one from which it never fully recovered. Prominent progressives who had been willing to be publicly associated with the PCA began drifting away. The Socialist Party had always been at the core of the Council, but after September 1917, its members were left as the only ones attempting to keep the national organization together.

The failure to hold a founding conference also had serious financial consequences for the People's Council. More than $5,500 had been spent on organizing the conference, which is more than $100,000 in current dollars. This expenditure represented a significant drain on the organization's resources. Nearing circulated a special plea for funds to cover the budget deficit caused by the Minneapolis fiasco, but funding remained a significant problem.[80]

Nearing's indictment in March 1918 provided another serious blow to the People's Council. He was released on bail until his trial, so he could continue to travel and speak. Still, Nearing had to be even more careful in publicly discussing controversial issues related to the war. Furthermore, he had to devote a great deal of time to preparing for his trial. In February 1920, Nearing was finally acquitted after testifying on his own behalf.[81]

The federal government understood that the PCA was in disarray after the disruption of its founding conference, but the relentless effort to quash the organization continued. In January 1918, Bielaski wrote a memorandum for the attorney general in which he concluded that the People's Council was "on the distinct downgrade." This downturn was due in part to the failed Minneapolis conference. Organizing the event had cost "a great deal of money and left them in considerable debt." Still, Bielaski castigated the People's Council as an "unsavory alliance of anarchists, pacifists, socialists and 'pro-Germans.'"[82]

The PCA was on a downward spiral, and yet the government continued its intensive surveillance. The San Francisco office of the People's Council was raided by Bureau of Investigation agents carrying out a search warrant. Soon afterward, this office was targeted with overnight break-ins. Agents of the Military Intelligence Division were almost certainly responsible for these illegal raids.[83]

In the summer of 1918, the Bureau of Investigation tapped the phones used by the PCA's San Francisco office. Agents placed the wiretap without the authorization of a search warrant. The U.S. Supreme Court had not specifically ruled that wiretaps could only be conducted after a search warrant had been obtained, but the Justice Department had to be wondering whether these surveillance methods violated basic constitutional rights.[84]

The U.S. Post Office also became involved in the government's campaign to disrupt the People's Council. By the fall of 1917, mail going to its New York office was being held by the Post Office, as was any literature it circulated. In December 1917, an internal memorandum confirmed this hold on the PCA's mail. William Lamar, the solicitor of the Post Office, was considering a blanket order "barring from the mails any and all" documents issued by the organization. In the view of an attorney on Lamar's staff, the People's Council had "published and distributed matter in clear violation of the Espionage Act." Furthermore, the PCA was "a growing menace."[85]

The actions of the Post Office were a significant factor underlying the rapid decline of the People's Council. Lochner circulated an open letter complaining that the Post Office was delaying mail coming into and leaving the PCA's office.[86]

The unrelenting pressure exerted by the federal government proved to be effective. By the spring of 1918, the PCA was in dire straits. As donations dropped to a trickle, Lochner was forced to halt the publication of the *PCA Bulletin* in August 1918. At about this time, Nearing accepted the Socialist Party's nomination for the U.S. House of Representatives from a Manhattan congressional district. He informed Lochner that he would be focusing on this campaign. By October 1918, the People's Council had virtually stopped functioning, although it did not officially disband until October 1919.[87]

The American Alliance for Labor and Democracy had always been a shell organization, propped up by large sums covertly provided by the Committee on Public Information. When the war ended in November 1918, the CPI wound down its affairs, so funding of the AALD ended. Once the PCA ceased to exist, the AALD lost its last reason to continue and officially dissolved in March 1920.[88]

In the summer of 1917, the People's Council appeared to have an enormous potential for rapid growth. Opposition to the war was widespread. Individuals holding a spectrum of political views were seeking an organization that could pose a credible opposition to the war, while resisting the enormous pressure being exerted by a federal government intent on suppressing any organized dissent.

The president was alarmed by the success of the PCA, so he authorized a covert operation involving an array of intelligence agencies. Although the Committee on Public Information and its front group, the AALD, were at the forefront of the attack, the Post Office, military intelligence, and the War Emergency Division of the Justice Department were also involved. Ultimately, the People's Council floundered, unable to effectively resist the government's assault.

CHAPTER 3

Intimidating Senator Robert La Follette

ROBERT LA FOLLETTE WAS THE MOST prominent and respected voice for progressive politics during the first years of the twentieth century. During his three terms as governor of Wisconsin, from January 1901 to January 1906, he compiled a record as a persistent reformer who boldly confronted entrenched corporate interests. Once in the U.S. Senate, he continued to push for measures restricting the monopolistic profits received by large corporations.

When the First World War enveloped Europe in a bloodbath, La Follette worked to keep the United States neutral and out of the war as a belligerent combatant. He continued to criticize the administration's policies even after the United States declared war on Germany in April 1917. In doing so, he left the mainstream of American politics and came closer to the leadership of the Socialist Party. La Follette aligned himself with a broad alliance of liberals and social democrats that sought to mobilize popular support for immediate peace negotiations and a speedy end to the war.

La Follette's willingness to speak out for an immediate peace made him a target of government repression. The federal government, with the president's approval, unleashed a concerted campaign of abuse and threats to isolate and discredit him. Unfortunately, this coordinated attack succeeded in its goal, and La Follette was silenced. During the last months of the war, La Follette gave muted support for the war effort, implicitly repudiating his previous position as an outspoken voice of dissent.

La Follette as Progressive Reformer

As governor of Wisconsin, La Follette sought to defend the interests of the small farmer by pushing for greater regulation of the railroads. He successfully pushed through legislation that significantly increased taxes on railroad lines operating in Wisconsin. His effort to regulate railroad tariffs was less successful, since the state legislature created a commission with only limited power to set rates. Nevertheless, these were significant reforms benefiting farmers, who were convinced that the railroad companies charged extortionate rates on freight shipments. In the face of venomous attacks from mainstream newspapers, La Follette held to his plan to curb corporate power. As a result, he gained enormous popularity, along with the nickname "Fighting Bob."[1]

In spite of the intense hatred he evoked from the corporate establishment, La Follette was far from a radical. Wisconsin was also the home of the Milwaukee Socialist Party, a mainstay of its dominant social democratic wing. Led by Victor Berger, the Milwaukee socialists advanced a program of structural changes that moved well beyond the limited measures advocated by progressives. La Follette believed in the virtues of capitalism, a system based on privately owned corporations that produced goods and services that sought to maximize profits. La Follette sought to modify the system by breaking up monopoly trusts and regulating corporations to ensure that they did not engage in collusive agreements limiting competition. These were fundamental principles held by most progressive reformers.

In contrast to this perspective, Berger and the Milwaukee social democrats hoped to bring about a socialist society through a series of incremental reforms, such as bringing key industries into public ownership. Progressives and social democrats held two distinct and conflicting perspectives. Wisconsin elections saw heated debates between the two political tendencies.[2] Still, the First World war would bring the two tendencies toward a close working relationship.

La Follette and Wilson

President Woodrow Wilson and La Follette had worked together on reform legislation before the war and Wilson had publicly expressed his admiration for the senator. As governor of New Jersey from January 1911 to March 1913, Wilson had sought to develop a record as an effective social reformer, while La Follette had already consolidated a reputation as a staunch progressive. During the last weeks of the 1912 presidential campaign, Wilson attempted to lure the progressive vote away from Theodore Roosevelt's Progressive Party. In a campaign speech, he praised La Follette as "an indomitable, unconquerable champion of progressive ideas." Indeed, Wilson insisted that he and La Follette had "been fighting the battle of progressive democracy."[3]

Once elected, Wilson invited La Follette to the White House, where the two discussed a variety of possible initiatives, especially "legislation on social reform," and "found themselves in agreement." It was most unusual for a Democratic Party president to consult with a Republican Party senator on a legislative agenda, but Wilson had "the highest admiration for the Senator."[4]

La Follette then worked closely with the White House in pushing through progressive legislation such as the Seamen's Act in March 1915, a first step in improving the working conditions of sailors employed in the merchant marine. The positive relationship between La Follette and Wilson held firm through the first years of the First World War despite the differences that arose as the war unfolded. In January 1916, a vacancy on the U.S. Supreme Court opened when Justice Joseph Lamar died. Having decided to propose Louis Brandeis for the post, the president was concerned that the nomination would be defeated by the U.S. Senate. Brandeis was a close friend of La Follette's and had become known as an attorney for progressive causes.[5] He was also the first person of Jewish descent to be nominated to a seat on the U.S. Supreme Court.[6]

Wilson prepared for the coming fight by ordering Attorney General Thomas Gregory to meet with La Follette to formulate a strategy to overwhelm the opposition. La Follette promised to gain the support of other progressive Republican senators for Brandeis's nomination. He then canvassed the entire Senate and reported to Gregory that the nomination would be approved. In the end, Brandeis's nomination was approved by a narrow vote of ten to eight in the Senate Judiciary Committee and carried the entire Senate by a vote of 47–22.[7]

La Follette Opposes the War

La Follette and Wilson had shown that they could work together on crucial issues of mutual concern. Nevertheless, this relationship ended in bitter disputes as the president moved to bring the United States into the First World War. La Follette vehemently opposed this decision while continuing to support a position of neutrality in the conflict. This was not simply the stance of an isolationist eager to keep the United States aloof from global concerns. La Follette had consistently opposed U.S. military intervention in Mexico and elsewhere in Latin America. He was a consistent critic of an aggressive foreign policy that he viewed as imperialist. La Follette was also disturbed by the continuing drift toward a more militarized society. His opposition to the president's decision to bring the United States into the First

World War was consistent with his overall stance on militarism and imperialism.[8]

As the United States drifted toward a formal declaration of war, the differences between La Follette and Wilson became more acute. In the middle of February 1917, leaks from the White House indicated that the president was preparing to agree to the arming of civilian merchant ships, including those carrying war materiel to Britain. Philip Franklin, the president of the International Mercantile Marine, formally applied to the Navy requesting the transfer of guns to arm the IMM's fleet of cargo ships. The International Mercantile Marine was a trust created by the investment bank of J. P. Morgan to control commercial shipping. The Morgan bank also acted as the UK government's purchasing agent for the huge supply of goods required to sustain the Allied war effort.[9]

La Follette was convinced that arming merchant ships would bring the United States into the First World War as a combatant. On February 12, 1917, he introduced a resolution designed to trigger a congressional debate on this crucial issue. His resolution held that "it shall be unlawful" for a merchant ship flying the U.S. flag "to be armed" whenever this country was at peace.[10]

La Follette's resolution never reached the Senate floor. Still, it was an important factor behind Wilson's decision to ask Congress for authorization to arm merchant ships rather than implementing this move on his own authority. On February 26, 1917, the president addressed a joint session of Congress and asked for authority to pursue a policy of "armed neutrality." Shortly afterward, his supporters introduced legislation to arm merchant ships. By the time this legislation reached the floor for debate, only three days remained before Congress was set to adjourn. When those senators opposed to the bill initiated a filibuster, the administration's supporters denounced the opposition for arbitrarily thwarting the will of the majority.[11]

In reality, the issue was more complex. Senator William Stone, a Democrat and chair of the Senate Foreign Relations

Committee, was a key figure in the filibuster, speaking continuously for four hours. (Stone died the next year, so this speech, which was met with intense hostility, was undertaken at a significant cost to his health.) During his speech, Stone offered to drop his opposition to the bill if its sponsors would accept an amendment that "expressly forbade" any armed merchant ship from carrying munitions as cargo.[12] The proponents of the bill, acting at the behest of the president, ignored Stone's proposal, and the filibuster proved to be successful.

Wilson was furious, denouncing those who had blocked a vote for derailing a crucial measure during a "crisis of extraordinary peril." The Senate majority had been rendered "powerless, helpless" by "a little group of wilful men representing no opinion but their own."[13] Of course, the president knew full well that those in Congress who opposed the bill to arm merchant ships had the support of many Americans who were concerned by the drift to war, thus the use of shrill denunciations to intimidate them.

La Follette and his allies were convinced that the Armed Ship Bill was intended as a devious step toward a declaration of war on Germany. They were certain that Germany would continue to attack ships laden with military supplies, and the resulting battle with U.S. troops defending these ships would be viewed as an act of war. The intense debate triggered by this bill was indicative of a deeper disagreement. Opponents of the war were sure they had the support of a majority of Americans. La Follette and the progressive opposition believed the president was using a combination of devious tricks and threats to ram through a policy that would otherwise be rejected under the pressure of an aroused populace.[14]

The leadership of the Senate, working closely with the White House, was adamant that La Follette would not be permitted to gain the floor during the debate on arming merchant ships. Thus, ironically, although the *New York Times* insisted that the filibuster had been "largely invented if not directed by Mr. La Follette," he did not actually speak during the extended debate.[15]

This was an unprecedented action. Senators had always had the right to speak, even if their views were in the minority. By covert agreement, Willard Saulsbury Jr., a Democrat from Delaware, acting as the presiding chair in his role as president pro tempore, refused to call on La Follette. The entire Senate upheld the chair's ruling, even though it violated every precedent and the Senate's rules of procedure. La Follette refused to be seated and began shouting his protest. Ollie James, a Kentucky Democrat and a zealous defender of the administration, began crossing the Senate floor, apparently to silence La Follette. Harry Lane, a progressive Democrat from Oregon, followed closely behind James, ready to defend La Follette. Lane later said that he had seen that James was carrying a gun.

A medical doctor, Lane was carrying a long file with a sharp point. He was ready to strike James if he saw any movement toward the gun. Lane had studied anatomy, and he was also terminally ill, so his willingness to use lethal force to stop James from attacking La Follette is plausible. Nevertheless, it is doubtful that James was preparing to shoot La Follette on the Senate floor. Instead, as a rather tall, large man confronting a shorter one, he was probably seeking to physically intimidate La Follette and stop him from further disrupting the proceedings. In any case, there was no altercation and La Follette soon quieted down.[16]

The incident indicates the passionate tensions that roiled Congress as the United States entered the war. As soon as the Armed Ship Bill was defeated by a filibuster, Wilson made it known that he was ready to call Congress into a special session. However, he would not do so until Senate rules were changed to block filibusters. In response, the Senate leadership pushed through a procedural motion that allowed a debate to be terminated by a two-thirds vote, thus ending one hundred and twenty years of unfettered debate.[17]

On April 2, 1917, Wilson addressed a joint session of Congress calling upon them to pass a declaration of war against Germany.

La Follette joined with a small band of senators in opposing the resolution. In a lengthy speech, La Follette rebutted the president's official reasons for abandoning the previous position of neutrality. Wilson insisted that Germany was engaged in indefensible actions in attacking merchant ships without warning.[18] He ignored the fact that these ships carried arms and munitions of direct military value. Furthermore, ships owned by British interests and carrying war materiel to the United Kingdom sometimes flew the U.S. flag to deter German submarine attacks.

La Follette sought to rebut the president's speech while opposing the push toward war. He pointed out that most Americans wanted to remain neutral as a non-combatant nation. Indeed, his office had recently received fifteen thousand letters, with 90 percent opposed to a declaration of war. La Follette challenged the administration to hold a referendum on the issue.[19]

Wilson cited the German submarine campaign as a significant factor that led him to call for a declaration of war. In response, La Follette condemned the British total blockade of Germany and its allies. He insisted that the United States had an "absolute right" to ship food to the German people. The British blockade had "wiped out the established rule of international law." As a result, the "sole responsibility for continuing the unlawful naval warfare rested upon Great Britain."[20]

La Follette then moved beyond an analysis of the immediate conflicts between Germany and the United States to an examination of the underlying causes of the war. In his view, the First World War had "originated in the selfish ambition and cruel greed of a comparatively few men in each Government" who had seen in the war an "opportunity for profit and power."[21]

This was a powerful speech that pulled few punches. The Justice Department prosecuted anyone who made similar comments once the Espionage Act became law in June 1917. Needless to say, the speech caused a furor and guaranteed the enmity of the White House. One issue that La Follette avoided was what led Wilson to bring the United States into the war after carefully sidestepping several incidents that could have provided a rationale for military intervention.

In the early morning hours of April 6, 1917, the Senate approved the declaration of war by a vote of 82 to 6, with the House of Representatives then giving its approval by a vote of 373 to 50.[22] Everyone understood that the president would not tolerate any opposition and that those who continued to raise objections would become the targets of a coordinated campaign of vitriol.

Three weeks later, Wilson returned to Congress to push legislation imposing conscription on men from the age of twenty-one to thirty-one.[23] Once again, La Follette was one of the few in Congress to resist the president. Public opinion, particularly in the Midwest and the West, was overwhelmingly opposed to the draft. Nevertheless, most members of Congress lined up behind the White House.

In a lengthy speech delivered in opposition to the draft, La Follette argued that the federal government had no authority to compel young men to fight in the trenches of the Western Front, thousands of miles from home. There was "no authority in the Constitution to raise an army by draft and send them across the seas." Although Congress had instituted a draft during the Civil War, the situation confronting the United States was an "entirely different proposition." This time, soldiers were being conscripted as "an expeditionary force to carry on a foreign war."[24]

La Follette then went beyond the legal arguments to address broader policy issues. He denounced the entire concept of a conscripted army since "the draft is the corollary of militarism and militarism spells the death of democracy." As he had during his speech opposing the declaration of war, La Follette proposed that an advisory referendum be held before a final vote on conscription. Of course, supporters of the administration's policies were unwilling to put the issue to a popular vote.[25] Finally, La Follette spoke to the broader issues raised by the conflict. The United States should seek to bring "the war to the earliest possible conclusion" based on an equitable peace that did not require the total defeat of either side.[26] La Follette was significantly more careful in the phrasing of this speech than he had been three weeks earlier in opposing the declaration of war. Nevertheless, this was another public challenge to the president's exclusive authority to determine the country's war policy.

The draft was extremely unpopular. Still, Congress approved conscription, and any organized opposition was harshly suppressed.[27]

The President Considers Prosecuting La Follette's Supporters

La Follette had openly defied the president three times in less than two months. There can be little doubt that Wilson had come to view La Follette as a grave threat who had to be neutralized. In early July 1917, Lucius Nieman traveled from Milwaukee, Wisconsin, to Washington, D.C., to confer with influential figures in Congress and the Wilson administration. Although he was unable to see the president, he did hold a meeting with Joseph Tumulty, Wilson's private secretary and de facto chief of staff.[28] An ardent supporter of the war effort, Nieman was deeply concerned by the strength of the antiwar opposition in Wisconsin and Minnesota.

Nieman was the owner and publisher of the *Milwaukee Journal*, the newspaper with the largest circulation in Wisconsin. In general, the *Journal* had aligned itself with the progressive opponents of the conservative mainstream. The *Journal* had supported the reforms proposed by La Follette during his term as governor. The paper's stance changed drastically in March 1917 as the United States edged into an entry into the war as a combatant nation. The *Journal* repeatedly and vociferously denounced La Follette for opposing the war and the draft.[29]

Shortly after returning to Wisconsin, Nieman wrote a memorandum to Senator Paul Husting, a friend and political ally. Nieman was deeply concerned with the growing strength of the opposition to the war, particularly in the German-American community of Wisconsin. Husting sent the memorandum on to Wilson, who read it with interest. The president enclosed it with a letter to the attorney general, Thomas Gregory, along with a warning that the memorandum examined "the activities of our fellow-citizens of German extraction."[30]

It would appear that the issue was left in limbo. The Bureau of Investigation was already closely monitoring the activities of the antiwar opposition in Wisconsin. Still, Nieman remained convinced that more drastic measures were required. He therefore sent Tumulty a letter enclosing clippings from several local newspapers serving towns that were largely composed of those of German descent, along with a warning of the danger posed by the articles. Tumulty passed on Nieman's letter to Wilson. This time, the president prodded Gregory to take action.[31]

Gregory responded that although there were newspapers that continued to print "disloyal matter," nevertheless, "in most cases" this could not be prevented "lawfully." Gregory reassured Wilson that "close attention" to the issue was being given and that the Justice Department would initiate prosecutions under the Espionage Act where warranted.[32]

Nieman's push for a harsher repression of the antiwar opposition in Wisconsin circulated among the administration's decision-makers. Secretary of War Newton Baker was one of those who rejected Nieman's calls. In a confidential letter to the president, Baker conceded that Nieman and Husting were "loyal men" working in "difficult conditions" in Wisconsin, where supporters of the war found themselves in a distinct minority. Nevertheless, their analysis of the situation in the state had been wrong "from the very beginning." Husting had advised Baker that there would be mass resistance to draft registration, and yet the process went smoothly. Indeed, Husting had forecast "riotous disorder" when soldiers were conscripted and yet the city remained calm.[33]

Although the president was warned by a key figure in the

administration to be wary of Nieman's predictions of turmoil in Wisconsin, he ignored this warning. Wilson was fearful of the German-American community's resistance to the war effort. He was also worried that La Follette could provide the leadership required for a popular insurgency.

Nieman's concerns went beyond the German-American press. He therefore followed up his initial letter with another letter to Tumulty that broadened the scope of his worries. Nieman decried the widespread opposition to conscription in Wisconsin and Minnesota led by socialists and "aided by German alliance men and La Follette politicians." There was even a report that La Follette would travel to Wisconsin to personally "campaign against the draft law." Nieman was convinced there was an urgent need to "make an example of traitors."[34]

Nieman enclosed a recent article from the *Milwaukee Journal* concerning an antiwar rally held in New Ulm, Minnesota. New Ulm was a small town ninety miles southwest of Minneapolis. Most of its residents were descendants of German immigrants. The rally, attended by five thousand, decided to circulate a petition opposing the decision to dispatch conscripted soldiers to the battlefields of France and Belgium.[35]

Tumulty passed on this second message to the president. Wilson was impressed by the letter and generally agreed with Nieman's perspective. He later wrote Baker praising Nieman's "extraordinary efforts" to "smoke out the hostile elements" in Wisconsin.[36]

Although the president agreed with the tenor of the letter, he was not prepared at that point to press for the prosecution of antiwar progressives. Wilson advised Tumulty to consult with Gregory to see if the government was doing all it could to deter those questioning the government's war policies. Wilson conceded that anyone was "entitled to make a campaign against the draft law provided they don't stand in the way of the administration of it by any overt acts or improper influences."[37]

The president's formulation granted the government considerable leeway in prosecuting those opposed to the draft. The phrase "improper influences" was so nebulous that it could be interpreted to ban virtually any opposition to the draft.

Gregory's response to this second letter from Nieman does not seem to be included in the archives. Still, it is clear that Gregory was reluctant to prosecute La Follette's progressive supporters in the summer of 1917. This was partly because the Justice Department had set higher priorities for immediate targets. The federal government was about to launch a coordinated assault on the Industrial Workers of the World. The prosecution of the progressive antiwar opposition was kept in abeyance, although La Follette and his supporters came under intense surveillance.

The interchange initiated by Nieman indicates that even in the summer of 1917, only a few months after the United States had entered the war, Wilson viewed La Follette as a credible threat. The president was convinced that the German-American community was sympathetic to imperial Germany. With this as a popular base, La Follette could lead a movement that could stymie the administration's intent to carry on the war to the bitter end. Still, Wilson's advisors understood that La Follette was enormously popular and that it was essential to move carefully.

La Follette Advocates an Immediate Peace

Once war was declared and conscription was imposed, La Follette shifted the focus of his efforts. He insisted that the United States needed to set the terms on which it would agree to a peace settlement with Germany and its allies and that it was incumbent upon Congress to make this determination. Although this argument seemed intended to avoid a confrontation by tacitly accepting the war and conscription, La Follette was actually on a collision course with the White House. Woodrow Wilson reserved the total right to determine every aspect of the U.S. war effort, and he refused to address the issue of peace terms in the months following the declaration of war.[38]

La Follette understood the president's position, but he refused to abandon his position. In June 1917, he wrote to Gilbert Roe, a close friend, and his personal attorney, that it was "important that Congress should not permit itself to be shouldered aside" by the president.[39]

This argument placed the focus of the debate on the power of the executive relative to Congress as mandated by the Constitution. Yet La Follette realized that far more was involved than a jurisdictional dispute within the federal government. Shortly after his letter to Roe, La Follette wrote to his family in Wisconsin that the United States must "not be dragged through years of war to establish imperialism and the exploitation of all the weaker nations of the world." He saw the need for a "campaign along constitutional lines" to achieve policies aimed at "bringing each country out of the war in an honorable and just way."[40]

La Follette's stance was very much in line with that of the leadership of the Socialist Party of America (SP). Leading members of the SP were instrumental in bringing together a loose coalition of progressives and socialists in the People's Council of America for Democracy and the Terms of Peace (PCA).[41] The People's Council and La Follette worked closely together on a campaign to persuade the government to set the terms for peace.

La Follette was convinced that the way to pressure Woodrow Wilson into negotiating an end to the war was by electing antiwar candidates in the 1918 congressional election. Although he was willing to address large rallies with a call to a speedy end to the war, La Follette rejected grassroots protests as a viable strategy. Of course, those who participated in peaceful antiwar protests risked arrest for allegedly violating the Espionage Act. On the other hand, La Follette's electoral strategy permitted the president to pursue his goal of a total victory over Germany unhindered until November 1918, by which time the war was over.

In any case, La Follette believed that the People's Council of America could become the sponsor of a coordinated campaign for antiwar candidates. On August 1, 1917, he cabled the PCA that he was in general support of its program. La Follette urged the organization to mobilize the effort needed to elect candidates opposed to the "war party."[42]

By working in tandem with the People's Council, La Follette and the Socialist Party drew closer. At the same time, the lines between those who supported the administration and those willing to criticize official war policies widened and hardened. In early July 1917, Seymour Stedman, a prominent attorney who would become the Socialist Party's vice-presidential nominee in 1920, joined Clarence Darrow, Gilbert Roe, and other influential figures in a delegation that met with Postmaster General Albert Burleson and top officials of the Justice Department. Congress had authorized the postmaster general to bar any item from the mail that he believed violated the Espionage Act. Burleson was ready to exclude newspapers allied with the Socialist Party from the mail. Government officials proposed that, as an alternative, the newspapers "submit proofs before marking up" an issue.[43]

Although Roe was concerned that the Socialist Party would be pressured into agreeing to this alternative proposal, the leadership of the SP rejected pre-publication censorship, and Burleson proceeded to block socialist newspapers from being delivered by mail. Stedman then went to La Follette to inquire whether he would agree to take over the subscriber list for newspapers aligned with the Socialist Party. Instead, readers would receive *La Follette's Magazine*. La Follette told Stedman that he would consider the proposal. Stedman promised to report back to the Socialist Party's National Executive Committee, but he told La Follette that, although socialists "differed" with him "on many things," the "big thing now was war and democracy." The SP would be "satisfied" with the perspective on the war being advanced in *La Follette's Magazine* "without any change in its policy."[44]

It would appear that nothing ever developed to implement this proposal, but the interchange is indicative of the close working relationship that had developed between La Follette and the leaders of the Socialist Party in the summer of 1917. This budding friendship provided a further reason for the administration to view La Follette as a significant threat. In the fall of 1917, with the Industrial Workers of the World (IWW) already in disarray with dozens of its leaders in jail awaiting charges of violating the Espionage Act, the government turned its attention to the Socialist Party and the People's Council of America.

Peace Terms and Secret Treaties

A further sign of the close links between La Follette and the People's Council occurred a few weeks later when La Follette introduced legislation that would set the terms of peace. His resolution was very similar to proposals already circulated by the People's Council, which in turn paraphrased the peace proposal of the Petrograd Soviet, the most powerful body in Russia following the overthrow of the tsar in March 1917. A few weeks after the czar had been overthrown, the Petrograd Soviet had issued a statement insisting that Russia would only continue to fight on a purely defensive basis. The new government was not interested in the "forcible occupation of foreign territories."[45] Both the People's Council and La Follette focused their proposals on the essential points made in that statement. The Petrograd Soviet had insisted that the war should end soon with a negotiated peace that did not entail punitive reparations or forced annexations of territory.

On August 11, 1917, La Follette introduced his resolution, which soon became the target of vitriolic debate denunciations. In presenting the resolution on peace terms, La Follette sought to counter the terms set by secret treaties signed by the United Kingdom and its allies. La Follette became more aware of these secret treaties in late June 1917 when Lincoln Steffens returned to the United States after a trip to Russia to report on the recent revolution. (Steffens was the most famous of the muckraking journalists.) Steffens came to Washington with a message from Alexander Kerensky to Woodrow Wilson. Kerensky was then the minister of war of the Russian provisional government, but he would soon become its prime minister. Kerensky told Steffens that the Russian people believed the secret treaties were "rotten." Until this issue was "cleared up, Russia will not fight."[46]

Britain, France, Italy, and Czarist Russia had entered into a series of secret agreements dividing territory previously occupied by Germany and its allies, the Austro-Hungarian Empire and the Ottoman Empire.[47] There were rumors in the world press that such agreements had been signed, but the specific provisions were unknown to the public. Kerensky urged Wilson to publicly renounce the treaties, and to then convene a conference of all of the Allied Powers to "abrogate the secret treaties." The Allies would then agree to offer the Central Powers peace terms based on a policy of no annexations and no reparations.[48]

Under pressure from the Allied governments, Kerensky was organizing an attack on German positions by the Russian army. Kerensky informed Steffens that the Russians were preparing to go into battle, but he also told Steffens that he expected the attack "to fail."[49] Indeed, the Russian army launched an attack in June 1917, but the attack soon became a rout as the German army counterattacked.[50] Kerensky was proven to be correct. The Russian army would no longer fight. Instead, soldiers in the trenches insisted on a quick peace and the nullification of the secret treaties.

Steffens and La Follette were close friends. Indeed, Steffens consulted with La Follette before leaving for Russia in April. When he returned from Russia, he immediately reported to La Follette on his trip. The two met on June 25, 1917, a day before

Steffens was to meet with the president. Steffens told La Follette of the message from Kerensky. It is not clear if Steffens knew the exact details of the secret treaties and, if he did, whether he informed La Follette of the specifics.[51]

The next day, Steffens saw the president, who insisted that the British government had not officially informed him of the secret treaties. He thus knew "nothing of those secret treaties" and could not make any public comment on them. In fact, Arthur Balfour, the British foreign secretary, had given the president a complete briefing on the treaties on April 30, 1917, shortly after the United States entered the war. Steffens immediately informed La Follette of his meeting with Wilson after returning from the White House, so La Follette knew the president had been told of the secret treaties and was unwilling to repudiate them.[52]

According to La Follette's daughter Fola, the information received from Steffens "intensified Bob's feeling" that it was necessary to move forward in presenting a resolution on peace terms. The resolution was written by La Follette with the help of Roe and Edwin Borchard, a professor of international law at Columbia University.[53]

In his resolution demanding that Congress set the terms of peace, La Follette indicated his concern that the Allies were determined "to continue the war until" Germany was forced to accept a treaty that imposed "punitive damages and territorial advantages" for the victors. La Follette argued that Congress should assert its "full authority" to determine "the objects and purposes" of the war. The United States should insist that the Allied Powers issue a public statement that they were not seeking "territorial advantages" and that the United States opposed "prolonging the war to annex new territory" or "to enforce the payment of indemnities to recover the expenses of the war." The resolution proposed that, instead of imposing reparations on a defeated Germany, all of the belligerent countries, including the United States, would contribute to a common fund to repair the enormous damage caused by three years of total war. This idea had been included in a version of the Russian Soviet's peace plan.[54]

La Follette went further by including a reference to the secret treaties. Since "the people of this country" had not been informed of "the terms of the secret treaties," these should be made public so everyone could understand the current situation.[55] Of course, the Allies refused to reveal their secret understandings. However, the Bolsheviks did publish the treaties shortly after coming to power in November 1917.[56] La Follette's peace proposal put the administration in an awkward situation since the president refused to define the U.S. goals in entering the war. Thus, the intention of the resolution was to add to the public pressure on Wilson to clarify his position.

Still, La Follette's resolution was fundamentally flawed. The UK government had already rejected the Russian Soviet's proposal. Even if Congress had approved the resolution, it would have been ignored by the other countries in the Allied Powers coalition. The only way such a proposal could have had a cutting edge is if it were accompanied by a willingness to leave the war should the proposal be rejected. La Follette was unwilling to put this threat forward as a part of his resolution.

Nevertheless, despite its limitations, La Follette's resolution met with the bitter opposition of the administration and its supporters. Senators sympathetic to the White House viewed it as a deliberate effort to "embarrass" the president. They were intent on overwhelmingly defeating it after the briefest of debates. Once La Follette introduced the peace terms resolution, Wilson was determined to make sure that he was silenced.

As a first step, the president called key Democratic Party senators to the White House to discuss how La Follette could be prevented from using Congress as a platform and how to ensure that the resolution was quickly defeated by an overwhelming vote. Senator William King, a Democrat from Utah, brought back Wilson's plan, and a closed meeting of Senate leaders from both parties was then convened to work out the details. If La Follette was recognized by the chair and began to speak on the need to define peace terms, the Senate would immediately vote to go into a secret executive session. Furthermore, once the peace terms resolution was defeated, any further motions along these lines by La Follette or any other senator would be tabled and would never reach the floor for a vote.[57]

Thus, by August 1917, efforts were already underway to silence La Follette. In the past, senators had been granted a great deal of leeway in presenting their views on controversial issues, even when those views represented a minority opinion. The Senate had already revised the rules so that a few senators could not block the enactment of legislation, but Senate leaders, under prodding from the president, were going even further by preventing La Follette from raising a critical perspective on a vital issue in a public session.

La Follette Speaks Out

As the most prominent voice for progressive politics, La Follette had a national reputation, and thus could attract a large audience by speaking at public forums. A key occasion arose in September 1917, when he was invited to address a mass rally at the Conference of Producers and Consumers in St. Paul, Minnesota. This event was organized by the Nonpartisan League (NPL) to pressure the president to rein in consumer prices while increasing taxes on corporate profits.[58] The conference would provide La Follette with a platform to reinforce his position as the leading voice for progressive politics while bolstering his status as a viable presidential candidate.

As the most popular progressive politician, La Follette had become the leading spokesperson for the loose network of liberals and pacifists who disapproved of the administration's war policies and were dismayed by the government's harsh suppression of dissenting opinions. Yet La Follette was more than this. The administration feared that he could become the presidential candidate of a new, independent party. The formation of such a party would place centrist Democrats such as Woodrow Wilson in a difficult bind. It could also ensure that the Republican Party became the dominant party at the national level.

La Follette had sought the Republican nomination for president in 1912. He was likely considering a campaign in 1920 as an independent candidate. Theodore Roosevelt had already shown that one could stand as an independent presidential candidate and still return to a mainstream party. After his 1912 campaign for president for the newly formed Progressive Party, Roosevelt rejoined the Republican Party. He worked for its presidential candidate, Charles Evan Hughes, in the 1916 election.[59]

Nevertheless, there is no reason to believe that La Follette was interested in leading a party truly independent of the two-party system. In 1924, he would stand as an independent presidential candidate and gain considerable support. During this campaign, La Follette made it clear that he opposed the creation of an independent progressive party, although he left such a step as a possible option for an indefinite point in the future. After the 1924 campaign had ended, he returned to the Senate as a member of the Republican Party's caucus.[60]

La Follette remained on the edge of the two-party system. Nevertheless, the Wilson administration was convinced that La Follette was intent on becoming the leader of a new party. An article in the *New York Times*, a newspaper closely aligned with the Democratic Party, stated incorrectly that La Follette was "at the head of a movement to found a new party."[61] After all, La Follette's speeches at mass rallies allowed him to directly connect with the grassroots activists needed to make a potential new party a reality.

The speech at the conference sponsored by the Nonpartisan League gave La Follette the opportunity to speak to thousands of progressive activists. Aware of the threat this posed, the administration and its congressional supporters were ready to pounce on any controversial comment made by La Follette, hoping that he could be intimidated into remaining silent. In doing so, they could suppress an influential critic of the president's war policies, while also blocking the effort to bring together an electoral coalition of antiwar congressional candidates for the 1918 election.

By the time of the St. Paul conference in September 1917, Arthur Townley and the NPL's leadership had already reached a confidential agreement with George Creel and the government's Committee on Public Information. The Nonpartisan League was committed to supporting the war effort, so its leaders were determined to exclude any criticism of the administration's war policies from the conference.

La Follette was scheduled to speak on the last evening of the conference, September 20, 1917. His talk drew a huge audience; ten thousand people filled the auditorium, and more listened to the speech on speakers set up outside. La Follette had prepared a lengthy speech on the need for free speech in wartime and the critical role of Congress in determining the terms of peace. The NPL's leadership was aware of La Follette's break with the president on the war, so they sought to keep La Follette on track and away from any mention of the administration's war policies. James Manahan, a progressive attorney who had served one term in the U.S. House of Representatives, was sent to La Follette with that urgent message. La Follette reluctantly agreed to confine his comments to issues related to the financing of the war. The two then worked together on a set of notes which were to provide the outlines of the speech.[62]

La Follette's speech was being closely monitored by the federal government. Several Bureau of Investigation (BI) agents attended the talk, along with agents from the Treasury Department's Secret Service. One of the BI agents took shorthand notes. Alfred Jaques, the U.S. attorney for Minnesota, reviewed these notes and concluded that La Follette's speech had been "contemptible," but that "no criminal law" had been "violated."[63]

La Follette would later claim that he had diverged from his intended message in response to hecklers in the audience. Yet the transcript of the speech, as approved by him, indicate that this is only partially true. The enthusiastic response from the audience led La Follette to depart from his prepared notes to address his criticisms of the administration's decision to enter the war and the heckling of a few pro-war zealots sparked even more controversial comments.

La Follette began by focusing on corporations that were reaping excessive profits from the wartime boom. He derided the administration's decision to finance the war largely through government bonds and proposed that Congress levy a steep tax on corporate profits instead. His speech was met with enormous applause. At that point, La Follette put away his notes and said he would speak more informally. He began by saying that he had not been "in favor of beginning the war." The right of a U.S. citizen to travel on a ship carrying munitions to a war zone was a privilege "too small to involve the government in the loss of millions and millions of lives."

Nevertheless, he conceded that the United States "had at the hands of Germany serious grievances." However, these grievances had provided an "insufficient" basis to go to war. (This statement would be distorted in some reports of the speech.) These comments brought a cry of "yellow" from a heckler. La Follette then responded that the United States should not "have gone into the war for that poor privilege."[64]

La Follette then returned to the primary topic of his speech, pointing to certain munition makers that were "making enormous profits" and who should be heavily taxed to fund the war effort. After a few minutes, he turned again to question the administration's war policies. If the primary reasons for the conflict were the "loans the house of Morgan make to foreign governments and the profits the munition makers will earn," then his doubts about the decision to enter the war had been correct.

La Follette had already gone well beyond the limits of dissent tolerated by the administration, but a heckler prodded him even further. In response to his comment on the underlying causes of the war, another member of the audience shouted: "How about the *Lusitania*?" La Follette countered that he would give the audience "some history" that had "not been given" to the public "here before."

The *Lusitania* had been carrying six million rounds of ammunition and a considerable quantity of explosives. According to La Follette, the German ambassador, Bernstorff, had gone to Secretary of State William Jennings Bryan to warn him that his government considered the Lusitania a legitimate target and that it was likely to be sunk by a German submarine. Bryan then contacted the White House to advise the president that the *Lusitania* was carrying munitions and to pass on Bernstorff's warning. La Follette reported that Bryan had gone even further, advising Wilson "to stop passengers" from sailing on the *Lusitania.*

Although La Follette's comments on the war were controversial in their entirety, it was his charge that Wilson had been warned beforehand that the *Lusitania* might be sunk that caused the most furore. Bryan claimed that he did not know the *Lusitania* was carrying munitions, and he vehemently denied that he had gone to the president with the warning that the German government was intent on sinking the *Lusitania.* Wilson confirmed Bryan's denial.[65] From this point onward, La Follette became a priority target for government repression.

The speech was met with a thunderous ovation. La Follette was fairly quoted in many newspapers around the country, but the Associated Press distributed an erroneous report around the country claiming that he had insisted that the United States had suffered "no grievances" in relation to German attacks on ships carrying U.S. civilians. For eight months, the AP refused to correct this mistaken report. Later, the AP claimed that it had not been aware that La Follette believed that he had been misquoted, a totally unconvincing excuse.[66] In fact, La Follette was quick to insist that there had been "wholly false reports" of his St. Paul speech.[67]

The entire incident can only be understood in the context of the campaign of vilification and distortion directed at La Follette and covertly coordinated by the government. Still, leaving the distorted phrase aside, it is clear that La Follette's speech challenged Wilson's decision to bring the United States into the war. Other opponents of the war who made similar comments were prosecuted under the Espionage Act.

After his speech in St. Paul, La Follette traveled to Toledo, Ohio, to address a forum sponsored by an organization affiliated with the People's Council of America. The speech had been scheduled before his trip to Minnesota.[68] The audience was sympathetic, and no hecklers marred the event. Nevertheless, La Follette continued to criticize the administration's war policies.

In his Toledo speech, La Follette emphasized the necessity of Congress determining peace terms. He also condemned the congressional vote to approve the declaration of war as "not the representative of a democratic government." Although La Follette neither discussed the sinking of the *Lusitania* nor the issue of conscription, he did argue that a popular referendum should be held before the United States entered into a future war, except in the exceptional circumstance that the country was threatened by an imminent invasion.[69]

The comments that La Follette had made in his speeches in both St. Paul and Toledo clearly exceeded the narrowly limited boundaries to free speech set by the Espionage Act as enforced by the Department of Justice. Virtually any criticisms of the administration's war policies were viewed by government attorneys as obstructions to the war effort and, therefore, not protected by the Constitution's Bill of Rights.

La Follette understood that his position had become tenuous

and that if he continued to challenge the administration's war policies in public speeches or articles in his magazine he could find himself indicted for sedition. The Toledo speech would be the last speech presented by La Follette in a public forum until the war ended with Germany's unconditional surrender fourteen months later. The decision to stop delivering public speeches indicates his awareness of the dangers he confronted.

La Follette was not being paranoid. Justice Department attorneys were closely monitoring his speeches. In January 1918, John Lord O'Brian wrote to the Post Office inquiring whether printed copies of La Follette's speeches were being permitted in the mail. (O'Brian was the director of the War Emergency Division, the section of the Justice Department charged with enforcing the wartime laws aimed at silencing opponents of the war.) O'Brian was particularly interested in copies of La Follette's speech on the Senate floor in April 1917 in opposition to the declaration of war. William Lamar, the solicitor of the Post Office, replied that copies of La Follette's speeches were still being allowed in the mail.[70]

O'Brian informed the Post Office that the Justice Department was "examining" whether the distribution of La Follette's speeches violated the Espionage Act.[71] This letter is ominous. It suggests that the Justice Department was seriously investigating the possibility of prosecuting La Follette for his speeches.

Under Article 1, Section 6, of the Constitution, members of Congress are "privileged from Arrest" for "any Speech or Debate in either House," and they "shall not be questioned in any other Place" concerning these speeches. Judicial rulings had confirmed that speeches made by a member of Congress during a floor debate on an issue of public policy concern were protected from prosecution. The issue of whether this immunity extended to speeches made in a public forum was still undetermined as of the First World War. The lack of clarity as to the law, as well as the political costs to the administration of prosecuting a popular senator, deterred the Justice Department from pursuing an indictment. On the other hand, had La Follette been expelled from the Senate, he would likely have been indicted if he had continued to speak out against the war.[72]

La Follette understood that the Justice Department was closely monitoring his activities. Shortly after returning to Washington from his trip to the Midwest, La Follette wrote to his family in Wisconsin that "we need to be very careful" in determining which articles to print in the magazine. The Justice Department "should not be given the slightest chance to complain."[73]

Thus, less than six months after the United States had entered the war, La Follette was already retreating from his position of open opposition. Self-censorship made it easy for the government to suppress dissent. Many newspapers aligned with the Socialist Party refused to buckle and, as a result, were shut down. La Follette understood that "the feeling against me" was "very bitter in administration circles," so he opted to pull back and seek a safer course.[74]

The Threat of Expulsion

As La Follette acted to censor himself in the public arena, he also found his position in the Senate under attack. Petitions from around the country were sent to Congress demanding his expulsion. Article 1, Section 5, of the Constitution allows both houses of Congress to expel one of its members by a two-thirds vote of that house. Most senators who have been expelled were charged with supporting the Confederate States during the Civil War. Several senators have resigned when confronted with the probability of expulsion based on corruption or a fraudulent election. La Follette's case was unique. He was threatened with expulsion for expressing a dissident point of view.[75]

At first, the Senate leadership was inclined to ignore the issue, believing that La Follette's expulsion would only increase his popularity and result in his reelection with an overwhelming vote of support. Nevertheless, on October 5, 1917, the Senate held a closed executive session to consider the matter. The Senate Committee on Privileges and Elections was authorized to hold hearings to determine what exactly was said during the St. Paul speech and to ascertain whether the assertions made by La Follette were accurate. In turn, the committee established a five-person subcommittee headed by its chair, Senator Atlee Pomerene, a Democrat from Ohio.[76]

La Follette demanded the right to respond to the calls for his expulsion publicly and was granted a three-hour time slot. His speech on October 6 took up most of the allotted time. It has come to be considered one of the most effective speeches ever made on the Senate floor. When it ended, most senators made a point of ostracizing La Follette, who was rapidly becoming an outcast among his congressional peers.[77]

Unlike the St. Paul speech, the Senate speech was carefully written and delivered. It incorporated much of what La Follette intended to say in St. Paul before being pressured by the leadership of the Nonpartisan League. Most of the speech focused on the repression directed at those who opposed the war and the threat this posed to the maintenance of civil liberties. According to La Follette, "the war party" had "sought to intimidate" those who criticized the government's war policies. As a result, "honest and law-abiding citizens of the country" were being "terrorized" with the explicit purpose being "to stifle criticism and suppress discussion of the great issues involved in the war."[78] Although La Follette did not directly link the president and his administration to this concerted assault on fundamental civil liberties, the inference was clear.

La Follette also presented a theoretical defense of free speech during wartime that directly contradicted the "clear and present danger" doctrine that would later be formulated by Oliver Wendell Holmes Jr. (The speech was written with the assistance of Gilbert Roe, an attorney who had presented briefs on this issue to the Supreme Court, and Edwin Borchard, a professor at the Columbia University Law School.)[79] In La Follette's view, both "the citizen and his representative in Congress must maintain his right of free speech." Indeed, it was even more true "in time of war" that one "must maintain his right of free speech."

Having described the wartime hysteria with its disregard for the rights of dissenters, La Follette then addressed the caustic attacks on him. In accord with "the general campaign of vilification and attempted intimidation," the proponents of the war were demanding his expulsion from the Senate. Still, despite the personal attacks, La Follette pledged to stand firm: "Neither the clamor of the mob nor the voice of power will ever turn me by the breadth of a hair from the course I mark out for myself." La Follette thus set a high standard for courageous behavior in the face of repression and personal attacks. It was a standard that La Follette would fail to meet.

La Follette moved from the issue of free speech to the questions raised by the war, specifically his belief that it was incumbent upon Congress to determine peace terms. It was essential that Congress "exercise in full the war powers" it had been granted by the Constitution if the United States were to "extricate" itself from the war and bring about "an honorable and lasting peace." In particular, the United States had to declare that it was "not seeking to dictate a form of government to Germany." (Wilson had made it clear that he would not negotiate with the German government for as long as the Kaiser held power.) Also, this country had to specify that it had not entered the war "to render more secure England's domination of the seas."

These were the two major themes of the Senate speech: a defense of free speech and a call for Congress to set the terms for a peace treaty. A speech along these lines fell along the outer limits of what was permitted under the guidelines set by the Justice Department in enforcing the Espionage Act. Still, La Follette made comments in passing that would have certainly led to his arrest had they been made by an activist speaking at an antiwar rally.

In general, La Follette avoided a public discussion of the sensitive issue of conscription. Nevertheless, in his speech to the Senate in October 1917, he asserted that the Constitution had assigned Congress the right to declare war because the U.S. House of Representatives was elected every two years, along with one-third of the Senate, so an aroused populace could quickly turn out of office those who had approved "an unwise declaration of war, especially a war of aggression."[80] La Follette hoped to do just this in the November 1918 election. He believed that a coalition that included his supporters and the organizations linked to the People's Council could provide the base of support needed to elect antiwar candidates to Congress, who could then force the president to rapidly conclude the war.

Still, a great deal of harm could be done in two years. La Follette held that the authors of the Constitution sought to protect against such a contingency by providing for a purely volunteer army. "Voluntary enlistment" was "the only system of raising an army for use outside of the country" that was even considered by the delegates at the constitutional convention. Thus, "the people could force a settlement of any war to which they were opposed by the single measure of not volunteering to fight it."[81]

Of course, Wilson was well aware of this potential roadblock to his plans for the war. The president had therefore pushed through Congress legislation implementing a draft that would force millions of men into the military and into the trenches of the Western Front. According to La Follette's own argument, given conscription, there was no "constitutional" means for bringing a rapid end to the First World War. The only possibility was a mass movement of organized protests to pressure Congress into calling for negotiations and an equitable peace treaty. La Follette always avoided this logical conclusion and, instead, remained committed to working within a system that had disastrously failed.

Although he did not explicitly state this in his speech, La

Follette was challenging the constitutionality of the legislation creating a conscripted army that would be sent overseas. The Supreme Court denied the challenge to the statute by a unanimous vote in January 1918, another indication that relying on the system would prove to be futile.[82] Since the administration understood that the draft was the most vulnerable link in the war effort, those who made arguments similar to those advanced by La Follette were frequently prosecuted for violating the Espionage Act and often wound up spending years in a federal penitentiary.

In his Senate speech on October 6, 1917, La Follette castigated the president for seeking total control over war policy. The framers of the Constitution had understood that giving anyone, be that person monarch or president, this kind of power "meant despotism." The result would be aggressive wars that necessarily arose from "secret diplomacy and secret treaties." This "system of secret diplomacy" had "plunged the helpless peoples of Europe in the awful war" that threatened "to engulf the world before it stops." If the United States were to "forestall the danger of being drawn into years of war," a conflict that was based on "imperialism and exploitation," it was necessary to campaign for a free discussion of the issue related to the war, culminating in "its conclusion on a just basis."[83] This analysis of the underlying causes of the war was similar to those often made by dissidents, who were then prosecuted for violating the Espionage Act.

La Follette's speech raised several important points and provided a rallying point for the antiwar opposition. Nevertheless, despite his insistence that he would not be intimidated, La Follette did not detail his vision of a just peace. Furthermore, La Follette did not reveal to the public that the president had been informed of the secret treaties and had refused to repudiate them. This in a speech that lasted more than two hours. Still, the speech went well beyond the circumscribed limits set by government authorities. It greatly increased the determination of the administration to silence La Follette.

Demonizing La Follette

The speech in October 1917 delivered on the Senate floor was the final event to convince the Wilson administration that La Follette was a significant threat and that he had to be silenced. Countering La Follette's influence required more than shutting down possible forums for his views. The government opted to discredit La Follette by initiating a coordinated effort to malign him through a covert operation of psychological warfare involving both government agencies and a private, non-profit organization funded and controlled by the wealthy and powerful.

The president had given George Creel and the Committee on Public Information the primary responsibility for molding public opinion. Creel worked closely with Woodrow Wilson, who personally supervised the CPI's activities.[84] Thus, the campaign of vilification and misinformation directed at La Follette could only have been implemented with presidential approval.

Creel opted to work through the American Defense Society (ADS) in leading a propaganda campaign to discredit La Follette. The ADS was an organization committed to seeing the war fought to the end, that is, to the total surrender of Germany. It believed that any opposition to the war, no matter how cautiously phrased, constituted treason and should be treated accordingly. La Follette's speech in St. Paul convinced the organization that he had become the leading spokesperson for the antiwar opposition and thus had to be harshly punished. On September 25, 1917, five days after the St. Paul speech, the ADS executive committee agreed that it would "devote all its energies to ensure La Follette's expulsion from the Senate." This would only be the first step. If La Follette and any other member of Congress continued to speak out against the war after their expulsion, the ADS would push for "their prompt imprisonment" as "traitors."[85]

The Committee on Public Information and the American

Defense Society had a common goal and were soon working together to implement a covert program. On October 13, 1917, a week after La Follette's Senate speech, an internal memorandum from the American Defense Society reported that Creel had asked the organization to move its publicity bureau to Washington, D.C., so that the bureau could be located near Creel's office at the CPI's headquarters. The move would enable it to "work in closest cooperation with him." ADS publicity bureau staff members, mostly former journalists, would be given access to certain confidential, secret government documents. They would then write statements to the press promoting the official war policy. Before their publication, these statements would be vetted by Creel.[86]

This project involved a dangerous blurring of the distinction between a government agency and private advocacy organizations. Creel had an even more important project in mind for the American Defense Society. Its publicity bureau "could handle many topics (such as an attack on Senator La Follette) which a governmental agency could not handle." The president was desperate to destroy La Follette's credibility. Still, he understood that his standing as a progressive reformer would be irrevocably tarnished if his role in promoting this personal attack were to become public. Instead, the American Defense Society was recruited by Creel to spearhead a secret campaign to destroy La Follette's reputation, a campaign that would also involve propaganda organizations directly controlled by the government. Several individuals involved in the covert campaign of slander aimed at La Follette were members of the group of pro-war socialists that was closely aligned to Gompers and the Committee on Public Information.

ADS executive officers sent the secret memorandum to a selected group of wealthy donors. Creel had suggested that the publicity bureau would need a budget of $100,000, presumably for the coming year, to put these projects into motion. (This would come to more than two million dollars today, enough to hire a considerable staff.) The purpose of the memorandum was to solicit funds from wealthy donors, but it is also possible that part of the cost was met by an allocation from the president's secret, unaudited national security fund, which provided most of the funds for the CPI. In any case, there can be little doubt that the ADS proceeded to implement Creel's proposal.

Every time that he had spoken out against the administration's war policies, La Follette had been subjected to vitriolic personal attacks. Still, these attacks were uncoordinated and soon subsided. This time, following the St. Paul speech, the personal attacks did not lessen over time, but rather became even more strident over the following months. One of the most prominent of these denunciations was a resolution approved by the Minnesota Commission of Public Safety. A state agency given wide authority to suppress dissent, the commission issued a statement condemning La Follette's St. Paul speech as "disloyal and seditious." La Follette should be expelled from the Senate since his speech had given "aid and comfort" to "our enemies" and was, therefore, the act of a traitor.[87]

The effort to destroy La Follette's reputation did not only rely on articles denigrating him at every level, political and personal. The ADS also organized a mass rally at Carnegie Hall in New York City on November 2, 1917. James Beck, the chair of the ADS Disloyalty Committee and a former assistant attorney general, gave the keynote speech. He held it a "matter of supreme and vital importance" that "no man, be he in the Senate" or the editor of a newspaper should be permitted to disseminate "the subtle poison of sedition." The crowd then approved a resolution denouncing La Follette as a "traitor" and demanding his expulsion from the Senate for promoting a "dishonorable peace."[88]

In organizing the rally, the ADS tried to coalesce a coalition that went beyond conservative corporate Republicans. Samuel Gompers, the president of the American Federation of Labor and a vociferous defender of the administration's war policies, was also a featured speaker. The rally was thus indicative of the informal network that started with Creel and the CPI and included Gompers and the American Defense Society.

By appearing at this rally, Gompers implicitly gave public support to the ADS and its bellicose attacks on those who questioned the administration's policies. In his brief speech, Gompers insisted that the AFL believed the war should continue until Germany was completely defeated. This policy of demanding total victory was justified because the Kaiser was the "new vampire of the world."[89]

The campaign to discredit La Follette also gained the assistance of former president Teddy Roosevelt. As honorary chair of the ADS, Roosevelt did not oversee the organization's daily affairs, but he did keep in close touch with its leadership. On a tour through the Midwest, he repeatedly demanded La Follette's expulsion, calling him a "neo-copperhead." In Kansas City, he condemned La Follette for "loyally serving one country—Germany."[90]

In private, Roosevelt stressed the necessity of discrediting La Follette. Writing to one of his sons in November 1917, Roosevelt wrote that La Follette was "the most dangerous leader" of those opposing the war effort, since he had become the spokesperson for the loose antiwar coalition that included the IWW, the Socialist Party, "and the professional pacifists."[91]

As strident as the American Defense Society was in its efforts to discredit La Follette, Creel understood the necessity of broadening the range of those joining in the attack. One key figure in this widening campaign of vituperation was Charles Edward Russell. A leading muckraker, Russell joined the Socialist Party in 1908. He raised money for La Follette during his 1910 campaign for reelection to the Senate. La Follette viewed Russell as a friend and yet once the First World War began the two moved in opposite directions. Russell supported the preparedness campaign in the fall of 1915, which the president had initiated with the aim of arming the United States in preparation for a possible entrance into the war. Until then he had been seen as the likely presidential candidate for the Socialist Party in the 1916 campaign. Once the United States declared war on Germany, Russell enthusiastically supported the war effort and bitterly condemned those who criticized the administration. He was then appointed by Wilson to the Root Commission that was sent to Russia in the summer of 1917 with the goal of keeping that country in the war.[92]

Upon his return, Russell spoke at the Union League Club on the need to aid the provisional government of Russia. The Union League Club had an exclusive membership that included most of the wealthiest capitalists in the country, such as J. P. Morgan Jr. and John D. Rockefeller. During his speech, Russell assailed those who opposed the war and called for an immediate peace. In particular, he condemned La Follette as "a disloyal American, a traitor in disguise" who was doing "the dirty work of the Kaiser."[93]

Although Russell had initially focused his attacks on his former comrades in the Socialist Party, he soon turned to La Follette as a primary target. In an extensive interview with the *New York Times,* Russell emphasized the necessity of supporting the provisional government in Russia led by Kerensky. Russell also criticized the peace movement for undermining morale. In passing, he denounced La Follette's peace resolution as a "strange and sinister outburst of pacifism." [94]

Once he began touring the country in the fall of 1917, Russell focused his attacks on La Follette. In September, he spoke in Minnesota, declaring that La Follette and Senator William Stone were "the most awful traitors" and should be "thrown out of Congress."[95]

The attacks on La Follette during the fall of 1917 were unrelenting. Newspaper articles published around the country assailed La Follette as a traitor. In an editorial, the *New York Times* denounced his Senate speech given on October 6 as "seditious" for "uttering words for the encouragement" of the "German enemies." Indeed, La Follette's actions as a senator were "nothing less than treachery to the national cause."[96]

In November 1917, the *New York Tribune* published two

lengthy articles of vituperative denunciations of La Follette. These articles were reprinted by other newspapers, including the *Wisconsin State Journal,* which reprinted one of them. Both articles were written by Samuel Hopkins Adams, a well-known writer and muckraking journalist. Adams had joined the staff of the Committee on Public Information as an unpaid volunteer. In this role, he wrote articles that the CPI's features bureau syndicated.[97] Creel and the CPI did not officially commission the articles for the *Tribune*. Still, they clearly represented the viewpoint of the Wilson administration.

In the first of the two *Tribune* articles, Adams condemned the "near-treason" of La Follette's speech in St. Paul and "his malign and potent influence against the Liberty Bond subscription." The second article went further. La Follette served as "the mouthpiece and the leader" of the "pro-German and pacifist elements" in Wisconsin.[98]

La Follette Under Attack

The coordinated campaign of personal attacks took its toll on La Follette. Although he had been a respected senior member of Congress, most of his colleagues began to avoid him. Having been an influential public figure, La Follette was now vilified. He had become a priority target of government repression.

The menace underlying the public attacks and the threats of expulsion also had economic implications. La Follette relied on thousands of dollars in fees received from speaking engagements to finance his luxurious lifestyle. In 1905, he purchased a large estate of sixty acres, complete with a mansion, located along a lake on the outskirts of Madison, Wisconsin. The property cost $30,000, substantially more than $500,000 at current prices. With a salary as a senator of $7,500, La Follette found it difficult to meet the costs required to maintain this estate and his house in Washington, D.C. He was, therefore, forced to seek a second mortgage on the Madison property.[99]

As a controversial figure under siege, La Follette found that fees from speaking engagements began to dwindle. Thus, part of the pressure to conform came from the threat to his economic status. In a letter in early January, La Follette claimed that there were people "who would ruin" him "financially and beggar my family if the slightest chance offered."[100] In reality, La Follette lived quite comfortably and was far from destitute. Nevertheless, had he been expelled from the Senate, he would have been compelled to sell his Wisconsin estate and live on a more modest scale.

The economic pressure on La Follette also involved his magazine. In 1909, La Follette had launched this venture with financial support from Charles Crane. A supporter of progressive causes, Crane had inherited a small fortune from his father who had founded a lucrative firm that produced plumbing fixtures. Crane later became a major contributor to Woodrow Wilson's presidential campaigns. As a staunch supporter of the war effort, he was not likely to continue subsidizing a journal that criticized the administration's policies.[101]

La Follette Threatened with Expulsion

Although the attacks on La Follette came from many directions, the one that most concerned him was the threat of expulsion from the Senate. Shortly after the speech in St. Paul had been delivered, Wilson summoned several influential senators to the White House. That morning, he met with John Sharp Williams, a Democrat from Mississippi. Williams was La Follette's most caustic critic. Although Senate rules prohibited personal attacks, Williams repeatedly did just that. For instance, in response to the April 1917 speech in opposition to the declaration of war, Williams derided La Follette for a presentation that was "pro-German, pro-Goth, pro-vandal," and "anti-American."[102]

That afternoon, the president met with Senator Atlee Pomerene, a Democrat from Ohio and the chair of the sub-committee that would consider La Follette's expulsion. After the meeting, Pomerene briefed reporters. Wilson had denied that Bryan had warned him before the sinking of the *Lusitania* that it was likely to be attacked since it carried munitions.[103] Obviously, the president found the charges made by La Follette to be highly damaging.

The specific basis for the move to expel La Follette arose when Senator Frank Kellogg, a Democrat from Minnesota, submitted the resolution from the Minnesota Commission on Public Safety to the Senate on September 29, 1917. The Senate then referred the resolution to the Committee on Privileges and Elections, which then established a special sub-committee to investigate the charge and report back to the full committee.[104]

The special sub-committee seemed ready to move quickly when it was first established. On October 16, 1917, La Follette was called before the sub-committee to testify as to exactly what he had said during the St. Paul speech. At first, La Follette was reluctant to testify, insisting that he should first be furnished with a list of the comments he had made that were being cited as the basis for the investigation. Despite his repeated requests, Senator Atlee Pomerene, as the sub-committee chair, refused to inform La Follette of the specific sections of the St. Paul speech that were in dispute.[105]

In his first appearance before the sub-committee, La Follette attempted to go on the offensive, demanding that those submitting evidence that claimed to contradict the validity of his version of the facts should appear in person before the sub-committee where he could cross-examine them. This proposal was aimed at former Secretary of State William Jennings Bryan. Furthermore, La Follette also insisted that he still believed "all the statements contained" in his St. Paul speech "to be correct." He was ready to present "witnesses and documents to substantiate every statement" he had made.[106]

Pomerene replied to these demands by agreeing that any witnesses before the sub-committee would be subject to cross-examination by La Follette's attorneys. Furthermore, Pomerene specified that the sub-committee's investigation would focus on the speech at the NPL conference in September and whether "the statements contained therein [were] accurate."[107]

Thus, Bryan would be subject to a hostile cross-examination on his knowledge of the events surrounding the sinking of the *Lusitania.* At first, it appeared that the sub-committee was prepared to move forward in implementing its mandate. On Saturday, December 1, 1917, Pomerene notified La Follette that Bryan was about to arrive in Washington, D.C., and that the sub-committee would hear his testimony that Monday, December 3.[108]

This would mark the furthest point that the expulsion process would reach. The hearing on December 3, 1917, was canceled. Clearly, Bryan was unwilling to testify that he had not known of any credible warnings concerning the *Lusitania* before its sinking and that he had not gone to the president with his concerns. Without Bryan's testimony, the expulsion proceedings were stymied.

Nevertheless, La Follette's continued assertion that his comments on the *Lusitania* were truthful gave the administration another salient reason to view La Follette as a hostile menace. It is unclear if La Follette had obtained the secret documents that could have proven that Wilson had been warned of the attack on the *Lusitania* before it happened, but the mere threat that he did would have caused consternation at the White House.

The matter seemed to reach a stalemate, with La Follette refusing to cooperate and the sub-committee unwilling to call witnesses. Yet this was only a surface appearance. In reality, the sub-committee had left La Follette hanging, fearful that his next public criticism of the administration would lead to his swift expulsion from the Senate. Following his initial appearance before the special sub-committee, La Follette spent "night after night" huddling with his closest associates, planning the next move in his defense.[109] Of course, this is exactly what the administration had been trying to accomplish. Previously, La Follette had taken the initiative in criticizing the administration's war policies. Threatened with expulsion, he devoted his time and energy to defending himself and protecting his position as a member of the Senate.

In December 1917, the American Defense Society submitted a lengthy brief to the Senate sub-committee investigating La Follette. The brief was given a great deal of favorable publicity, thus adding to the pressure on the Senate to expel La Follette. An extensive extract from the ADS brief was printed in the *New York Times*. La Follette had been "disloyal to the government" in questioning the administration's war policies. Indeed, "regardless of his intent," La Follette was "giving aid and comfort to the public enemy," that is, he was guilty of treason.[110]

At the end of 1917, the sub-committee submitted a report to the Senate blasting La Follette and suggesting that his actions were treasonous. The sub-committee argued that anyone who uttered seditious comments during a time of war had taken actions that might "constitute him a traitor."[111]

In a written response, La Follette, through his attorney Gilbert Roe, reiterated his belief that his St. Paul speech had been based on the facts and should not be censured. He then went on to point out that La Follette had "remained silent" during the previous months, believing that the sub-committee investigation was "quasi-judicial" and that its findings "should be arrived at uninfluenced by anything except the facts."[112]

Thus, La Follette had entirely retreated, abandoning his role as the leading critic of the administration's war policies. He had stopped giving public speeches after the crescendo of venomous attacks following the St. Paul speech. Repressive legislation, in particular the Espionage Act and the Trading with the Enemy Act, convinced him to avoid printing any controversial comments in his magazine. Finally, the threat of expulsion had kept him from speaking on the Senate floor in opposition to the administration.

Targeting the Capital Times

By November 1917, La Follette had been effectively silenced. Nevertheless, the federal government continued to look for ways to discredit him. Mainstream newspapers, particularly those in Wisconsin, printed a steady stream of articles denouncing La Follette, insisting that he was pro-German in his position on the war. The *Wisconsin State Journal* was at the forefront of this campaign of vilification.

The *State Journal was* published in Madison, the second largest city in Wisconsin and the state capital. Madison was La Follette's home and the place where most of his closest friends lived. Although the *State Journal* had a long history, its recent past was closely linked to La Follette. In 1911, Richard Lloyd Jones raised $100,000 from a group of La Follette's supporters to purchase the papers. Once again, Charles Crane provided much of the money, investing $40,000 in the venture, a sum worth more than $500,000 in current dollars.[113] The *State Journal* then became a staunch supporter of social reforms and a media outlet friendly to La Follette.

As the United States drifted into the war, Jones became a fervent supporter of the war effort. In the fall of 1916, the paper's editorial policy drastically changed as it enthusiastically endorsed the president's preparedness program. When the United States entered the war in April 1917, the *State Journal* vociferously supported the war effort and castigated those who criticized the administration.[114]

La Follette became a target of venomous abuse. Editorials frequently marked the senator as a traitor who frequently supported the German position in the war. In an editorial printed in August 1917, the *State Journal* argued that La Follette's statements critical of the government's war policies "lend aid and comfort to the sympathizers with the enemy." Indeed, "every move" La Follette made was "designed to bring behind him the pro-Germans of this country."[115]

In response, several key members of the *State Journal* staff began planning the creation of a new, alternative newspaper. The journalists behind the new venture were united in their commitment to the agenda of progressive reforms that La Follette had promoted as governor. Still, they were split on the issue of the war.

At the head of this effort to launch a new newspaper was William Evjue. Jones had hired Evjue as managing editor soon after purchasing the *State Journal*. Evjue was an experienced journalist, having worked at a Milwaukee newspaper. He was also a progressive and a fervent supporter of La Follette. Although Evjue supported the government's war policies, he continued to support La Follette and the campaign for social reforms. This put Evjue and Jones on a collision course.[116]

Evjue resigned from the *State Journal* in September 1917, and word of the appearance of a new paper began circulating shortly afterward. Needless to say, Jones and the management of the *State Journal* viewed the *Capital Times* as a direct threat. They began warning government officials that the new paper would encourage Wisconsin's "disloyal" elements and should be suppressed. Since the federal government already considered La Follette a dangerous threat, the Justice Department was prepared to closely monitor the new paper even before its first edition had been issued. This surveillance would make it possible for its editors to be prosecuted under the Espionage Act at the slightest sign that the paper was ready to print articles critical of the war effort.

In early November 1917, Bielaski wrote to George Mayo concerning reports he had received of a new newspaper. Employed by the Bureau of Investigation as an accountant, Mayo was an expert in tracing funds through bank accounts. He was already looking into the source of funds for *La Follette's Magazine*. Bielaski informed Mayo of rumors that the "purpose of the paper" would be to "advance the German-American ideas." Furthermore, it was possible that the newly launched newspaper would be "financed with money of the German government."[117]

Mayo proceeded to travel to Madison. On December 13, 1917, the *Capital Times* began printing daily. With Evjue as publisher and editor, the new newspaper consistently supported the war effort, although it did stress the need to defend civil liberties. In one of its first issues, the *Capital Times* printed an editorial declaring that it was "in favor of the war." Furthermore, the editors asserted their independence from La Follette, although all of them had been his close associates. Nevertheless, the editorial insisted that La Follette had "nothing to do with the *Capital Times*."[118]

Despite the newspaper's pro-war stance, the Bureau of Investigation maintained its intrusive investigation. Mayo spent several days of the week in Madison monitoring the editorial policy of the *Capital Times* and investigating its source of funds. At times, Mayo had an agent follow Evjue to see who his contacts were. Indeed, the newspaper and its editors were "under surveillance for some months."[119]

Mayo's primary aim was to determine who was financing the new paper. He soon discovered that it was operating at a deficit of $3,000 a month, a considerable sum. (This would be equivalent to a monthly deficit of more than $60,000 in current dollars.) The goal of uncovering the names of the wealthy donors behind the *Capital Times* would "demand the closest surveillance of all accounts."[120]

Mayo succeeded in gaining access to the paper's bank accounts. He soon realized that the *Capital Times* was being subsidized by Wisconsin progressives. The paper's largest contributor was Alfred Thomas Rogers, a former law partner of La Follette and a successful real estate developer.[121]

Nevertheless, Mayo pursued intense surveillance for several months after initiating his investigation. In early March 1918, he wrote a lengthy report to Bielaski in which he concluded that if there were "any truth" to the claim that the *Capital Times* received funding from pro-German sources, it would surface during the election campaign to fill the seat caused by the death of Senator Paul Husting. According to Mayo, the upcoming election would be "a straight-out loyal and disloyal fight." Furthermore, the *Capital Times* would be the only newspaper in Madison that would "support the disloyal candidates."[122]

At roughly the same time Mayo wrote this report, Bielaski sent a message to William Lamar, the solicitor of the Post Office and the official primarily responsible for determining which newspapers and journals would be allowed through the mail. Enclosing the front page of the *Capital Times* from February 27, 1918, Bielaski pointed out that its front page included three articles from the Associated Press describing recent battles won by the German army. Bielaski believed this was "evidence of pro-Germanism" and could provide the basis for declaring the paper to be non-mailable.[123]

This was a step too far for Lamar. AP articles were carried by mainstream newspapers around the country, most of whom zealously supported the war effort. Furthermore, editorials in the *Capital Times* supported the administration's war policies. Still, the fact that the chief of the Bureau of Investigation was willing to advance such a flimsy argument to harass the paper is indicative of how far the government was willing to go in its effort to silence La Follette and his supporters.

Of course, La Follette was aware of the *State Journal*'s incessant attacks on his reputation. He, therefore, initiated a lawsuit against Jones, contending that the *State Journal* was guilty of libel by repeatedly accusing him of being a traitor acting in the interests of the German government.[124]

As the lawsuit moved toward a trial in March 1918, Emerson Ela, a prominent Madison attorney acting as counsel for the *State Journal*, travelled to Washington to gain the federal government's assistance. Ela met with Attorney General Thomas Gregory, a most unusual event. The attorney general of the United States did not usually intervene in civil disputes. Clearly the campaign to discredit La Follette continued well after he had been silenced, with the active participation of those at the highest levels of the federal government. Ela asked Gregory to instruct the Bureau of Investigation to provide him with information in its files that could bolster the *State Journal*'s defense in the libel suit. The Bureau of Investigation had a strict policy prohibiting the sharing of information with private citizens. Gregory responded by requesting Ela to write a memorandum specifying the information he was seeking.[125]

Ela knew of this policy, so he understood that he was "asking for favors" that were "unusual." Still, since the administration was "concerned" with La Follette's stature within the antiwar movement, the government would benefit by opening its books on this exceptional occasion. Ela then listed an extensive series of charges that had been levied against La Follette in the pages of the *State Journal*. These included the claims that La Follette was unpatriotic and that he "was in favor of Germany." Indeed, the paper had insisted that "he was a traitor to his country."[126]

Gregory was persuaded, and Ela's request was passed onto Bielaski. By this time, Mayo had not completed his investigation into the funding sources being tapped by the *Capital Times*. Nevertheless, Mayo understood that the paper was not funded by pro-German sources. The Bureau of Investigation had closely monitored La Follette's speeches at St. Paul and Toledo, but the essence of these talks had been reported in the press and was hardly a secret. Thus, Bielaski responded to Ela's request by stating that there was no information in the files that could support the charges being made by the *State Journal*.[127] (Bielaski did pass on to Gregory a report that La Follette had been instrumental in forming the People's Council.) The Bureau of Investigation could not provide Ela and the *State Journal* with evidence that La Follette was a traitor because none existed. Bielaski did not mention that his agents had searched for evidence indicating that La Follette or the *Capital Times* was receiving money from

German sources, but had failed to find any evidence to substantiate this charge.

In early April 1918, Mayo filed his final report on the *Capital Times*. Contrary to his expectations, German money had not flooded into the paper during the primary election. Indeed, Mayo conceded that his many months of intensive surveillance had shown that there were "no traitors" among the editors of the paper or its donors. The charges of disloyalty had "originated chiefly from the established newspapers," that is, the *Wisconsin State Journal*, and from the political opponents of La Follette. The editors of the *Capital Times* were "all loyal to the government," and the editorial line of the paper supported the war effort.[128]

The effort put into investigating the *Capital Times* was only partly driven by the concern that La Follette was trying to circumvent the tight restrictions that had been placed on him and *La Follette's Magazine* by using a newspaper controlled by his supporters. Beyond this was pure vindictiveness. Even after La Follette had been silenced, government officials despised and feared him as a symbol of the antiwar opposition, a public figure who could coalesce the progressive opposition into a viable third party. This vindictive hatred began at the top with the president. Woodrow Wilson did not forgive or forget those who publicly challenged him.

The Wisconsin Senate Election of 1918

La Follette might have entirely withdrawn from the public debate on the course of the war following his October 1917 speech had not an unforeseen incident occurred. On October 21, 1917, Senator Paul Husting was accidentally killed by his brother while duck hunting.[129] Husting was a Democrat and the other senator from Wisconsin. He had been an enthusiastic supporter of the war effort, so the president was eager to have him replaced by someone also fully committed to the administration's policies.

In Wisconsin, popular opposition to the war was widespread. The Socialist Party dominated politics in Milwaukee, the state's largest city. Indeed, Victor Berger had been elected to the U.S. House of Representatives on the Socialist Party ticket. In the rural farm areas, voters had rallied behind La Follette and the progressives. A candidate that could unify these two strands of the antiwar opposition had an excellent chance of being elected to the vacant Senate seat.

Husting's unexpected death triggered an intense political battle in Wisconsin. Governor Emanuel Philipp, a conservative Republican, was anxious to avoid a special election in which the question of the war could become the central issue. He therefore sought to convene a special session of the state legislature to push through a law authorizing the governor to appoint a replacement when an incumbent member of Congress died in office. This law would have reversed a statute enacted by progressive legislators that called for a special election in these circumstances. A wide range of legislators, including those supporting La Follette and the progressives, rejected the governor's maneuver, and the entire process came to a stalemate for nearly four months.[130]

During this stalemate, La Follette sought to reassure Philipp that a special election would not become a test of public support for the war. In an editorial in his magazine, he wrote that Husting's death had left a void that was "deep and abiding." Furthermore, there was "no difference in Congress about supporting the war until [an] honorable peace may be obtained."[131] Of course, La Follette had opposed the decision to enter the war and afterward had insisted that Congress establish peace terms based on a policy of "no annexations, no reparations." Instead of pursuing this policy of opposition, La Follette was pledging that his wing of the Republican Party would downplay any discussion of the war and would, instead, focus on the levying of higher taxes on profits as the means of funding the massive expenditures on armaments.

With both sides entrenched in their positions, Wisconsin's progressives looked to La Follette for leadership. Gilbert Roe, a key confidante, wrote to a leading progressive in Wisconsin arguing that La Follette needed to return to his home state to hold public rallies. This would inevitably lead La Follette "to discuss [the] war," and that might "start something." Nevertheless, it was essential "to show" that he was "still a leader in Wisconsin." Roe sent La Follette a copy of this letter, but with no result. The senator remained in Washington D.C., having little to say about the war.[132]

Finally, on February 19, 1918, the legislature convened to debate the governor's proposed statute and defeated it. Three days later, Philipp set March 19 as the date for the primary election and April 2 for the general election. Very few elections for national office were held after the United States entered the war in April 1917, and the Wisconsin special election for the Senate was by far the most important.

Progressive Republicans quickly rallied behind James Thompson, a prominent attorney from La Crosse, Wisconsin, who had supported La Follette during his unsuccessful bid to be the Republican presidential nominee in 1916. Given the intensity of antiwar sentiment in Wisconsin, Thompson should have been an easy winner in the primary election. Still, his campaign proved to be timid and tentative at every level. He gave only two public speeches during the three weeks between filing for the nomination and the primary election date. One of the key issues that arose during the election campaign was La Follette's possible expulsion, and yet Thompson, his ally, refused to state his position. In his platform, Thompson equivocated, urging support for the war effort while also calling for the United States to delineate its war aims.[133]

Irvine Lenroot, Thompson's opponent in the Republican primary, toured the state, rallying his supporters. He had the support of Governor Philipp and the major newspapers in the state. Ironically, Lenroot had risen to prominence in Wisconsin politics by being a loyal supporter of La Follette and his progressive program. After several terms in the state legislature, he was elected to the U.S. House of Representatives in 1908. In Washington, Lenroot remained close to La Follette, a political ally and a personal friend. As the United States drifted into the war, Lenroot vacillated. Nevertheless, once the United States entered the war, Lenroot became an enthusiastic supporter of the war effort and publicly broke with La Follette.[134]

During the primary campaign, Lenroot placed support for the war as the most important point in his program. He argued for "the stamping out of all seditious speech and propaganda." The constitutional guarantee of free speech did not ensure "the right to give aid and comfort to the enemy." There was only "one plank" in Lenroot's platform, "LOYALTY." In a speech before five hundred students at the University of Wisconsin in Madison, Lenroot conceded that although Thompson was a person of "high character," his support came from those who were "pro-German in their sympathies." The vote of those who were "disloyal" was being divided between Berger and Thompson. Lenroot concluded his speech by warning that "he who is not openly for America in the war is against America." Four days before the primary, Lenroot went further, advising those unwilling to support him to vote instead for Joseph Davies, the candidate of the Democratic Party, since a vote for Thompson would "lengthen the war."[135]

The breach between La Follette and Lenroot was both political and personal. La Follette had no intention of endorsing Lenroot, and yet he made little effort to keep him from being elected to the Senate. Despite the obvious importance of the special election, La Follette did not make a single public appearance for Thompson, who was left to campaign on his own. A few days before the primary election, La Follette finally endorsed Thompson. Most of his statement focused on the need to tax the wealthy to pay for the huge costs of the war. The few words commenting on the war emphasized the need for Congress to play an "authoritative" role in defining peace terms. Still, La Follette gave his reluctant support to the war effort, with the proviso that the United States should more clearly define its peace terms. He then urged his supporters to "vote for Mr. Thompson" as the candidate who opposed the "tax-dodging profiteers and the war-hogs."[136]

Everyone understood that the Wisconsin special election was a critical test of support for the president's war policies, as well as an opportunity to assess the extent to which the deluge of attacks on La Follette had eroded his popular support. The campaign was closely scrutinized by the White House and around the country.

On March 15, 1918, Woodrow Wilson wrote to Vice-President Thomas Marshall pointing out that the "attention of the country will be centered" on the Wisconsin election. To the president, the election would demonstrate whether Wisconsin was "really loyal to the country in this time of crisis." As usual, Wilson tried to convince himself that his policies had the support of most Americans, claiming that there was a "universal feeling against Senator La Follette."[137]

The president correctly believed that Lenroot would carry the Republican primary to be held four days later, but he was also convinced that Lenroot's victory would "by no means demonstrate that loyalty." Thus, it was of the "utmost importance" that Davies be elected in April's general election. Marshall was, therefore, requested to "make some speeches" for Davies while touring Wisconsin.[138] Despite Thompson's lackluster campaign and the token support he received from La Follette, the contest for the vacant Senate seat was very close. Lenroot defeated Thompson by 2,400 votes out of more than 140,000 total votes cast in the Republican primary. A cogent antiwar campaign from a candidate prepared to bring the message to communities across Wisconsin could have led to an easy victory in the Republican primary.

Instead, the general election featured a three-way contest, with the candidates from both major parties providing unstinting and enthusiastic support for the administration's war policies. The Democrats sought to portray Lenroot as pandering to those opposed to the war despite Lenroot's repeated affirmation of his "loyalty." Following the president's directive, Marshall traveled around Wisconsin condemning the Republicans as "half for America, half for the Kaiser and all against Wilson." Lenroot was "bidding for the vote of the German sympathizers, for the vote of the seditionist, for the vote of the pacifist," those seeking to "make an inglorious peace." Instead of seeking the support of these voters, Marshall promised that Davies would "scorn them."[139]

Lenroot knew that he had to attract some of the votes that had gone to Thompson in the Republican primary and that might go to Berger. Nevertheless, he remained steadfast in his unwavering support for the war effort. Lenroot softened his criticism of progressive Republicans, holding that it "would not be fair to judge" everyone who voted for Thompson as "disloyal." At the same time, he still believed there was a "presumption of disloyalty" for those who backed Berger. After all, "if the Kaiser were writing a platform," the one advocated by Berger would be "the one he would write."[140]

Victor Berger was the only candidate for the Senate seat who questioned the president's policies and called for an immediate start to peace talks. His platform held that the "American people did not and do not want the war." In a speech during the brief campaign, Berger told a sympathetic audience that he wanted the United States "out of the war as quick as we can." This goal could be reached by beginning with an "immediate armistice looking forward to a general and permanent peace." His platform further detailed this proposal by calling for a peace treaty based on no "forcible annexations or punitive indemnities."[141]

Berger did not support the call for the United States to unilaterally withdraw from the war. Instead, he hoped that the United States had sufficient influence to pressure the Allies into accepting a negotiated peace. His platform also included a provision that U.S. troops should be withdrawn from Europe following a negotiated agreement ending the war.[142] These were hardly radical demands, and, indeed, Berger's position on the war was very similar to that which La Follette had advocated until October 1917, when he became a target of a concerted campaign of intimidation and vilification.

By March 1918, La Follette had ceased to be a defiant symbol of resistance. He was no longer willing to stand up to the president and the establishment. In an editorial in his magazine, La Follette recognized that Berger's sizable vote affirming his nomination as the Socialist Party candidate, 38,000, or 15 percent of the total vote in the primary, was evidence of a "profound and radical dissatisfaction" with "some of the war policies of the present Administration."[143]

Yet La Follette no longer saw himself as a spokesperson for this current of dissatisfaction. Instead, he sought to counter the antiwar opposition and thereby buttress support for the administration's policies. La Follette falsely claimed that Berger advocated that the United States unilaterally withdraw from the war. Berger was, therefore, putting forward "a demand impossible to seriously consider." The U.S. government had "lawfully assumed" an "obligation" to fight the war with Germany, and it could not "repudiate" its "obligation to prosecute the war efficiently." La Follette had taken a further step away from his initial position as a crusading progressive reformer. He was now joining the Wilson administration in launching misleading attacks on a leading opponent of the war.

In the end, Lenroot defeated Davies by a vote of 163,000 to 149,000. The president was not pleased. He congratulated Davies on putting up "a good fight," but he still believed that Lenroot was not "a satisfactory choice." In Wilson's view, Lenroot's "early record" of equivocation in the period leading up to the U.S. entry into the war had "showed a very serious weakness."[144]

Berger came in a respectable third, garnering 110,000 votes, or 26 percent of the total vote. This after he and several other Socialist Party leaders had been indicted on charges of violating the Espionage Act.[145] Despite the indictment and the many articles in the mainstream press labeling him a traitor, Berger attracted far more votes than any other socialist candidate had recorded in previous statewide elections.

Wisconsin voters were eager to see the war come to a quick end. They were left in the lurch when La Follette attacked Berger and thus implicitly indicated his support for Lenroot in the final election.

La Follette Supports the War Effort

During the last months of the war, following the Wisconsin special election, La Follette kept a very low profile. He declined every offer to speak publicly on the controversial issues of the day. As a final move away from any public role, La Follette opted to not make a single appearance at the Senate for eight months starting in January 1918. Once he returned, he refrained from making substantive speeches on the Senate floor, confining his activities to contributions to the Senate Finance Committee as it crafted a budget to cover the enormous costs of the war.[146] Until the end, La Follette remained fearful that he might be expelled from office.

La Follette's sole form of expression during these last months of the war was writing editorials for his magazine. He ignored the assaults on civil liberties perpetrated by the Wilson administration. There was, for instance, no mention of the prosecution of Eugene Debs in the summer of 1918 for allegedly violating the Espionage Act by voicing his opposition to the war. Indeed, *La Follette's Magazine* had little to say about the war beyond the conviction that the rich should pay a larger share of the cost.

Yet, there were a few passages in editorials that did address the broader issues. In January 1918, Wilson finally agreed to set out his views on U.S. war aims. This was the famous Fourteen Points speech to Congress, one full of nebulous promises but short on specifics. La Follette's response was ambivalent. He viewed the speech as "evidence of progress," and he was eager to "rejoice" at the willingness of the president to define the terms of peace. Still, there was a tone of muted criticism in La Follette's analysis of the speech. Specifically, no "satisfactory reason" had been given as to "why the terms should not have been stated" when the United States first entered the war in April 1917.[147]

La Follette also pointed out that Wilson had not addressed the sensitive issue of reparations. This omission would prove to be a major problem arising from the Versailles Treaty. La Follette objected to Germany being forced to pay punitive indemnities since these would not be paid by "the people who caused the war," but rather by the "plain people" who had suffered the consequences.

Despite the cautious criticisms in this article, La Follette had significantly shifted his perspective. Initially, he had distrusted Wilson, a distrust that was heightened when the president rammed through conscription and silenced dissidents. By January 1918, La Follette had come to view the president as an ally against the hawks. Unfortunately, he argued, the length and intensity of the war "would depend on" the most extreme demand insisted upon by the most extreme of the Entente Allies. Instead of a hardline stance premised on crushing Germany, the United States should seek an "honorable peace by requiring Great Britain and the Entente Allies to modify their terms."

Although Wilson would make a half-hearted effort to convince the Allies to limit their punitive demands once the war had ended, the president was adamant during the war that it be fought to the bitter end. Ultimately, the war ended when a popular revolution toppled the Kaiser and Germany unconditionally surrendered.

During the last months of the war, La Follette shifted from cautious criticism to open support for the war effort. In a June

1918 editorial, La Follette wrote that there had been "serious and dangerous delays in equipping" the U.S. expedition to France. Nevertheless, U.S. troops were "giving a good account of themselves." Since these soldiers were willing to sacrifice their lives, those "at home" should be willing to make sacrifices "in the same spirit."[148] This was pro-war propaganda, not a serious analysis of a complex situation.

An unsigned editorial in the September 1918 issue of *La Follette's Magazine* heaped praise on the troops fighting in the trenches of France: "The American soldier has a proud record." U.S. forces were "brave and generous" and acted as "defenders of the weak." La Follette concluded that he was "proud" of their successes.[149] This, at the end of four years of a global bloodbath that had caused the death and serious injury of millions of combatants and civilians and would pave the way to the Second World War.

La Follette's decision to continue to criticize the administration's war policies even after the United States entered the war had been risky. He quickly became the leading spokesperson for the antiwar opposition. His supporters were ready to organize behind him as an independent candidate for president in the 1920 elections. Woodrow Wilson was determined to silence La Follette. The administration launched a coordinated assault on La Follette that operated on several levels. La Follette was threatened with expulsion from the Senate and repeatedly denounced as a traitor in the mainstream press. The threats and vitriolic denunciations had their effect. La Follette withdrew from public forums. During the last months of the war, he even wrote editorials endorsing the war effort. His defection from the antiwar movement was a major blow to the progressive opposition.

CHAPTER 4

The Nonpartisan League: Cooptation and Repression

THE NONPARTISAN LEAGUE (NPL) represented a unique phenomenon in U.S. history. It recruited small farmers into a mass organization that was both a social movement and an electoral force, and it did so based on a program of progressive reforms.

The league was formed in North Dakota in 1915 and spread rapidly to Minnesota and other adjoining states. At its peak, it enrolled 245,000 farmers as paid members in thirteen states.[1] The NPL provided an alternative culture for progressives in isolated rural communities. Local groups held regular meetings with speakers who crisscrossed the region. The league also produced a weekly newspaper, the *Nonpartisan Leader*, as well as a series of pamphlets.

Yet its most important activity was in the electoral arena. The NPL endorsed candidates for state and local offices within both the Democratic and Republican parties. These candidates campaigned for a legislative program aimed at improving the conditions of small farmers.

Threatened by this popular upsurge, corporate interests in the region began attacking the league as a corrupt clique of dangerous revolutionaries. The conservative government of Minnesota initiated a coordinated effort to quash the league. Despite this, George Creel, the chair of the government's Committee on Public Information, opted to reach out to the leaders of the NPL. As a result, the league became an ardent supporter of the First World War, working closely with the Committee. Nevertheless, the Justice Department kept the NPL under intensive surveillance by agents of the Bureau of Investigation. Distrustful of the league, President Wilson refused to be drawn into the bitter conflict that unfolded in Minnesota. Although state authorities flagrantly trampled on fundamental constitutional rights in their effort to crush the NPL, the federal government refused to intervene.

Origins of the League

The Nonpartisan League was created by Arthur Townley and Albert Bowen. Born on a farm in northwest Minnesota, Townley owned a flax farm in western North Dakota. In the winter of 1912, he went bankrupt when an early frost ruined his crop at the same time as speculators drove down the price of flax.[2]

Angry and disillusioned, Townley joined the Socialist Party of America (SP) in early 1914. In June 1914, Townley proposed the formation of an Organization Department to recruit farmers based on a program of immediate reforms, with no mention of creating a socialist society in the future. Party leaders agreed to this suggestion, and Townley began touring the rural areas of North Dakota in a car.[3]

Townley was a "genius for organization" who remained calm in the midst of an emergency. Although "not much of an orator," he was persuasive in individual conversations. With his "magnetic personality," Townley quickly recruited thousands of new members. The Socialist Party's state leadership soon became concerned that the recruits would dilute the party's commitment to fundamental change, so in January 1915, the Organization Department was dissolved. Townley then quit the Socialist Party in disgust.[4]

Townley had worked with Albert Bowen in organizing farmers into the Socialist Party through its Organization Department. Bowen was already a prominent member of the North Dakota SP, having been its candidate for governor in 1912. Nevertheless, he also quit the party in protest of the decision to dissolve the Organization Department.[5]

Townley and Bowen jointly developed the fundamental premises of the Nonpartisan League. They started with the specific demands included in the section of the immediate program of the North Dakota Socialist Party directed at farmers. These demands included a state-owned grain elevator, hail insurance guaranteed by the state, and a state bank that would provide low-interest loans to small farmers. Bowen came up with the idea of endorsing candidates within both mainstream parties pledged to implementing the immediate program. Although Bowen agreed to let Townley act as the public spokesperson for the new organization, he remained an influential figure behind the scenes.[6]

By the spring of 1915, Townley, Bowen and a few early recruits began touring North Dakota, recruiting members to the newly formed organization. League locals were established around the state. Organizers found a ready response, and the NPL grew rapidly.

The new organization operated as a personal autocracy. Townley determined the NPL's policies and strategies, hired each staff member, and set the editorial line of the league's newspaper, the *Nonpartisan Leader*, as well. A pragmatist rather than an ideologue, Townley later commented that socialism was "too far off" in the future. Instead, he wanted to create an organization that could put into practice measures that would quickly aid the region's small farmers.[7]

The NPL Sweeps North Dakota

Initially, the Nonpartisan League was organized on a statewide basis. North Dakota had open primaries, so any registered voter could vote in either party's primaries. The NPL endorsed candidates pledged to their program and then mobilized its membership to vote for that candidate. In general, the league placed its candidates in the primary of the party that was the strongest in that district. Once having won the primary, the NPL-endorsed candidate had an excellent chance of being elected. Since the Republican Party was the dominant party in North Dakota, the league's candidates in that state usually appeared on the ballot as Republicans. Once in office, those endorsed by the NPL worked together across party lines to implement the legislative measures called for in its program. Voting membership in the organization was limited to small farmers. Furthermore, members of its paid staff were not permitted to seek office.[8]

By the spring of 1916, a year after its formation, the NPL had become a serious force in North Dakota's politics. In virtually every precinct in the state, members were encouraged to attend a meeting to choose delegates to a nominating convention held in each district in the state legislature. Candidates were chosen from among the membership to represent the league in the November elections for the state legislature. NPL members were committed to supporting that candidate, no matter what their political affiliations were. Thousands of farmers participated in this grassroots process to select candidates for the North Dakota state legislature.[9]

Candidates endorsed by the league won most of the primary elections contested in the election for the state legislature in June 1916. Its candidate for governor, Lynn Frazier, won the Republican primary as well. In November 1916, the NPL swept to power in the general election. Frazier was elected to a two-year term with nearly 80 percent of the vote. The results for the state legislature were nearly as impressive. Of the 113 seats in the State House, candidates endorsed by the NPL won 81. The state was overwhelmingly Republican, but there were pockets of support for the Democratic Party. The league endorsed Democrats in those districts; as a result, thirteen of those elected to the State House were Democrats committed to the league's program.[10]

The only hitch to this tidal wave of support for the NPL was the state senate. The North Dakota state constitution provided four-year terms for state senators, with half elected every two years. Of the twenty-five seats open in 1916, eighteen were filled by candidates endorsed by the NPL. Despite this tremendous victory, the NPL could not enact its legislative program. A majority of the state senate rejected any legislation opposed by business interests. It was only two years later, in 1918, with Frazier reelected and the NPL in control of both houses of the state legislature, that the league could begin to implement its program.[11]

By the fall of 1916, the Nonpartisan League had established a solid base of support in North Dakota. It then began to spread its influence into adjoining states, in particular Minnesota. Still, the league's leadership understood that many of the issues confronting the region's farmers could only be confronted at the national level.

The Progressive Coalition

Townley hired former activists and leaders of the Socialist Party to become NPL organizers.[12] Many of them retained their belief in independent politics, that is, the need to build a political party independent of either the Democratic or Republican parties. They convinced Townley that the league could be more than the organized expression of discontent among the farmers of the Upper Midwest. Indeed, it could become a critical component of a progressive coalition that could become a force at the national level. A successful progressive coalition would bring together farmer organizations, militant trade unions, and consumer advocates around a program of structural reforms that could challenge corporate control of the economy.

The former members of the Socialist Party who developed this strategy viewed the prospective progressive coalition as a first step in the move toward an independent third party. Many of them had supported the formation of a labor party during their time in the Socialist Party.[13] In the aftermath of the First World War, Minnesota's farmers joined with progressive unions to form the Farmer-Labor Party (FLP). Former socialists who had been involved in the NPL would go on to play significant roles in the FLP.[14]

Townley accepted the strategic concept of building a broadly based progressive coalition, but only as an effective pressure group within the two-party system. In an interview with the *New York Times* in March 1917, just before the United States entered the war, Townley concluded that the NPL "surely must enter national politics." This would be done by using "the primaries of both parties to elect candidates for Congress" pledged to support a progressive platform.[15]

Woodrow Wilson knew of the NPL's activities at the national level and the potential problems this could cause for the Democratic Party. In June 1918, Antoinette Funk, a leading figure in the movement for women's suffrage and an ardent supporter of the war, wrote a report on the current situation. As an attorney in Chicago, Funk had good contacts in the region the league was organizing. She informed Wilson that farmers were becoming increasingly disenchanted with the war and were looking for an alternative to the two mainstream parties. Funk warned the president that many people believed the NPL could become the nucleus of "the Labor Party of the future."[16]

Funk doubted that such a formation would be possible given the "inherent antipathy" of farmers toward urban industrial workers. Nevertheless, she was worried, as was the president.

Woodrow Wilson's distrust of the league partly came from his concern that a nationally based progressive coalition could become the basis for a progressive third party. The formation of a third party would have created serious difficulties for centrist Democrats such as himself.

The Nonpartisan League and the IWW

The decision to enter the war in April 1917 left the nation's farmers in a difficult quandary. The demand for war materiel greatly outstripped the capacity to produce these goods. Food was desperately needed to feed the huge army being sent overseas while at the same time sustaining the armies of Britain and France that were already deployed. Even the unskilled labor required to harvest crops was in short supply. Farmers who had joined the NPL were eager to ensure sufficient migrant workers for the upcoming harvest.

To resolve this problem, the league sought an agreement with a union of migrant workers affiliated with the Industrial Workers of the World. This was a risky course of action. The NPL emerged from those in the most moderate wing of the Socialist Party, while the IWW stood for a militant and radical political perspective. The Wobblies, as they were nicknamed, also had a history of active opposition to militarism and imperialism and were harsh critics of Woodrow Wilson and his administration.[17]

The IWW was rapidly growing in the summer of 1917. Workers throughout the western states were ready for militant action to defend their wages and working conditions. At the same time, the mainstream unions affiliated with the American Federation of Labor (AFL) were hesitant to act because of their enthusiastic support for the war effort and their close ties to the Democratic Party.

In this context, Townley authorized Arthur Le Sueur to travel to the Kansas City convention of the IWW's Agricultural

Workers' Industrial Union #400. Formerly a prominent member of the North Dakota Socialist Party, Le Sueur had also acted as defense counsel for the IWW. After joining the NPL in early 1917, he quickly became a trusted advisor to Townley.[18]

Le Sueur informed the delegates to the AWIU conference that the league was interested in reaching an "understanding" with the union. In return for farmers granting a wage rate of $5.00 for a ten-hour day, the AWIU would agree to provide a steady supply of workers for the coming harvest season. With no dissent noted in the minutes, the AWIU conference agreed to the offer of the NPL, with an amendment that overtime beyond the ten hours would be paid at double time, or $1.00 an hour. The delegates elected a negotiating team to work out a contract and called upon the league to do the same.[19]

A few days later, on June 7, 1917, Townley reported to the annual conference of the North Dakota Nonpartisan League on the AWIU proposal for a negotiated agreement. Townley urged the delegates to approve this proposal since by "working in cooperation" with the AWIU, "instead of fighting it," farmers would be ensured an adequate supply of workers for the harvest. With the conference's approval, Townley then appointed a three-member negotiating team.[20]

The two negotiating teams met several times in various towns around North Dakota during June and July of 1917, with Townley personally participating in some of the negotiating sessions. A tentative agreement was finally reached, which was then approved by the AWIU's executive committee. By August 1917, the NPL was moving in a very different direction, seeking to gain the confidence of the Wilson administration. Townley opted to veto approval of the tentative contract, claiming that farmers within the NPL felt that the proposed wage rates were too generous.[21] More likely, he had come to understand that the IWW was becoming a prime target of government repression, and thus it was dangerous to be publicly associated with it. The mainstream press would frequently cite the negotiations with the IWW and its Agricultural Workers' Union as proof that the league was led by dangerous and unpatriotic radicals.

The Nonpartisan League and the U.S. Entry into the War

Wilson's decision to bring the United States into the war in April 1917 left the NPL in an awkward bind. Townley had devised a successful formula. By the spring of 1917, the NPL seemed poised to become a major factor in the politics of several states. Yet this success also attracted the intense hatred of the region's business interests.

Once Congress declared war in April 1917, the league became even more vulnerable to repression. Townley understood that open opposition to the war would bring harsh repression from the federal government. Still, he also realized that the farmers of the western states were ardently opposed to the war and expected the NPL to reflect that position.[22]

The Nonpartisan League moved carefully in defining its stance on the war. An editorial that appeared in the *Leader* shortly after the declaration of war confined itself to a call for unity in a time of "emergency."[23]

This vague formulation was not enough to satisfy the league's members, who insisted on a more critical perspective. Henry Teigan, the executive secretary of the NPL and a former secretary of the North Dakota Socialist Party, wrote to Carl Thompson, a pro-war socialist, that the farmers in the Upper Midwest who were sympathetic to progressive politics were "practically a unit in opposition to the war." Indeed, an NPL organizer had recently reported to Teigan that he had not found "a single farmer this spring who seemed enthusiastic about America's entry into the conflict."[24]

Thus, the league's leaders understood that its members were solidly opposed to the war and that they expected the organization to reflect that position. Throughout May 1917, local meetings of the league in North Dakota discussed and approved a resolution criticizing the war. It had been formulated by two leading NPL figures who had been active members of the Socialist Party for many years before becoming influential advisors to Townley.

Joe Gilbert served as the NPL's organizing director and directed the delegates' activities in the field. He had been the secretary of the Washington State Socialist Party and the editor of its newspaper before joining the league. Gilbert wrote most of the resolution, although part of it was also written by Arthur Le Sueur.[25]

The NPL Questions the War Effort

On June 7, 1917, the North Dakota NPL convened its annual conference. This meeting would mark the high point of the NPL as a dissident force. Delegates overwhelmingly approved a resolution holding that the league was "opposed to waging war for annexation," whether by the United States or its allies, and that it was opposed to "demanding indemnity as terms of peace." The North Dakota NPL also went on record calling for the "abolition of secret diplomacy" and a rejection of secret treaties.[26]

These were controversial positions, but another section of the resolution proved to be even more dangerous for the NPL. To clarify the underlying causes of the war, the resolution held that the conflict was "a convulsive effort" of the "rulers of warring nations for control of a constantly diminishing market." Rival imperial powers were "playing a deadly game for commercial supremacy."

In his speech to the North Dakota conference, Townley supported the antiwar resolution. However, he focused on the economic implications of the wartime mobilization and avoided discussing the broader issues relating to the war. Yet Townley also presented an argument justifying conscription.[27]

During the summer of 1917, the *Nonpartisan Leader* generally avoided any discussion of the war. Nevertheless, an editorial in August 1917 suggested that "all the nations at war, including the United States, [should] state the terms on which they will make peace."[28] The editorial raised a sensitive topic since the United Kingdom and its allies had repeatedly refused to delineate the terms of a possible peace treaty with Germany. President Wilson held to this same position during the first months after the United States entered the war.[29]

Two weeks later, an editorial in the *Leader* followed up on this point. The reluctance of the administration to define its aims was "discouraging." The people of the United States "intend to have more of a voice in the war than the rulers of Germany have permitted the German people to have."[30] This call for popular control of the country's war policy raised a critically important point, but it was also a position that could lead the NPL into a direct confrontation with the federal government. The president was certain that he alone had the legal and moral authority to make the crucial decisions that would shape the policies of the United States during the war.[31] Furthermore, he firmly believed that those who questioned his authority were deliberately disrupting the war effort and, thus, must be harshly suppressed.

As late as August 1917, some of its leaders still viewed the league as an informal component of the network of organizations calling for negotiated peace. The Nonpartisan League declined to join the People's Council of America because the PCA opposed the draft and called upon Congress to repeal it.[32] Nevertheless, Teigan wrote to a leading supporter of Irish independence that, although the NPL had "no official connection" to the People's Council, their policies were "much the same." Furthermore, the victory of candidates endorsed by the league in local elections scheduled for November 1917 who were "pledged to a constructive program along the lines of peace" could pressure Wilson into presenting a peace proposal that "would be acceptable to the Teutonic allies."[33]

Creel Cajoles the NPL

Despite these tentative moves toward cautious opposition to the government's policies, George Creel, as chair of the Committee on Public Information, saw the opportunity for a crucially important clandestine operation. The league commanded the loyal support of tens of thousands of wheat farmers in North Dakota and the neighboring states. Grain was essential to the war effort. Creel hoped to persuade the NPL to uncritically endorse the government's policies. Such an endorsement would boost the war effort by encouraging farmers to increase their harvests to feed the millions of soldiers in the trenches.

Creel understood that Townley and a small coterie around him made decisions in the NPL. Townley had demonstrated consistent pragmatism by quitting the Socialist Party to form the NPL on the basis of a minimum program of reforms lifted from the SP platform. Furthermore, Townley had endorsed the draft, the weakest point in the government's wartime mobilization. During the late spring and early summer of 1917, Creel invited several leaders of the league to Washington for extended confidential discussions. Charles Lindbergh, the father of the famous pilot, joined the NPL leaders in these confidential discussions.[34]

Although no detailed record of these secret meetings has survived, the general outlines are clear. Governor Joseph Burnquist of Minnesota was a conservative Republican who despised the league and viewed the wartime crisis as a perfect opportunity to disrupt its activities. In addition to this, even the most cautious criticism of the war effort could lead the Justice Department to initiate a prosecution of NPL leaders for allegedly violating the Espionage Act.

In this context, Townley and the league's leadership understood the advantages of having an influential member of the administration acting as its advocate. Convincing Creel that they had swung behind the government's war policies could provide some protection from prosecution by the Department of Justice. NPL leaders were also anxious to convince Creel to use his influence to persuade the president to pressure the Minnesota state government to curtail its repression of the league.

In return for Creel's efforts to deflect repression, the Nonpartisan League was ready to consider shifting its stance from cautious opposition to the war to ardent public support for the administration. While wooing the NPL, Creel worked through John Thompson, a journalist on the league's public relations staff. Before the war, Thompson had been on the editorial staff of *Pearson's*, a populist magazine. In this role, he had become a friend of Chester Wright, then the editor of the *New York Call*. With Wright on the staff of the Committee on Public Information, this friendship provided a ready contact between Creel and the league.[35]

Creel later noted that "as a result of many conferences" the NPL position changed, and that "no organization" had become "more loyal" to the war effort.[36] The meetings held by Creel and Townley during the summer of 1917 led the league to drop its cautious, hesitant criticism of the war and, instead, to provide an enthusiastic endorsement of the administration's war policies. Once this shift in position had been made, the league never wavered, although it continued to be a target of government repression and vigilante violence.

La Follette's Speech

By September 1917, the NPL had adopted a pro-war stance and insisted that it loyally supported the administration. Nevertheless, it became entangled in a controversial incident that enabled its opponents to portray it as an integral part of a broader coalition of organizations opposing the war. The conflicting pressures on its leadership became apparent during a national conference organized by the NPL in September 1917.

The Producer's and Consumer's Convention brought together an array of farmers' organizations, consumer advocates, cooperatives, and friendly trade unions with the primary purpose of consolidating an effective lobby to pressure the administration to control the prices of essential consumer goods and to sharply increase the tax on excess profits. At the same time, the NPL was determined to demonstrate its newfound support for the president's war policies.[37]

A week before the conference began, Townley wrote to Woodrow Wilson informing him of the upcoming event, while also conveying "deep assurances" of the league's "loyalty." Townley asked the president to either send a message to the conference or dispatch a representative. Wilson was persuaded by Townley's request. He, therefore, told Joseph Tumulty, the president's secretary and de facto chief of staff, to transmit to William Colver the president's request that Colver speak to the conference as the unofficial representative of the administration. Colver held the post of editorial director of the Scripps-Howard newspaper chain. The Scripps papers were loyal supporters of the war effort and the administration. Wilson had appointed Colver to the Federal Trade Commission. In this role, he criticized the excessive profits of the meat packers, thereby gaining the NPL's approval.[38]

Creel's plan to cajole the league into supporting the war effort seemed to be working beautifully. The conference convened on September 17, 1917, in Fargo, North Dakota, and moved to St. Paul, Minnesota, for the final three days. In his address to the conference, Colver warned that this would be "a long war" requiring every American "to sacrifice heavily." When Townley spoke on September 18, he defended the government's efforts to greatly increase tax revenues since the United States sought "to win the war for Liberty and Democracy." Still, Townley warned the delegates that profiteers were "influencing the government in too large a measure."[39]

The conference approved resolutions calling upon the government to fix prices on essential goods, increase the tax on excess profits, and bring key national resources, in particular the railroad system, into government control. (In December 1917, three months after the St. Paul conference, the president placed the nation's railroad system under direct government control for the duration of the war.) The delegates also approved a motion to "pledge our lives, our fortunes" in "this OUR WAR."[40]

Everything appeared to be under the tight control of the NPL leaders until a farewell session featuring a speech by Senator Robert La Follette. Outspoken in his opposition to the decision to enter the war, La Follette had continued to call upon the United States to define its war aims. In his speech to the St. Paul conference, La Follette emphasized the need to control prices and tax excess profits, but he also reiterated the arguments behind his opposition to the decision to go to war with Germany.[41] A distorted version of his speech was circulated in the mainstream press, setting off a huge uproar. The intense controversy that ensued put the NPL on the defensive.

Townley was eager to disassociate the NPL from La Follette's speech, although relations between the league and La Follette had been extremely cordial. In an article providing a report on the St. Paul conference, the *Leader* excused La Follette by claiming that he had been "goaded" by hecklers. Still, "the senator said things he should not have said," and for which the NPL took "no responsibility whatsoever."[42]

This was followed by a letter from Thompson to Creel confirming that the league was "loyal to the government of the United States." As a result, the *Leader* agreed to accept advertisements for war bonds without charge while printing editorials urging farmers to purchase as many bonds as possible.[43]

Townley Meets the President

Creel was willing to overlook the debacle around La Follette's speech and continued to seek out ways to use the Nonpartisan

League to promote the war effort. The president was scheduled to address the annual conference of the American Federation of Labor on November 12, 1917, in Buffalo, New York. Wilson used the opportunity to present the official line on the war, insisting that the war had been "started by Germany" and that the United States was "fighting for freedom." According to Wilson, the root of the problem was Germany's determination "to dominate the labor and the industry of the world."[44]

Creel understood that the AFL convention could be used as more than a convenient forum for the president. Before the convention, he telegraphed Samuel Gompers, pressing him to invite Townley to speak. Gompers was not eager, both because of Townley's background as an organizer for the Socialist Party and because the NPL operated on the edge of the two-party system. Nevertheless, Creel was "convinced of [the] importance" of Townley's appearance in Buffalo. Townley, therefore, spoke to the AFL convention on November 16, four days after the president's appearance.[45]

Townley's speech focused on the economic issues confronting farmers during wartime mobilization. These were topics not likely to interest delegates at a trade union convention. Townley did reassure the delegates that the farmers he represented were "second to none" in their "loyalty to the people of the country and the nation."[46]

Although Townley's speech was not well received, Creel remained convinced that the league's adherence to the administration's policies was of vital importance. He, therefore, convinced Townley to travel to Washington. On November 30, 1917, Creel arranged for a brief White House meeting between Wilson and Townley.[47] The president generally avoided such meetings, preferring to let his trusted aides handle such negotiations. Wilson's willingness to see Townley indicates the importance given to persuading Townley to provide enthusiastic support to the government's war policies.

From the White House, Creel escorted Townley to a three-hour meeting with Herbert Hoover, the government official in overall charge of food production. Townley and Hoover worked out a plan to boost grain production in the Upper Plains states where the NPL was strongest. This meeting was of special importance since it validated Townley and the NPL as intermediaries between the small farmers of the Midwest and the administration.[48]

The meetings with the president and Hoover were the culmination of a sustained campaign by Creel to cajole the Nonpartisan League into becoming uncritical defenders of the war. After these meetings, Townley "pledged the full support of his organization to the war," and, according to Creel, "these pledges were kept."[49]

The NPL Expands into Minnesota

Despite its efforts to mollify the federal government through its increasingly strident support for the war effort, the NPL would find itself in the midst of an acrimonious conflict in Minnesota, a conflict from which the Wilson administration deliberately remained aloof.

In the summer of 1916, Townley decided the league should expand into states adjacent to North Dakota. A new organizational framework was created as the organization developed a regional presence. The National Nonpartisan League, with Townley as its president, sent organizers into several states. To further confirm its commitment to expanding beyond its initial base, the NPL moved its headquarters to St. Paul in January 1917.[50] Minnesota was viewed as the priority target for organizing. More than ninety organizers were soon traveling throughout that state's rural areas recruiting new members. By early 1918, the league had enrolled fifty thousand members in Minnesota.[51]

The rapid rise of the NPL in Minnesota convinced powerful corporate executives that the league was about to gain control

LIBRARY OF CONGRESS

Abraham Cahan

LIBRARY OF CONGRESS

Scott Nearing

NATIONAL ARCHIVE AT COLLEGE PARK, MD.

Louis Lochner

LIBRARY OF CONGRESS

Lola La Follette

LIBRARY OF CONGRESS

Robert La Follette

STATE HISTORICAL SOCIETY OF NORTH DAKOTA

Arthur Townley

LIBRARY OF CONGRESS

George Creel

LIBRARY OF CONGRESS

John Lord O’Brian

LIBRARY OF CONGRESS

Alfred Bettman

NATIONAL ARCHIVE AT COLLEGE PARK, MD.

A. Bruce Bielaski

NATIONAL ARCHIVE AT COLLEGE PARK, MD.

Ralph Van Deman

LIBRARY OF CONGRESS

General Marlborough Churchill

of that state's government as it had in North Dakota. An alliance of business interests and conservative Republicans were determined to prevent such a takeover, whatever the cost. The result was a bitter conflict.

Although adjacent to North Dakota, Minnesota had a distinctive character. It was far more urbanized than its western neighbor. There were no major urban centers in North Dakota. Indeed, every city in North Dakota had a population under thirty thousand. In contrast, 45 percent of Minnesota's residents lived in cities. The Twin Cities of Minneapolis and St. Paul, the largest metropolitan area, had a population of roughly 700,000 during the First World War, nearly a third of the state's total count. Unions represented a significant sector of the workforce in the Twin Cities.

In North Dakota, the NPL had challenged a business community composed of small-town merchants and bankers. In contrast, large corporations dominated the scene in Minnesota, with the flour mills of the Twin Cities the most significant. The executives who controlled these corporations were entrenched and powerful. They were closely aligned with Governor Joseph Burnquist and the Republican Party's majority in the state legislature. The wartime crisis would provide a convenient rationale for corporate interests to develop a coordinated campaign of repression that would effectively counter the league's drive into Minnesota.

The Minnesota Commission of Public Safety

Burnquist's chances of being reelected governor depended on disrupting the emerging alliance between the NPL and progressive trade unions. In April 1917, two weeks after the declaration of war, the legislature approved a bill establishing a Commission of Public Safety. The commission was given a broad mandate to do whatever was necessary to mobilize Minnesota's resources for the war effort. It was funded with an appropriation of one million dollars, a considerable sum at the time, more than $20 million at current prices. Burnquist and Attorney General Lyndon Smith were given seats on the commission by virtue of their positions. In addition, Burnquist appointed five members. All were men and most were corporate executives or lawyers representing corporations.[52]

The most influential member of the commission was John McGee. A corporate attorney, McGee was bitterly hostile to the left and to the formation of trade unions of any sort. He was convinced that the Commission of Public Safety should seek to suppress any group that challenged the domination of the business community. Burnquist provided McGee with the backing he needed.[53]

State militias had been integrated into the U.S. Army by order of the president in August 1917. With the backing of the Commission of Public Safety, McGee created an alternative militia, the Home Guard.[54] Most of those who volunteered were local businessmen who were ardent supporters of the war. Home Guard units were used to break strikes and as an armed force to disrupt NPL activities.

Although most of Burnquist's appointments to the commission adhered to the same conservative political perspective, there was one exception. John Lind had served one term as governor of Minnesota from 1899 to1901, having been elected as a liberal reformer. A Democrat, his campaign gained the support of populists as well. Lind resigned from the Commission of Public Safety in January 1918, but initially, he joined with the other members in their efforts to suppress dissent.[55]

The commission's initial campaign targeted the Industrial Workers of the World. Wobbly organizers were busy recruiting miners in northern Minnesota and migrant farm workers harvesting the wheat crop throughout the state. The IWW was far more radical than the NPL. It sought to form industrial unions of unskilled workers with the goal of organizing a general strike that would end the existing system and replace it with an economy based on worker control of publicly owned industries. Furthermore, in December 1916, the IWW voted at its national convention to engage in militant resistance to the war effort, culminating in a general strike. Once the United States declared war in April 1917, the union's leadership opted to downplay its opposition to the war and to ignore the convention resolution.[56]

The Minnesota Commission of Public Safety was particularly concerned that the Agricultural Workers Industrial Union #400 (AWIU), an affiliate of the IWW, would call a strike of migrant workers during the upcoming harvest season. Lind wrote to Secretary of Labor William Wilson, warning that the situation in the wheat fields was "menacing." One of the commission's first acts was to place informants in the union's Minneapolis headquarters. This enabled the commission to obtain a complete list of IWW organizers and activists in the state.[57]

With those in hand, the commission formulated a model for an amended version of a vagrancy statute. The proposed bill was drafted by Lind and Ambrose Tighe, a corporate attorney who served as lead counsel to the commission. The proposed bill made it illegal to advocate syndicalism and defined those who did as vagrants. The amended law was clearly aimed at the IWW.[58] Although the IWW denied that it was a syndicalist union, it was significantly influenced by French syndicalist unions.[59]

Dozens of town councils adopted the model vagrancy law. Local police or sheriff deputies then arrested IWW organizers and forcibly deported them from their jurisdiction as vagrants.[60] This was a flagrant violation of free speech rights guaranteed by the First Amendment, and yet it was written, in part, by Lind, a liberal reformer. Lind would strongly object to the commission's trampling on fundamental civil liberties when it targeted the NPL. Still, he had no difficulty aiding its ruthless effort to crush the IWW.

In the summer of 1917, the Minnesota Commission of Public Safety was one of several organizations that lobbied the president to initiate a coordinated nationwide campaign to quash the

IWW.[61] By September 1917, the Justice Department had set the suppression of the Wobblies as one of its highest priorities, so the commission turned its attention to the Nonpartisan League.

The Commission of Public Safety Targets the NPL

The Producer's and Consumer's Convention organized by the NPL in St. Paul in September 1917 attracted thousands to hear various speakers, including Senator Robert La Follette. The conference's success demonstrated that the Nonpartisan League was becoming a serious force in the politics of Minnesota. In response, the Commission of Public Safety shifted its focus from the IWW to the league.

As NPL organizers recruited members, they held rallies in small towns where farmers shopped. The rallies helped break down the isolation felt by those living in sparsely settled rural areas. Speakers were dispatched from the league's headquarters. The Commission of Public Safety decided to ban these rallies as a first step in suppressing the NPL.[62]

The commission decided to build on the strategy it had used to quash the IWW, but this time, the target would be the NPL. At the request of Governor Burnquist, Lyndon Smith, the state attorney general, issued an opinion on October 10, 1917, that was then distributed by the commission to its local affiliates throughout the state and to local authorities as well. The opinion held that sheriffs could ban public meetings of the league on the basis of a statute that provided that "the sheriff shall keep and preserve the peace." Sheriffs acting on this basis, Smith argued, would be "acting in good faith" to prevent "discord, strife and division." At a meeting of sheriffs from around the state, the governor's representative advised those attending that "if a riot was imminent," they could ban the holding of an NPL rally. Indeed, even the threat of a disturbance would provide an excuse for sheriffs in several counties to prohibit the league from organizing any public event.[63] NPL organizers who proceeded to hold a rally that had been banned were arrested for unlawful assembly.

Smith's legal opinion blatantly contradicted the First Amendment guarantee of free speech. State officials cannot prevent public meetings from being held because speakers will make controversial comments. This principle holds even in wartime. A more accurate reading of the Minnesota statute would be that one responsibility of a sheriff is to protect the free speech rights of citizens from those who seek to disrupt the speeches of those with whom they disagree. State authorities were telling sheriffs the exact opposite.

Furthermore, Smith ignored a Minnesota statute that addressed this very topic. This statute provided that anyone who "shall willfully disturb any assembly" was guilty of a misdemeanor. Of course, this statute was not enforced.[64]

The commission's effort to disrupt NPL meetings was quite successful. By early 1918, twenty-one counties had banned all league meetings. In fourteen of these counties, the orders prohibiting league meetings had come from the local Commission of Public Safety, usually a group of local businessmen. These orders had no legal validity even by the dubious guidelines set by Smith's opinion. Local sheriffs issued orders forbidding all NPL meetings in the remaining seven counties.[65]

The commission's campaign to disrupt NPL meetings had a significant impact. The league's newspaper, the *Nonpartisan Leader*, reported in March 1918 that forty out of 250 scheduled in the previous weeks had been banned by sheriffs or mayors.[66]

Vigilante Violence and the Nonpartisan League

Local authorities soon discovered that the commission's efforts to disrupt the NPL were ineffective. Organizers found it difficult to hold public meetings in towns, but they could still travel by car to individual farms to recruit new members. Small gatherings could be held quietly at the homes of friendly farmers.

The next step was to move beyond even nominal compliance with the law to blatantly illegal actions and vigilante violence. These mobs were not spontaneous outbursts of popular anger. On the contrary. Vigilantes were often meticulously organized, and the level of violence was carefully orchestrated. Local officials such as the mayor, sheriff and county attorney were usually directly involved, with the Home Guards providing many of those who participated in the mob. In most cases, the attacks on NPL organizers arose from decisions made at a secret meeting attended by the community's leading merchants and bankers.

The mob violence in Minnesota began in October 1917 and lasted through the summer of 1918. In general, the level and scope of vigilante violence escalated over this period. At first, the league's organizers were intimidated and harassed. Nine months later, the aim was to terrorize an entire community of NPL supporters, with individual activists singled out for beatings and deportations.

On October 4, 1917, the league attempted to organize a rally in Lake City, a town of 2,900 residents located seventy-five miles southeast of Minneapolis. The town's mayor joined the sheriff of Wabasha County in banning the meeting. Deputies then used a fire hose to disperse the crowd of farmers gathered to hear the speakers.[67]

Two weeks later, two NPL organizers, N. S. Randall and Perry Aronson, tried to address a meeting in the Rock Creek district, located sixty-five miles northeast of Minneapolis in Pine County. At the time, it was a village of less than nine hundred inhabitants. Pine County would become a focal point for mob violence. Before the meeting could begin, a mob that included several members of the local Home Guard stormed the hall. Randall and Aronson were assaulted and threatened with lynching. They were then forcibly deported from Pine County and warned not to return.[68]

During November and December of 1917, there was a lull in vigilante actions, perhaps reflecting a decision by the league to keep a low profile for the time being. In any case, beginning in January 1918, arbitrary arrests and mob violence escalated. One set of incidents occurred in Hubbard County, located in northern Minnesota, 175 miles northwest of Minneapolis.

On January 25, 1918, two NPL organizers, Charles Barnes and Robert Hamilton, attempted to hold a meeting in a local hall in the small town of Akeley. Six armed members of the Home Guard held the two organizers and forcibly deported them from Hubbard County.[69]

Six weeks later, on March 4, 1918, Barnes returned to organize a meeting in Park Rapids, the largest community in Hubbard County. Barnes met with Sheriff Dan Petrie, who agreed that the NPL could hold the meeting during the following week. (Petrie had been sheriff since 1901 and was closely linked to the local business community.)

Barnes returned to Park Rapids on the day of the planned event, March 11, 1918. Upon arrival, he was told by the mayor that the meeting could not be held because the league had a reputation for being "unpatriotic." Barnes then went to a street corner where sixty local farmers were gathered waiting for the start of the rally. Petrie warned the crowd that the meeting had been canceled because of the threat of a riot, citing the advisory opinion of the state attorney general authorizing sheriffs to prohibit NPL meetings when there was a threat of violence. Of course, the threats came from those opposed to the league.

Several members of the Home Guard surrounded the gathering of farmers with the determination to enforce the ban. One of them informed Barnes that a secret meeting of local merchants and bankers had insisted that no NPL meetings would be held in Park Rapids. There had been a division within the secret meeting, with a minority calling for "drastic action," that is, a physical assault on Barnes and his forcible deportation. Instead, the "moderates" had prevailed, and the gathering of farmers was dispersed by the threat of vigilante violence rather than its actual use.

Similar incidents occurred in towns around Minnesota during the fall and winter of 1917. League meetings were banned, organizers were forcibly deported and, in some instances, beaten. Despite this campaign of mob violence, the NPL continued to grow. It had become a significant factor in Minnesota's politics, bringing together farmers in support of a program of progressive reforms. State authorities began looking for further methods of suppressing the league. One of these paths involved bringing the federal government into the dispute.

Charles Ames and the Nonpartisan League

One of the members of the Commission of Public Safety, Charles Ames, was so disturbed by the NPL's growth that he decided to devote most of his time to devising ways to disrupt its activities. Ames owned and operated the West Book Company, one of the largest publishers of law books in the United States. A caustic critic of unions, he succeeded in keeping his firm an open shop without any union.[70]

By the fall of 1917, Ames had decided that the NPL represented a serious threat to the established order and that the highest priority of the commission should be its suppression. Indeed, Lind later commented that Ames was "absolutely hysterical on the subject of the Nonpartisan League." On October 2, 1917, the Commission of Public Safety formally delegated the responsibility for monitoring the NPL to Ames.[71]

At first, Ames focused his efforts on the state and local level, but he was soon involved at the national level. In the last week of November 1917, he traveled to Washington to meet with officials at the Department of Justice. This trip would be the first of several to Washington made by Ames in an effort to persuade the administration to charge the league's leadership with violating the Espionage Act.[72]

The primary responsibility for enforcing wartime legislation was entrusted to the War Emergency Division of the

Department of Justice. As deputy director of the division, Alfred Bettman made the day-to-day decisions on who would be prosecuted.[73] Initially, he was wary of becoming directly involved in a domestic political dispute within Minnesota. Still, Bettman took Ames's charges seriously, prodding Ames to provide the Justice Department with credible information proving that the NPL continued to oppose the war effort even after the summer of 1917.

Ames returned to Washington at least once a month for the four months from November 1917 through February 1918.[74] In spite of this continuing pressure, the issue remained in limbo during the fall of 1917, with Bettman still unwilling to authorize intensive surveillance of the NPL.

Ames and the Transit Strike

In December 1917, as the Minnesota Commission of Public Safety turned its efforts away from the IWW to focus on other perceived enemies, internal differences deepened, and splits became public. Although Lind was eager to join the campaign to quash the IWW, he was unwilling to use the same autocratic methods to suppress mainstream unions and the Nonpartisan League. At the same time, Ames believed that the suppression of the league was of the utmost importance, and he was, therefore, wary of using the commission to break strikes. Lind and Ames soon found themselves marginalized within the commission, albeit for different reasons.

Strains within the commission reached a breaking point during a militant strike of transit workers. In September 1917, organizers from the Amalgamated Association of Street and Electric Railway Employees, a business union aligned with the Gompers wing of the AFL, began developing a base of support among the tram workers in the Minneapolis-St. Paul area. The Twin Cities Rapid Transit company held a monopoly on streetcars in the metropolitan area. Its president and owner, Horace

Lowry, was determined to prevent any union from representing its workforce.

Initially, the tram workers demanded a small increase in wages and the recognition of the Amalgamated as their bargaining agent. Lowry granted a small pay increase, but he refused to recognize the union, and he fired fifty-seven workers for being troublemakers. This action triggered a bitter, lengthy conflict that kept the Twin Cities in turmoil for months.[75]

Lowry created a company union as a docile alternative to the Amalgamated. The company then issued blue buttons to be worn by workers aligned with the company union. The Amalgamated responded by issuing yellow buttons to be worn by its members. The ensuing battle of the buttons further heightened tensions and left the question of union recognition unresolved.[76]

At this point in late November 1917, the Commission of Public Safety stepped in with a ruling that banned the wearing of either button and prohibited any union organizing while on the job. This ruling clearly favored management. In response, the Amalgamated called a strike on the trams and organized a mass rally for December 2. James Manahan of the NPL joined several local labor leaders as speakers at the rally. All of the speakers urged those attending to engage in peaceful protests to show their support for the strike. Two thousand at the rally left and began attacking trams operated by strikebreakers. Burnquist deployed the Home Guard, militia units created by the commission, and order was restored.[77]

Ames happened to be in Washington while these events occurred, once again seeking to convince administration officials to prosecute the league for allegedly violating the Espionage Act. Although Ames scorned unions, he was concerned that the transit strike was propelling Twin Cities unions into a closer alliance with the NPL. For Ames, the most urgent task was the suppression of the Nonpartisan League. The actions of the Commission of Public Safety were making this more difficult by helping to forge a broader progressive alliance that could more effectively repel the state's repressive measures. Ames, therefore, urged the federal government to intervene in the strike in order to broker a settlement that could bring a rapid end to the dispute. While in Washington, Ames participated in an informal meeting that included Secretary of War Newton Baker and Gompers. Those at the meeting discussed possible compromise solutions to the transit strike.[78]

Burnquist rejected any intervention by the federal government. He was ready to fully align the state government with those intent on breaking the strike and preventing the transit workers of the Twin Cities from organizing. In attending the informal conference, Ames had acted directly contrary to the orders of the governor, who proceeded to fire Ames from his post on the commission.[79]

The transit strike led to an additional split within the Commission of Public Safety. On December 5, 1917, the day after Ames had been fired, the commission held another meeting to discuss the strike. McGee proposed that the commission use its powers to dismiss Thomas Van Lear from his elected position as mayor of Minneapolis. A member of the Socialist Party and a former official in the machinists' union, Van Lear had been reluctant to deploy the city's police force to protect trams operated by strikebreakers. When Lind opposed McGee's proposal, McGee denounced him, and the two got into a shouting match. Burnquist attended the meeting but remained silent. Lind walked out in disgust, never to return. The commission wisely opted to leave Van Lear in office, but it continued to act as an ally of the transit company in a coordinated effort to break the strike.[80]

In spite of Burnquist's hostility, Baker agreed to appoint a mediation commission, which sought to facilitate a compromise solution to the dispute. The transit company then rejected the proposal of the mediation commission. With the support of Burnquist and the Commission of Public Safety, the Twin Cities Rapid Transit Company broke the strike and remained an open shop. Transit workers in the Minneapolis-St. Paul area were only able to organize in 1934 during the wave of militant strikes that took place during President Franklin D. Roosevelt's New Deal.[81]

To the public, it seemed that Ames had been dropped from his role in the state government. The actual situation was more complicated. Burnquist provided the Commission of Public Safety with the authority to take the actions needed to crush the transit workers' strike. At the same time, the governor gave Ames the sole responsibility for dealing with issues related to the NPL. On December 10, 1917, Burnquist appointed Ames to the post of special commissioner with total control over the state government's efforts to quash the league.[82]

Thus, after December 1917, Minnesota's state government worked on two distinct tracks. On the one hand, the Commission of Public Safety focused on suppressing the strike of tram workers, a conflict that dragged on through much of 1918. On the other hand, Ames directed the coordinated campaign targeting the NPL. In the end, Ames was proven to be correct. Although the league did not survive the blows it received during and immediately after the war, the Minnesota Farmer-Labor Party emerged out of the broad alliance of unions, farmers and other progressives that had, in part, been built during the transit strike.[83]

Ames did not limit his contacts to the Justice Department's War Emergency Division. In January 1918, he also met twice with Bruce Bielaski, the director of the Bureau of Investigation.[84] Ames also met with Henry Hunt, who served as the chief advisor on counterintelligence matters to Marlborough Churchill, the director of the army's Military Intelligence Department. Hunt had served a term as the progressive mayor of Cincinnati, Ohio, before joining the army.[85]

Ames and the Nonpartisan League

As Burnquist's special commissioner, with total authority for suppressing the NPL, Ames was granted the power to subpoena witnesses and to take testimony under oath. Indeed, Ames notified a county attorney that the governor had ordered that "all matters connected with the Nonpartisan League" should be referred to him.[86]

Ames sent written reports to Burnquist detailing his covert activities. He also met regularly with the governor to update him on the effort to disrupt the NPL. In a written report dated February 1918, Ames warned Burnquist that the league was "a very dangerous organization." Ames had employed "several" private detective agencies to infiltrate the NPL in Minnesota and he was receiving reports from other detective agencies with informants in other states.[87]

Based on these investigations, Ames concluded that the NPL's leaders were "planning a social revolution." The Nonpartisan League was firmly embedded in a network of radical groupings, with "close and constant contact with the IWW, with the Socialist Party" and with "pacifist agitators." Ames was convinced that Townley was intent on gaining power in order "to destroy all property guarantees in the Constitution and the laws." Ames informed the governor that this drive for power would "involve the use of violence," if necessary. Of course, it was the Minnesota authorities who were inciting violence by encouraging vigilante actions against the NPL.

Ames presented Burnquist with a paranoid fantasy of the league. He offered no proof of his charges since none existed. This is not to say that Ames did not believe that the NPL was a dangerous group of violent revolutionaries. After all, he also believed that there was a global conspiracy of wealthy Jews who were determined to control the world. Indeed, after reading *The Protocols of the Elders of Zion*, an infamous forgery, Ames became even more wary of "the troublesome activities of the Chosen People." Although the *Protocols* might not be a genuine document, there were "many apparent confirmations of the tale."[88]

Ames was not a marginal right-wing extremist. On the contrary, he was a respected corporate executive with a considerable standing in the business community of the Twin Cities. Furthermore, Burnquist delegated substantial power to Ames and the governor continued to regularly meet with him even after receiving the bizarre report of February 1918. One can only conclude that Burnquist also believed the hysterical scare rhetoric being spread by the mainstream press. Apparently, Burnquist and Ames were convinced that the Nonpartisan League was preparing to overthrow the government, and that it had close ties to radical organizations such as the IWW. The league, therefore, had to be crushed by any means necessary, even mob violence and a conspiracy to solicit perjured testimony.

Ames and Bettman

Ames's repeated trips to Washington to consult with Justice Department officials had a significant impact. Although Ames did not convince the Justice Department to authorize the prosecution of Townley and other NPL leaders for violating the Espionage Act, he did succeed in persuading them that Townley and the league were untrustworthy and should be carefully monitored. Ames was certain that the NPL leadership was still opposed to the war, and that the league was only issuing pro-war statements to avoid prosecution. This assessment was probably accurate, certainly as it applied to those influential NPL figures who had been active in the Socialist Party for many years and who continued to view themselves as socialists. Nevertheless, Townley's orders were clear and consistent. No one representing the NPL could criticize the administration's war policies.[89] In fact, the league was fully committed to the war effort.

Although Bettman was initially unwilling to order the Bureau of Investigation to conduct an intensive surveillance of the league, his position changed in January 1918. It is hard to ascertain the underlying reasons for this shift, but it may have resulted from Ames's meetings with influential figures in the Wilson administration.

Ames was intent on persuading the administration that the NPL posed a nationwide threat to public order; thus, a coordinated response from the federal government was required. He conveyed this viewpoint "to some of the closest advisors to the president." On January 9, 1918, he met with Edward House, Wilson's closest confidant.[90]

In any case, Bettman became convinced that there was a credible possibility that confidential guidelines had been issued allowing NPL organizers to make statements critical of the war when such a position would facilitate the recruiting of new members. Since most farmers in the Upper Midwest opposed the war and the draft, aligning the league with the antiwar opposition was bound to make organizing easier.

At the end of January 1918, Bettman sent a memorandum to Bielaski confirming that Ames had provided the War Emergency Division with "voluminous data" demonstrating that the league had, at one time, been "obstructive to the war."

Indeed, NPL organizers "did not hesitate" to express antiwar sentiments during the first months after the U.S. decision to enter the war. Furthermore, even though Townley had "at least superficially abandoned his antiwar tactics" and was "supporting the government," agents from the Bureau of Investigation should intensify their surveillance of the league to ensure that Townley did not "repeat his old tactics."[91]

Bettman followed up this memorandum with another one written in February 1918, that was more specific in its directives. Ames had visited Washington again and had engaged in a further discussion with Bettman and the Justice Department. In the memorandum, Bettman conceded that the NPL's leadership had issued "instructions to the organizers expressly warning them against any antiwar or disloyal sentiments." Still, he was concerned that "secret verbal instructions" advised the organizers that they "may use antiwar sentiments when approaching" those "known to be against the war." Bettman directed the Bureau of Investigation to discover what NPL organizers were "saying to the individual farmers."[92]

The Bureau of Investigation had already been monitoring the public speeches of NPL organizers and leaders, but the type of information Bettman was now requesting could only be ascertained by a more intensive and intrusive surveillance.

The Minnesota Corporate Conspiracy

Since Ames had already briefed Bielaski on the supposed threat posed by the Nonpartisan League, he was ready to act quickly after receiving Bettman's memorandum authorizing closer surveillance of the league. Bielaski ordered Hinton Clabaugh, the agent in charge of the Bureau of Investigation's Chicago office, to send the "best qualified agent" to confer with Ames.[93]

Upon his arrival in the Twin Cities, Julius Rosin met with Ames, who referred him to Charles Patterson, a corporate executive who served as treasurer and member of the board of directors of the largest shoe manufacturer in Minnesota. The O'Donnell Shoe Corporation owned a large factory in St. Paul, employing nearly a thousand workers. Of course, the shop was non-union. Ames informed Roisin that Patterson kept close tabs on the NPL and its activities.[94]

Based on his discussions with Ames and Patterson, Rosin decided that the two were working closely together in an "intimate relationship." The dividing line between the state government and the business community had become entirely blurred. Ames was gathering information to counter the league as a special commissioner reporting to the governor, while Patterson was collecting information on the NPL as a private citizen and a representative of the business community. The two worked together as a seamless unit.

Rosin met with Patterson in an unmarked office in the Merchants National Bank in St. Paul's city center. Most of the offices in the building were occupied by lawyers with their names on the door. Patterson was not a lawyer, and the two adjacent rooms he and his assistant used had no names on the door.

Patterson informed Rosin that a confidential meeting of leading business executives from the Twin Cities had been convened in September 1917. Since then, further meetings of this informal organization had been held. Still, the shadow organization had neither a name nor an official structure or slate of officers.

Patterson did not name those involved in this secretive organization, although Ames must have been one of them. The secrecy surrounding this organization began to crack in the summer of 1918 when one of the group's efforts at counter-propaganda imploded. Clarence Johnson believed there was a place for a progressive organization that acted as an alternative to the NPL. He launched a newspaper, *The Nonpartisan*, that was covertly funded by the Patterson group. The league's newspaper, *The Leader*, denounced the paper as a fraud. This led to a rapid collapse of *The Nonpartisan*, as funding was terminated.

Johnson then sued the Patterson group, claiming he had not been paid as promised. More important, he provided the NPL with inside information on the shadowy organization of corporate executives. Johnson reported that the group had a five-person executive committee, all St. Paul business executives. In addition to Patterson, Eli Warner sat on the executive committee and took an active role in creating *The Nonpartisan*. Warner was also active in the Minnesota Republican Party, serving as its representative to the Republican National Committee.[95]

Johnson also provided the NPL with information on the wider group of bankers and corporate executives that funded and directed the Patterson group. He was instructed to send a copy of every issue of *The Nonpartisan* to a special list of individuals. The list included Fred Snyder, an influential figure in the Minnesota Republican Party. Snyder was an active member of the University of Minnesota regents. He had also been married to one of the founders of the Pillsbury Mills, an important link to the largest industry in Minnesota.[96] The flour mills of Minneapolis processed the wheat produced by the farmers of North Dakota and the surrounding region.

Yet the list given to Johnson included an even more influential figure, Louis Hill, the son of James Hill, the iconic figure who had led the push to build the Great Northern Railroad. Even before James Hill died in 1916, his son had taken over as president of the railroad, with personal investments in copper mining and California real estate. James Hill had been "closely identified" with J. P. Morgan, Sr., and was thus closely linked to the most powerful network of investment bankers in the country. Louis Hill maintained the connection to the Morgan interests. He, therefore, acted as a link between the Patterson group based in the St. Paul business community and Wall Street.[97]

During the initial meeting, the shadow group's members concluded that "they would not tolerate a condition in Minnesota akin to that in North Dakota." Implicit in this decision was the commitment to take whatever actions were deemed necessary to prevent the league from gaining control over Minnesota's state government. This secretive group had set this as its goal since the NPL was "a menace because of its socialistic ideas." Patterson advised Rosin that the members of the group believed that "secrecy, of course" was "the essence of their methods."[98]

Those at the September 1917 founding meeting of the clandestine group were prepared to use their considerable resources to ensure the NPL's defeat. Patterson had been "delegated the task" of implementing a covert program of disruption. For the six months following this meeting he "devoted practically all of his time" to defeating the NPL. Patterson, along with an aide, scanned every newspaper in the state. They then compiled a complete record of the league's activities and assessed its strength in all of Minnesota's eighty-three counties. Of course, this information was funneled to Ames and the Commission of Public Safety.

This was only one aspect of the shadow organization's coordinated effort to discredit, disrupt, and demoralize the NPL. Private detectives were paid to infiltrate informants into the NPL, to act as provocateurs, and to exacerbate divisions. Patterson's organization employed its own detective force, which was in all likelihood drawn from private detective agencies such as Pinkerton's. When Thomas Campbell, the agent in charge of the St. Paul office of the Bureau of Investigation, visited Patterson in June 1918, he reported that Patterson was the "leading businessman in the city," and that he was acting as "the representative of their interests." During this visit, Patterson received a report concerning the activities of the league from the head of this private detective force and passed it on to Campbell.[99]

Patterson told Rosin that the organization's detective force had established contact with an informant in the NPL's St. Paul headquarters. Although the informant was "not of the inner council," that is, one of Townley's closest advisors, he could still provide "valuable inside information."[100]

Using reports from this informant, Patterson compiled a list of the NPL's organizers and speakers operating in Minnesota. The list included information as to where and when the league was sponsoring speaking engagements. This information made it easy for Patterson's organization to notify local Public Safety Committees so NPL meetings could be banned or disrupted.

The full extent of the activities undertaken by the secret organization remains unknown. It is very likely that it raised funds to finance the campaigns of Burnquist and his conservative Republican allies. Furthermore, small-town bankers and merchants tied to the large corporations headquartered in the Twin Cities may have been prodded to initiate mob violence and to provide perjured evidence to help convict the league's leaders of making seditious speeches.

It has long been known that Burnquist and the Commission of Public Safety targeted the NPL and that they acted to protect the interests of their corporate sponsors. Yet Rosin's report took a step beyond this. Behind the politicians and the commission stood a secret group of powerful corporate executives who planned and financed a coordinated campaign of repression.

This was truly an insidious conspiracy to deprive Minnesota's citizens from exercising their constitutionally guaranteed rights. In May 1918, Bielaski sent Bettman a copy of the Rosin report. Bettman, therefore, knew of this conspiracy, and yet he and the War Emergency Division did nothing to counter it.[101] Bettman and the Department of Justice were unwilling to challenge those who held the real power in Minnesota and the surrounding states.

Patterson was well informed about the internal affairs of the NPL. He would have had access to the informant reports from agents paid by Minnesota's corporations to infiltrate the league as well as other organizations on the left. As a result, Patterson told Rosin that the specific purpose of his trip was bound to lead nowhere. Since the fall of 1917, the NPL had given specific orders to its field organizers to avoid any criticism of the war.[102] Those who violated this order were promptly fired. Patterson and the corporate executives he represented knew well that Townley supported the war effort. Furthermore, they should have known that NPL's leaders were far from revolutionaries. Nevertheless, the league had grown into a popular insurgency that threatened corporate control over the state government, and therefore, it had to be crushed.

The President Wavers

As the conflict between the NPL and the Minnesota authorities intensified, the administration found itself in the middle of a bitter dispute. Creel remained committed to Townley and the league, but he found himself increasingly vulnerable to attack.

In late January 1918, Creel urged the president to ignore the vociferous assault on the NPL since it had consistently been "behind the government" and its war policies. Furthermore, the attacks on the league came from "machine politicians" who were beholden to corporate interests.[103]

The president was not sympathetic to Creel's position as he began to distance himself from the NPL. Wilson instructed Tumulty to query a friendly journalist for his view of the situation. Louis Seibold was a well-known journalist for the *New York World*, a pro-war newspaper friendly to the administration. Seibold conceded that the NPL had "ceased its open antagonism to the Government." Nevertheless, Seibold insisted that the league was not "frankly loyal." Seibold charged that the "propaganda of the League" was "of the Bolsheviki sort," and that its program of economic reforms constituted a "get-rich-quick scheme."[104]

Seibold was not criticizing the NPL for its stance on the war, but rather attacking it for its advocacy of populist measures that would aid small farmers. There was no way that the league could satisfy these critics. Dropping its demand for measures such as a state-owned network of grain elevators would have been suicidal, a sure way for the NPL to lose the backing of its primary base of support.

The president then passed on Seibold's letter to Creel, with the warning that the White House had been "getting evidence from many quarters" that Townley and the other NPL leaders were "self-seeking and untrustworthy." Furthermore, Wilson advised Creel that it would be "worthwhile to learn what Mr. Ames" had learned "about the League." Creel was not convinced, and he remained a supporter of Townley and the NPL.[105]

Lindbergh Campaigns for Governor

The decision of the War Emergency Division to actively seek evidence that the NPL was secretly acting to encourage the antiwar opposition coincided with a decision by the president to avoid any entanglement with the league. The conflict within Minnesota sharpened after Charles Lindbergh announced he would challenge Burnquist in the Republican Party primary for governor. Lindbergh had the support of Townley and the NPL. This challenge led Wilson to seek a third alternative between the Nonpartisan League and the conservative politics of Burnquist.

Lindbergh was a popular politician. He had been elected as a Republican to the U.S. House of Representatives from 1906 to 1916, when he ran as a candidate for the U.S. Senate and lost.[106] Thus, Lindbergh had developed a significant base of support among progressives well before the NPL came into existence. He therefore posed a significant threat to Burnquist, who bitterly attacked him and the league for not being "loyal" to the war effort.

Burnquist's campaign took a few sentences out of context from a short book Lindbergh had published in the spring of 1917, immediately following the declaration of war. Most of the book dealt with how a few large corporations dominated the economy and extracted excessive profits through their control of markets. In terms of the war, Lindbergh insisted that the United States "must fight to the limit" of its capacity to ensure that a peace agreement did not "leave the country at a disadvantage." Still, only "war hysteria" prevented a reasoned discussion of peace terms. The United States needed to "plan the terms upon which peace can be negotiated."[107]

This was hardly a radical analysis of the president's war policies. Lindbergh did argue that the "greed" of "speculators" had led to the transporting of arms to the Allies on ships that also carried passengers. The German decision to sink some of these ships had provided the immediate rationale for the United States to declare war on Germany. Lindbergh's position was an indirect critique of the administration's policy in the months leading to the decision to enter the war. Still, Lindbergh was prepared to fully support the war once it was declared. Indeed, he held that once war was declared, it was everyone's "duty" to work "incessantly to supply the means required" to ensure that the United States emerged victorious.[108]

The reality is that Lindbergh supported the war effort, as did the NPL. His support did not stop Burnquist from questioning Lindbergh's patriotic loyalty. The attacks on Lindbergh constituted only one aspect of a systematic assault on the league initiated by Minnesota's state government and its corporate backers.

The Lindbergh Campaign Under Attack

The primary election for the Republican Party's nomination for governor was held on June 17, 1918. It bitterly divided Minnesota. Both candidates traveled around the state, giving dozens of speeches. Still, there was a critical difference between the two campaigns. Lindbergh tapped into a genuine popular enthusiasm by putting forward a platform that appealed to both small farmers in isolated rural areas and the industrial workers of the Twin Cities and Duluth. Lindbergh supported the standard demands of the NPL, calling for a state-owned grain elevator and a state insurance plan for small farmers. In his appeal to industrial workers, he also spoke for the eight-hour day, except for farmhands, old-age pensions, and government mediation of strikes.[109]

Lindbergh and the league sought to address the issues that had arisen during the war. The huge costs incurred by sending hundreds of thousands of soldiers overseas should be paid from taxes levied on the tremendous profits being gained by the wealthy few. In addition, Lindbergh called for state ownership of key industries such as munition factories and grain mills for the duration of the war.[110]

This was a popular program that could attract the support Lindbergh needed to win the primary election. Burnquist understood this, so he avoided any discussion of substantive issues. Instead, Burnquist toured the state, talking exclusively of the need for total support for the war effort and the necessity of harshly suppressing anyone who dissented from the administration's war policies. He also sharply condemned all those who had criticized the U.S. decision to enter the war. Of course, his audience knew that Burnquist was indirectly attacking Lindbergh for his initial hesitancy in backing the war effort in the spring of 1917.[111]

Even with his status as the incumbent governor and the vitriolic backing of the mainstream newspapers, Burnquist was unable to attract the crowds that his opponent did. Lindbergh's first rally occurred on April 25, 1918, in Willmar, a small town of five thousand about ninety-five miles west of Minneapolis. From there, the candidate gave similar speeches in numerous farming communities, drawing increasingly large crowds as the election approached. On June 14, three days before the primary, Lindbergh spoke to the largest crowd of his campaign. Fourteen thousand supporters attended a rally in Wegdahl, a small village 130 miles west of Minneapolis.[112]

In addition to the many rallies, the campaign organized large mobile parades during which hundreds of cars tooted their horns and waved signs supporting Lindbergh. Similar car caravans took place in many rural communities around the state, with the parades growing larger as the campaign progressed.[113]

Lindbergh's primary support came from farmers, many of whom were NPL members. He also drew support from many unionized workers in the Twin Cities and Duluth. Lindbergh found it almost impossible to rally his supporters in Minnesota's cities. Lindbergh was prevented from speaking in Duluth. In May 1918, he was scheduled to speak at the Shrine Hall in Duluth, but his talk was canceled when the Shriners buckled under pressure. At the last moment, the speech was moved to Woodman's Hall, a building owned by a fraternal life insurance company serving lumberjacks. Although eight hundred people quickly assembled to hear him, Lindbergh was blocked from speaking when the police chief threatened the managers of this venue.[114]

Vigilante Violence Escalates

Lindbergh proved to be a popular candidate with an attractive personality and a program that captured the imagination of Minnesota's voters. As a result, Burnquist and his corporate sponsors grew worried that they were losing control. Their response was to intensify the campaign of mob violence aimed at demoralizing the NPL and intimidating its supporters. During the fall of 1917, NPL organizers had been subject to beatings and forcible deportations. Mob actions in the spring of 1918 further escalated vigilante violence. Lindbergh was a well-known and well-respected public figure. Nevertheless, he was assaulted while his supporters were beaten and clubbed in violent confrontations involving hundreds of people.

As Lindbergh toured Minnesota, he was often pelted with eggs as he spoke. At times, he was dragged from the platform and physically prevented from completing his speech. In one case, he returned from a rally to find that a local sympathizer who had driven him to the event had been severely beaten. As Lindbergh left the scene, shots were fired at his car by members of the mob. Lindbergh was lucky that he avoided serious injury during the campaign, but the same could not be said of his supporters.[115]

Pine County was one of the areas where the conflict between the league and its opponents sparked mob violence. The county is located seventy-five miles northeast of Minneapolis and remains largely rural. In October 1917, two NPL organizers had been forcibly deported after being threatened with lynching. Despite the threats of violence, local activists continued to organize. Shortly after Lindbergh's nomination in March 1918, Niels Hokstad, a farmer and a league activist, was waiting at the train station in Rock Creek for the arrival of an NPL speaker.

(Rock Creek was a village of eight hundred in 1918.) He was surrounded by an angry crowd that threatened to kill him if he continued to work for the league. Hokstad understood that the violence he confronted did not originate at the local level. Indeed, there was a conspiracy that included state and county officials. Their aim was to keep Burnquist in power "by terrorizing" the poor farmers of Minnesota to prevent a democratic election.[116]

Hokstad was not intimidated. He continued to organize in Pine County, urging local farmers to join the NPL and to vote for Lindbergh. On May 2, 1918, he tried to deliver a speech in Hinckley, a village of about seven hundred residents. A mob beat Hokstad and then tarred and feathered him. The vigilantes then deported him and warned him not to return. Hokstad was courageous. He was back in Pine County in two days, where he remained an active NPL supporter.[117]

As election day drew near, the attacks on the Lindbergh campaign became more desperate. On June 14, the campaign organized a huge car caravan in Anoka, a town of fourteen thousand located twenty miles north of Minneapolis. As the caravan wended its way through the town, a mob of three hundred attacked. Car windows were smashed, and fifteen hundred NPL supporters were clubbed, men, women and children. All of this took place in broad daylight, and with no effort by the local authorities to stop this outrage.[118] None of the state's mainstream media provided any coverage of the incident.

Lindbergh and the Espionage Act

In early May 1918, Ames made another trip to Washington and met with Bettman. Lindbergh's campaign was gaining momentum as large crowds greeted him as he traveled around Minnesota. Ames was certain that Lindbergh was disloyal, although his speeches stressed his enthusiastic support for the war effort. The local media was already attacking Lindbergh by lifting excerpts from his book, so Ames left a copy with Bettman. Ames believed the book contained passages that would ensure Lindbergh's conviction in federal court.[119]

After reading the book, Bettman wrote to Bielaski that the book "verges on the line, if it does not actually cross it." As a starting point, Bettman queried Bielaski for information on "other antiwar activities" previously engaged in by Lindbergh. Bielaski replied that the Bureau of Investigation did not have a file on Lindbergh. That would soon change.[120]

Bettman then wrote two memorandums to Bielaski, setting out the guidelines for the investigation of Lindbergh and his book. In the first message, Bettman asked Bielaski to ascertain whether there had been any "systematic distribution of the book" since the United States entered the war in April 1917. If so, this might "warrant prosecution."[121]

This memorandum was followed by one that further clarified his position. Bettman advised Bielaski that legal action against Lindbergh "would be unwise" unless there was "a good case." Still, if Lindbergh continued to "permit" the book's distribution, this would provide sufficient grounds to initiate a prosecution under the Espionage Act.[122]

With Bettman's messages as guidelines, the Bureau of Investigation launched an investigation of Lindbergh that lasted several months. Lindbergh's book remained the focus of the investigation, but agents also monitored Lindbergh's campaign speeches to ensure that he continued to voice his unstinting support for the war effort. On June 5, 1918, Bielaski ordered Campbell to report on the "method, extent and time of distribution of the book," and the "character of statements" recently made by Lindbergh.[123]

Campbell quickly determined the basic facts concerning the book. It was written in November and December of 1916 and revised in April 1917, soon after the United States declared war on Germany. Five thousand copies had been printed by a publisher in Washington, D.C., with a publication date of May

1, 1917. Of these, six hundred copies had been distributed to bookstores or given to friends.[124]

Campbell assigned M. J. Murray, an agent in the St. Paul office of the Bureau of Investigation, to go beyond these basic facts. Murray proceeded to go to bookstores around the Twin Cities looking for copies of Lindbergh's book. Most stores reported that none were available. The Northwestern Publicity Bureau, an NPL adjunct, had ordered one hundred copies of the book and still had a few on hand. Still, Murray was told that the store could not order more copies.[125]

Murray then met with Lindbergh, who told the BI agent that he had "no intention of distributing" the remaining copies. Lindbergh was convinced that his work was not illegal or seditious, but he said his opponents were "making trouble" by taking selected excerpts from the book. Murray concluded that Lindbergh was being truthful and was willing to remain within the guidelines set by Bettman.

Once the primary election was over and Lindbergh was no longer a candidate for governor, the BI investigation remained dormant over the summer. Then, in August 1918, Bettman revived the issue. In a message to Bielaski, Bettman asked Bielaski to find out whether Lindbergh was "willing to place" the remaining unsold copies of his book "in [the] Department's custody during the period of the War."[126]

Bielaski passed this message to Campbell, who notified Lindbergh of Bettman's query. Lindbergh came to the St. Paul office of the Bureau of Investigation, where he told Campbell that he was "perfectly agreeable" to Bettman's request. Lindbergh pointed out that he had promised Murray three months previously that he would not distribute any more copies of his book, and "he had kept his word." A few days later, several boxes of the book arrived at the BI office in St. Paul, where they were stored for the duration of the war.[127]

With the war coming to an end, Bettman wrote to Bielaski that the "voluntary suppression" of Lindbergh's book meant that "no additional steps" were "necessary."[128] The case was finally closed.

Bettman was more sympathetic to issues of civil liberties than most influential members of the administration, including the president. Still, he was intent on preventing a former member of Congress from circulating a book he had written that contained a few passages that were mildly critical of the U.S. decision to enter the war.

Bettman's threat to prosecute the Lindbergh book is very troubling. The book had been published before the Espionage Act came into effect. Furthermore, the passages that were allegedly seditious had been written before the United States entered the war. Logically, anyone circulating a book containing a paragraph suggesting that the war arose out of imperialist rivalries could be subject to prosecution. Book dealers and publishers would have had to closely review their stock, withdrawing any item that could possibly be viewed as illegal under the Espionage Act. Even books published during the first months of the war in 1914 could be included in this ban. Bettman was already closely monitoring the NPL, and Lindbergh's book became an issue in that context. Bettman never extended the scope of his argument. Nevertheless, his warning to Lindbergh represented a serious threat to the freedom of the press.

Lindbergh Defeated

The Minnesota Republican primary of June 1918 was tumultuous. As Lindbergh mobilized his supporters, conservative Republicans backed by local and state authorities organized mobs to disrupt rallies and events. NPL leaders were placed on trial for sedition and sentenced to prison. Minnesota's mainstream newspapers ran countless articles denouncing the Nonpartisan League as seditious and pro-German.

It was in this context that Minnesota's voters went to the polls in June 1918. Everyone understood that the winner of the

Republican primary was almost certain to be elected governor in the November general election. When the votes were counted, Burnquist had defeated Lindbergh by fifty thousand votes.[129]

The number of votes cast in the Republican primary was far greater than expected. Indeed, the total vote in the Republican primary in 1918 was nearly twice the total counted in the 1916 Republican primary.[130] The enormous increase in the 1918 primary was even more surprising considering that the election occurred during the influenza epidemic, when many people were staying home and avoiding public spaces such as polling places. Furthermore, thousands of Minnesota's young men were serving in the military, frequently overseas. The number of soldiers who voted in the primary was minuscule.[131]

The 1918 primary election vote totals were truly an anomaly. Indeed, the total votes cast in the 1918 general election held in November were significantly less than the total cast in the 1916 general election.[132]

The huge and unexpected jump in voters participating in the 1918 Republican primary election startled contemporary observers and led many to believe the election had been rigged. Prior to the Minnesota primary, the NPL leadership was confident that Lindbergh would carry the primary. On election day, June 18, 1918, Townley was on a speaking tour of North Dakota. At a rally in Hillsboro, he declared, "We have won the election unless big business with its crooked methods counts us out." After the primary election, Lindbergh accepted the results in public statements, and yet privately he was convinced the election had been stolen.[133]

Nevertheless, a close examination of the election results indicates that the official count was valid. An analysis of each county's results indicates that the increase in votes in the Republican primary in June 1918 took place throughout the state. Furthermore, there was a vast increase in the number of votes cast in those counties where Lindbergh garnered a substantial majority. For instance, in Pipestone County, a rural area located along the southwestern border of Minnesota adjoining South Dakota, Lindbergh defeated Burnquist by a significant margin. The total Republican primary vote in the county more than tripled from the 1916 election to the 1918 election, so the proportionate increase in the primary vote was higher in Pipestone County than statewide.[134] This outcome was directly contrary to the result that would be expected if there was a deliberate effort to inflate the Burnquist vote.

The bitter controversies and divisions within the Republican Party brought out voters to the primary election across the state. Both sides mobilized supporters who might have otherwise abstained from voting.

Although Burnquist won the primary and went on to be elected governor, the 1918 elections hardly provided a popular mandate for his zealous support for the war or his suppression of dissent at home. Burnquist won the Republican primary in 1916 by a wide margin, and he easily defeated the Democratic candidate for governor in that year's general election. In 1918, Burnquist had to overcome a significant challenge from Lindbergh in the primary election, and he failed to win a majority of the vote in the general election. Had the opposition vote not been split between the Democratic Party and the Farmer-Labor Party, Burnquist would have been defeated in his bid for another term as governor.[135]

Nevertheless, the 1918 primary election results were a major blow to the NPL. The organization had put a great deal of time and resources into the Lindbergh campaign. Until this point, the league had been gaining momentum in Minnesota. Lindbergh's defeat and Burnquist's reelection reversed this upward swing. Lindbergh's campaign would mark the high point for the league in Minnesota.

The War Program

Lindbergh's book would not be the only published work to come under intense scrutiny by the Justice Department. In September 1917, the National Nonpartisan League published a lengthy brochure explaining its early history, its program of reforms to help small farmers, and its position on the war. Appended to the end of the main text was a compilation of resolutions approved by the league, including the resolution adopted by the North Dakota NPL in June 1917. One paragraph of that resolution proved to be a focal point for controversy.

The June resolution questioned the entrance of the United States into the war and asked for a clarification of the terms of peace being sought. In this context, the NPL asserted that a key cause underlying the advent of the war was "an economic system based upon exploitation." Wars arose as "rival groups of monopolists" sought to play "a deadly game for commercial supremacy."[136]

Although the great bulk of the brochure could in no way be considered in violation of the laws curbing opposition to the war, opponents of the league focused on that one paragraph to find a plausible basis for legal action.

Ames was certain that the decision by the league to continue printing the *War Program* brochure was further proof that its public support for the war effort was only a sham, and that its leaders were still committed to sabotaging any chance for a U.S. victory. He continued to pressure Bettman into prosecuting the NPL, but Bettman was also receiving pressure from Bielaski along the same lines. In April 1918, Bielaski ordered Campbell to ascertain whether the NPL was still circulating the brochure.[137] Campbell then wrote to Arthur Le Sueur, the league's legal counsel, who reported that the *War Program* brochure was still being distributed in response to requests. With the understanding that a query by an agent of the Bureau of Investigation indicated that the government found the brochure offensive, perhaps even seditious, he offered to withdraw the brochure from circulation. Le Sueur insisted that the league sought to avoid "any act or word" that might be "embarrassing to the government."[138]

When Campbell reported that the brochure was still in print,

Bielaski queried Bettman about the possibility of a prosecution under the Espionage Act. In May 1918, Bettman responded that the brochure contained "one paragraph which is rather close to the line."[139] This comment demonstrates how far the federal government had gone toward quashing even the mildest expression of opposition to the war. The distribution of a lengthy pamphlet that contained a single paragraph suggesting that one of the causes underlying the war was the imperialist rivalries of the European powers was sufficient to raise the genuine possibility that one could spend several years in a high-security federal penitentiary.

Still, Bettman advised Bielaski that, taken as a whole and in the light of the NPL's decision to provide uncritical support for the war effort, he had concluded that the league's actions did "not warrant any prosecution at this time." Instead, the NPL's leaders should be advised "confidentially" to "withdraw the present edition of the War Program," which included the "objectionable paragraph."

Bielaski then ordered Campbell to quietly propose to Le Sueur that the league should cease distributing the brochure. He advised Campbell that this maneuver should be "handled in a very diplomatic manner." The NPL acted quickly to heed Bettman's advice. All copies of the brochure were withdrawn from circulation and those holding copies were ordered to destroy them.[140]

Stalking the NPL

In May 1918, the NPL's opponents initiated a plan to directly enlist the Department of Justice in their effort to suppress it. A complaint was filed with Melvin Hildreth, the U.S. attorney for North Dakota, alleging that Townley had violated the Espionage Act in a speech he had given the previous summer at Buffalo Lake. The complaint was signed by seventeen residents of Milnor, a small town near Buffalo Lake.[141]

Townley was quoted as saying that while U.S. soldiers were "being killed, red-necked American plutocrats, ten times worse than the German autocrats, coin the blood of our young men" in their greedy search for maximum profits.[142] Hildreth passed the complaint on to O'Brian, although he doubted its veracity. O'Brian was "inclined to agree" with Hildreth, but he ordered an investigation just to be sure.[143]

An agent of the Bureau of Investigation then proceeded to interview eight of the seventeen individuals who had signed the complaint. Most of those interviewed had only hazy memories of Townley's speech and did not remember the quotes presented in the complaint. One of those interviewed was an NPL member, who insisted that Townley had confined his remarks at Buffalo Lake to a call for the war to be funded by income taxes on the rich rather than through the sale of war bonds. This demand was a frequent theme in NPL propaganda.[144]

O'Brian was incensed by the use of completely fabricated quotes to support the prosecution of the league's leadership on false charges. Shortly after receiving the report from the BI agent, O'Brian wrote Hildreth requesting him to investigate "to what extent" these accounts of Townley's speeches were "being manufactured and worked up." O'Brian followed this message with another one in which he again stated that he wanted Hildreth to ascertain whether there was an organized effort that led to false charges "being systematically manufactured."[145]

O'Brian's query was a potentially explosive query. An investigation along these lines could have exposed a conspiracy that crossed state lines and involved powerful corporate executives and influential politicians. Still, Hildreth had no intention of becoming involved in this dispute.[146] Furthermore, there was no way that the Justice Department would authorize such an investigation, particularly given the president's decision to remain aloof from the controversies swirling around the Nonpartisan League. Nevertheless, it is clear that O'Brian knew that there was a concerted effort to ensure that Townley and other NPL leaders were prosecuted on the basis of statements that they had not, in fact, made.

O'Brian Objects

O'Brian had been following the early stages of the Gilbert case. The Milnor complaint reinforced his belief that there was a pattern of bringing charges against the NPL's leaders based on perjured testimony. This was only one aspect of a broader campaign of repression. Dismayed by the illegal and autocratic actions being used to suppress the league, O'Brian wrote to Burnquist in the hope that the governor would act as a check on Minnesota's local authorities. The "lawless attacks upon residents" by local vigilante groups and the "suppression of meetings" held by the NPL constituted a "reign of terror." O'Brian was convinced that these repressive actions were "essentially unpatriotic."[147]

Of course, Burnquist was not persuaded. O'Brian's quiet attempt to counter the attacks on the NPL ran against the administration's policy of neutrality. The Justice Department frequently claimed it had no authority to intervene in the conflict. For instance, Gregory responded to a query as to why no actions were taken to deter vigilante violence by claiming that while such incidents were "particularly deplorable" during wartime, the federal government had "only very limited jurisdiction" in these matters. Instead, state authorities "should be dealing with the situation."[148]

The fundamental problem was that state authorities, especially the Minnesota Commission of Public Safety, were complicit in the encouragement of mob violence, while actively urging local authorities to suppress the league. In fact, laws enacted during the Reconstruction era could have been used by the Justice Department to bring charges against those responsible for actions designed to suppress the civil rights of NPL members.

The Enforcement Act of 1871 had given the president the power to counter paramilitary organizations such as the Ku Klux Klan. President Ulysses Grant had used this authority to undermine the Klan.[149] The North's commitment to Reconstruction soon faded. That became apparent in 1883 when the U.S. Supreme Court narrowed the scope of the Enforcement Act to the actions of the state and its representatives.[150]

This was exactly the situation in Minnesota. The Minnesota Commission of Public Safety encouraged local authorities to use force to prevent NPL organizers from engaging in activities protected by the First Amendment. Bettman and the War Emergency Division could have sought indictments of state and local officials under the Enforcement Act. This would have made it far more difficult for Minnesota to continue its campaign of vigilante violence targeting the NPL.

O'Brian could have gone public at the time by voicing his concerns to the press. Instead, his efforts to counter the illegal repressive measures in Minnesota always remained behind the scenes. Of course, had O'Brian publicly expressed his concerns, he probably would have been replaced as the head of the War Emergency Division.

After the war ended, O'Brian delivered a speech in which he criticized the situation in Minnesota. In January 1919, O'Brian spoke before the New York State Bar Association and reviewed the extent to which the right to dissent had been preserved during wartime. Justifying the policies of the Wilson administration, O'Brian insisted that the Justice Department had understood that "free expression of public opinion is the life of the nation." U.S. attorneys had been instructed to "bear in mind at all times the constitutional guarantees" codified in the Bill of Rights.[151] The reality had been very different. The federal government had instituted a relentless repression of those who stated their opposition to the war, accompanied by the imposition of harsh penalties on those convicted under the Espionage Act and other wartime laws.

Still, O'Brian deplored the situation in Minnesota, where "state laws of a sweeping character were passed and enforced with severity." Minnesota's "policy of repression" had led to "increased discontent." Furthermore, "the most serious cases of illegal interferences with civil liberty were reported to the federal government from that state." O'Brian knew that Minnesota's authorities had been complicit in a systematic effort to convict NPL leaders of violating the Espionage Act through perjured testimony. Yet he avoided this specific issue in his speech.

The efforts of O'Brian and the War Emergency Division to defend the civil liberties of the Nonpartisan League were ineffectual, too little and too late.

Prosecutions and Legal Harassment

State and local officials continued to ratchet up the pressure on the NPL. Within a few months in the spring and early summer of 1917, league organizers and activists were arrested nearly fifty times on charges related to allegedly "disloyal" activities.[152] Most of these cases were filed in Minnesota's district courts, either for unlawful assembly or for violating the state's sedition law.

The NPL was committed to providing a defense for those charged, even if this meant appealing verdicts through the judicial system. Only a few cases were reviewed by the Minnesota Supreme Court, which had a mixed record in terms of its decisions.[153]

In the end, very few of the league's organizers spent significant time in jail. Only Townley and Gilbert were prosecuted on felony charges upheld by the Minnesota Supreme Court and had to serve extended prison sentences. Nevertheless, the arrests caused major problems for the NPL. Legal resources diverted resources from the treasury. The state's mainstream newspapers repeatedly pointed to the convictions obtained in district courts as proof that the league was a seditious organization that opposed the war effort. The NPL's leaders had to spend many days in court and considerable time preparing to give testimony as defense witnesses. Crucially, the prosecution of its leading figures exacerbated underlying differences in political perspectives, leading to destructive splits and resignations.

Many of the charges arose from holding meetings in defiance of the ruling by the state attorney general giving sheriffs the right to ban meetings that might lead to disorder. In these cases, NPL organizers were arrested as they began to speak. Most often, they were held overnight and then escorted out of town. Sometimes, organizers would be charged with unlawful assembly and released on bail. When their trial date came, charges would be dropped, and the matter dismissed. Very few of these cases reached the appellate courts. In general, arrests for speaking at a banned meeting were made to harass the league and not with any real intent to imprison those detained.

Arrests for allegedly violating Minnesota's Sedition Act occurred less frequently, but they had more significant consequences. The NPL leadership was targeted, and county prosecuting attorneys were often assisted by an attorney from the state attorney general's office during the trial. Sedition cases led to lengthy trials, with the league providing defendants with more than one attorney. Guilty verdicts were appealed to the State Supreme Court, with mixed success.

Sedition was a difficult charge for the state to prove since Townley had ordered all NPL organizers and speakers to act as boosters for the war effort.[154] Only by fabricating perjured testimony could the authorities hope to persuade a jury to bring in a guilty verdict. The sedition trials demonstrated the extreme measures the Burnquist administration and its allies were prepared to take to suppress the Nonpartisan League.

In March 1918, Joe Gilbert was indicted for sedition for a speech he had given in August 1917 in Kenyon (a village in Goodhue County, located seventy miles southeast of Minneapolis). The prosecution's case depended on the testimony of witnesses who swore that Gilbert had made several provocative statements during his speech. Each of these witnesses insisted that Gilbert had used exactly the same words in his presentation. Gilbert was convicted of sedition and sentenced to one year in jail, the maximum sentence allowed under the state's sedition act.[155]

Once Gilbert was convicted of sedition, Townley began to view him as a liability. Mainstream newspapers pointed to Gilbert's conviction under the state sedition act as proof that the NPL continued to oppose the war effort. Furthermore, Gilbert had been the primary author of the league's resolution from June 1917, that had raised concerns about the U.S. decision to enter the war that April.

Before Gilbert's trial, the inner core of the NPL met and decided that the legal cases needed to be appealed through the judicial system. Gilbert volunteered to have his case be a test case and Townley agreed. Once Gilbert was convicted, Townley began to waver on his promise. Gilbert was furious and confronted Townley, who reluctantly agreed to finance an appeal. Townley retaliated by demoting Gilbert to a job in North Dakota. In July 1918, Gilbert and seventeen other league organizers and staff wrote a letter calling for greater democracy within the organization. Those who signed the call were also demoted.[156]

The sedition case against Gilbert was appealed and, in December 1918, the Minnesota Supreme Court upheld his conviction. In a decision written by Myron Taylor, the Minnesota Supreme Court ruled that those who listened to Gilbert's speech "would naturally and reasonably conclude" that the United States had entered the war "needlessly."[157]

Taylor did not directly address the question of how four members of the audience at the rally could repeat the same phrases months after the event had occurred. Instead, Taylor arbitrarily shifted the terms of the argument, thereby avoiding an embarrassing issue. It "was for the jury to determine" the "weight to be given" to the testimony of each witness. Since the jury had "found the testimony presented by the prosecution to be true," there was "no ground" for the court to question this.[158]

This would be the only case arising from the efforts of Minnesota authorities to quash the NPL that would be reviewed by the U.S. Supreme Court. In its December 1920 decision, the majority opinion delivered by Justice Joseph McKenna upheld Gilbert's conviction in terms that were similar to those made by the Minnesota Supreme Court.[159] The dissent by Justice Louis Brandeis would mark a crucial turning point in constitutional law.

Brandeis held that the Minnesota Sedition Act was unconstitutional. He pointed out that the act did not specify that it was only valid at a time when the United States had declared war on another country. In a time of peace, Brandeis argued, the state could not make it illegal to present opinions that might discourage someone from joining the military.[160]

The constitutionality of a state law was only relevant if federal courts had the jurisdiction to determine this. Federal courts had declined to extend the rights guaranteed by the Bill of Rights to state legislation since a ruling by the U.S. Supreme Court written by Justice John Marshall in 1833.[161] Even after the Fourteenth Amendment had been enacted during Reconstruction, the U.S. Supreme Court had ruled that its due process clause protected businesses from arbitrary state regulation. However, the court declined to extend this coverage to questions of civil liberties.[162]

In his dissent in the Gilbert case, Brandeis challenged this entire train of thought. He wrote, "I cannot believe that the liberty guaranteed by the Fourteenth Amendment includes only liberty to acquire and to enjoy property."[163] Within five years, this argument would be accepted by the entire court. In *Gitlow v. New York*, both the majority opinion of Justice Edward Sanford and the minority opinion of Justice Oliver Wendell Holmes, Jr., agreed that First Amendment rights were covered by the Fourteenth Amendment.[164] Thus, the legal cases arising from the bitter struggle in Minnesota would have a major impact on constitutional law and the defense of civil liberties.

Gilbert's conviction for sedition in Goodhue County represented a critical moment for the NPL. One of its leading figures could now be denounced as a convicted felon in the mainstream press. Under the pressure of this legal barrage, the league's leadership began to unravel.

The other sedition case that had important implications for the league began in May 1918, when Townley and Gilbert were charged with conspiracy to violate the state sedition law. The indictment in Jackson County contended that the NPL's leaders were engaged in a concerted and deliberate effort to undermine the war effort. In support of the conspiracy charge, the prosecution pointed to the circulation of the *War Program* and to a brief speech given by Gilbert in Litchfield, Minnesota, in January 1918. Once again, the prosecution relied on perjured testimony to bolster its case.[165]

The prosecution also introduced several speeches by Townley. In these speeches, Townley denounced the excessive profits made by corporations producing munitions.[166] The NPL had always believed that the underlying motive for the state's campaign of repression was the protection of corporate interests that had dominated Minnesota's politics rather than issues related to support for the war effort. The prosecution's use of Townley's speeches in the conspiracy case proved this point all too clearly.

The trial took place in July 1919. Townley and Gilbert were found guilty, and the judge then sentenced them to the maximum penalty of three months. The conspiracy case was appealed to the Minnesota Supreme Court. In April 1921, the court upheld the conviction of Townley and Gilbert, and the U.S. Supreme Court then declined to review this decision. Minnesota's authorities had finally succeeded in having Townley convicted of sedition and sentenced to prison.[167]

Ames Attacks the Administration

By the fall of 1918, Ames had realized that the Justice Department would not agree to prosecute the NPL's leaders. Instead of further efforts along this line, Ames began attacking the administration for protecting the league. He wrote to Judge Martin Wade, a federal district judge in Iowa, complaining of the refusal of the Justice Department to launch a campaign of repression targeting the NPL comparable to the one that had been "conducted against the IWWs." Wade was renowned for imposing lengthy prison sentences on opponents of the war who had been convicted of violating the Espionage Act.[168] Ames told Wade that he had presented O'Brian with copious evidence of the league's seditious activities, and yet nothing was done. In Ames's opinion, "The most obvious explanation" for this lack of action was "the manifestations of approval and cooperation by the administration with the Townley League."[169]

Ames was wrong at every level. O'Brian was a mainstream corporate attorney and a staunch Republican. He objected to mob violence, particularly when it was directed at those supporting the war effort, and he also found the use of perjured testimony to be abhorrent. Nevertheless, as director of the War Emergency Division, he zealously prosecuted those who organized to protest the war effort. In addition, by the fall of 1918, the Wilson administration had established its distance from the NPL and was trying to create a third, centrist alternative between the league and the conservative corporate interests that Ames represented.

Wade was hostile to the Nonpartisan League, but he was not prepared to join the vocal opponents of the administration. He, therefore, sent Ames's letter to Claude Porter at the Department of Justice. Porter had worked with Wade from 1914 to 1918 as the U.S. attorney for Iowa. He had then served as one of the attorneys assisting in the prosecution of IWW leaders for allegedly violating the Espionage Act before being appointed assistant attorney general in September 1918.[170]

In June 1919, Porter wrote a memorandum on the NPL for Mitchell Palmer, who had recently replaced Thomas Gregory as attorney general. Porter enclosed the letter from Ames that Wade had sent him. He also pointed out to Palmer that Arthur

Le Sueuer had worked as a defense counsel for the Wobblies, while also acting as an advisor to Townley. These facts convinced Porter that "Le Sueuer and Townley and the whole crowd were sympathizers with the I.W.W." Even so, there was "no evidence for a criminal suit."[171]

The Wilson administration kept the league under intensive surveillance, but it had no intention of openly aiding the alliance of conservative Republicans and corporate executives intent on destroying it. Still, the administration also refused to take any action to curb Minnesota's authorities and their allies as they flagrantly violated the law. The president refused to become directly involved in the conflict and, instead, watched the two sides battle it out, as he sought a safe third way.

The Military Intelligence Division and the NPL

The NPL continued to be a target of the intelligence community, and, in particular, of the Army's Military Intelligence Division (MID). Within the intelligence community, Townley was viewed as a dangerous radical. In December 1917, S. M. Canby, the assistant director of the Office of Naval Intelligence, wrote to Ralph Van Deman, the director of MID, that the league was "opposed to war [and] conscription." Furthermore, there was "more than a suspicion that German intrigue" was "behind" the league's activities.[172]

Officers of the Military Intelligence Division were continually advised by business leaders such as Charles Ames that the NPL posed a revolutionary threat to the established order. Marlborough Churchill replaced Van Deman as director of the MID in June 1918. Shortly after assuming this position, Churchill sent a circular to MID intelligence offices around the country, informing them that the league was "suspected of Bolshevist tendencies and of connections with the I.W.W." He also warned Creel that Townley and Gilbert were "radical socialists."[173] Needless to say, Creel ignored this warning.

Colonel Frederick G. Knabenshue operated out of San Francisco, where he coordinated the activities of the MID's intelligence officers stationed in the western states. He informed Churchill that the Spokane, Washington, office was "cooperating with the Department of Justice and the Secret Service in the investigation of the League."[174]

By the summer of 1918, the MID had come to view the NPL as a credible threat to the war effort that should be suppressed. Churchill wrote to Robert Maddox, the chair of the Censorship Board, asking him to "intercept all mail" sent to Townley, Le Sueur, Lindbergh and Gilbert. These letters were to be held until MID censors cleared them. This flagrant violation of the Fourth Amendment was justified because the NPL had been "suspected of disloyalty." The targets of this order included a recent member of the U.S. House of Representatives who had nearly gained the nomination of the Republican Party for governor of Minnesota. Edward White, the deputy chief of the postal censorship bureau, quickly responded that instructions had been sent to seize the mail of the NPL leaders and that these documents would then be sent on to the Censorship Board and the Military Intelligence Division.[175]

The Army's Military Intelligence Division was thus working at cross purposes to the Committee on Public Information. Creel and the CPI viewed the NPL as an ally in the effort to promote the war effort. At the same time, the MID was aligning itself with those business interests that saw the NPL as an integral component of a wider network of radicals and, thus, an organization that should be crushed. The president refused to fully accept either position as he sought a third alternative.

Creel Defends the League

The attacks on the NPL, and President Wilson's willingness to accept them, placed Creel on the defensive. Still, he was not prepared to abandon his effort to integrate the league into the war effort. In a letter to the president, Creel pointed out that the NPL had become one of the administration's "foremost supporters" in backing the war because he had made it "his business to see Townley." Furthermore, Creel denied that he was aiding the NPL in promoting a program of social reform, but rather that he was "simply making it a point to get" the league "behind the war." He also reiterated that mainstream politicians "hate the League" and were "trying to destroy it."[176]

Creel had placed himself in an untenable position. His political background as a crusading muckraker had been that of a progressive sympathetic to the league and supportive of its anti-corporate reforms. He had also criticized the wing of the Democratic Party most closely aligned with business interests. Yet Creel had given enthusiastic and uncritical support to Woodrow Wilson, a Democratic Party politician with close ties to certain corporate interests. For the last months of the war, Creel continued to support the NPL, while remaining a trusted advisor to the president.

Nevertheless, strains started to appear in that relationship. Wilson viewed the NPL's disdain of both major parties with suspicion, fearing that its leaders were preparing to initiate the formation of a progressive third party. He also rejected the populist program of the league as far too radical. The president was predisposed to distrust the NPL, although he understood that Creel's success in persuading it to give unqualified backing to the war effort represented a considerable boon to his administration.

In the end, Creel and the CPI quietly continued to work with the NPL. In February 1918, the league came to an agreement with the Committee on Public Information that it would organize public events featuring pro-war pep talks. Thompson reached an "understanding" with Arthur Bestor, the head of the CPI's division coordinating speakers, under which the NPL would "arrange for large audiences" and would pay the travel costs and living expenses incurred during the speaking tour.

In return, the CPI would "secure speakers" prepared to deliver talks in German, Swedish and Finnish.[177]

Woodrow Wilson Seeks a Third Way

By the spring of 1918, the president had become convinced that the administration could not be seen as giving tacit support to the NPL. When Townley wrote to the White House in March 1918 that the delegates at the NPL convention had "wholeheartedly" endorsed the war aims set out by the president, Wilson wrote to Tumulty that he "would like to proceed carefully" before responding to Townley's letter. Tumulty then referred the letter to David Houston, the Secretary of Agriculture. Houston did not equivocate in his denunciation of the league. Townley was "a radical socialist." Furthermore, the NPL had grown to be a significant force in the Upper Midwest "through the cultivation of class hatred."[178]

A barrage of hostile reports from the business community of Minnesota continued to pressure the White House to end all its links to the NPL. Two local businessmen, James Caldwell and Christian Wendt, from Lakeford, Minnesota, cabled the White House, insisting that NPL leaders were "disloyal." It was for this reason that the Minnesota Commission of Public Safety had acted to suppress the league's meetings. Caldwell and Wendt criticized the CPI for furnishing speakers for pro-war rallies organized by the NPL.[179]

The president passed this cable on to Creel, finding it "pretty convincing." Since the NPL had unnecessarily antagonized the corporate interests of Minnesota, the administration "had better pull away from them."[180]

Wilson continued to receive distorted reports concerning the Nonpartisan League from local business interests bitterly hostile to it. Yet he also received accurate reports on the situation in Minnesota from sources aligned with his administration. In the latter part of March 1918, Dixon Williams traveled to Minnesota at the behest of the Committee on Public Information to give loyalty speeches at NPL rallies. Williams, the vice-president of a construction firm based in the Chicago area, was an avid Democrat.[181]

Upon arriving in Minnesota, Williams was informed by Arthur Le Sueur that the sheriffs of three counties where Williams had been scheduled to speak had banned all gatherings of the NPL, even those that were to include loyalty speeches. The three sheriffs claimed that they were acting at the behest of the Minnesota Commission of Public Safety.[182]

Williams then received a message from Henry Libby, the secretary of the commission, and Charles Mills, the vice-president of the Midland Bank of Minneapolis. Mills was acting as chair of the Liberty Loan Speakers Bureau, and Williams was informed that he could speak under that organization's auspices, but only if he agreed that he would not deliver any talks under the sponsorship of the NPL. Williams refused to agree to this arrangement.[183]

This led Williams to hold a meeting at the state capital with Libby and Charles Henke, the publicity agent for the commission. Williams was told that he would only be permitted to speak in Minnesota if he agreed that none of his talks would be held under the auspices of the Nonpartisan League. Furthermore, Libby declared that the "declared purpose" of the Commission of Public Safety was "to prevent any meeting the League might attempt." The commission was intent on suppressing the league because it was "a disturber of the established order" and was "disloyal."

Williams was not persuaded by this argument. On the contrary, he became convinced that the Commission of Public Safety was acting on behalf of Governor Burnquist, who was in "great fear" of being defeated in his effort to be reelected. This had led to the commission's determined effort to "crush the League absolutely or cast a doubt on the loyalty of the organization."

Williams was a staunch supporter of the war effort and the

administration. The president, therefore, had received information from a friendly source that state authorities in Minnesota were using the opportunity provided by the wartime crisis to suppress and disrupt their political opponents. Instead of intervening to uphold basic democratic rights, Wilson opted to stay out of the conflict, while seeking an electoral alternative to both the NPL and the corporate executives backing Burnquist.

The president was receiving mixed messages on how to handle the league. Conservative elements within the Democratic Party were ready to stand with Burnquist and the Minnesota Commission of Public Safety in utilizing legal and extra-legal methods to quash the league. In direct contrast, Creel and the more liberal Democrats insisted that the NPL was fulfilling its pledge to support the war effort, and that the administration should consider implementing some of the reforms proposed by the league.

Wilson was not comfortable with either of these positions. In mid-March 1918, Colver, the Scripps-Howard editor, sent the president a lengthy analysis of the situation in Minnesota that proposed a third position between the polar opposites. Colver informed Wilson, through Tumulty, that Democratic Party state officials were organizing to ensure that the party officially endorsed Senator Knute Nelson's reelection bid in the November election. Nelson was a stalwart Republican and a staunch supporter of the war.[184]

Colver warned Wilson that this endorsement "would be a disaster to progressive development in the Northwest." This maneuver would bring together "the reactionary elements in both parties" and would also "drive many over to the extreme movements represented by the Socialists and the Nonpartisan League." His prediction proved to be correct.

Instead of endorsing Nelson, Colver proposed that "while the extreme reactionaries and the extreme radicals contest [for] the control of the Republican Party," the Democratic Party should appeal to the "sane and progressive" voters by nominating a popular candidate for the Senate seat who would campaign on a platform that combined support for the war effort with a program of limited reforms. Colver suggested that a former governor, John Lind, would make the perfect candidate.

Wilson was impressed by Colver's letter. He wrote to Vance McCormick, the chair of the Democratic National Committee, enclosing Colver's letter and asking him to "very carefully consider" it. Although the president retained a "warm feeling" for Nelson, he still believed Colver was "right about his political analysis." Wilson expressed his willingness to ask Lind to be a candidate for the Senate seat, although it is unclear if he did so. In any case, Lind was not interested in reviving his career as an elected official, so he refused to enter the contest.[185]

A few days after Colver's letter was written, the Democrats convened their state conference. Lind was able to block an official endorsement of Nelson, but the conference also voted not to present a candidate to oppose Nelson in the general election. At the end of April, the state Democratic central committee endorsed Nelson, infuriating Minnesota's liberals and further strengthening the drive for a progressive third party. Lind wound up endorsing Nelson's sole opponent, Willis Calderwood, who stood as the candidate of the National Party, a short-lived third party. Nelson won the election, but Calderwood gained 40 percent of the vote, a strong showing for a relatively unknown candidate of a small alternative party.[186]

Wilson's response to Colver's letter indicates that by March 1918 the president had decided to distance himself from the NPL. He would not join Burnquist in actively targeting the league, but he would also refrain from protecting it from the vindictive actions of the Minnesota Commission of Public Safety. The president was ready to assist the Minnesota Democratic Party in presenting candidates that could provide a centrist alternative to the program of social reforms advocated by the NPL on the one hand and to Burnquist and the conservative Republicans on the other.

Creel Parts with the President

As he sought to create a centrist alternative, Wilson did not want his administration to be seen as a friendly ally of the NPL. Creel understood this shift in policy and reluctantly modified the CPI's relations with the league. The Committee on Public Information would no longer directly provide the NPL with pro-war speakers. Although Creel "deeply" resented "the terrorism" inherent in the approach of Minnesota's authorities, he had to agree with Wilson that the federal government could not "afford an open break with State authorities." Still, Creel was adamant that, contrary to the claims of the Minnesota Commission of Public Safety and its business allies, the league had "been loyal absolutely."[187]

Creel was caught in the crossfire between the Nonpartisan League and its enemies. Under intense pressure, he blundered, undercutting his credibility. In early May 1918, Creel traveled to New York City, where he spoke at the Church of the Ascension and answered questions. During the question period, he was asked whether he thought every member of Congress was loyal. Creel's answer was flippant: "I don't like slumming, so I won't explore the heart of Congress."[188]

These remarks caused a furor in Congress. Creel was indirectly criticizing the Republican politicians who were constantly sniping at the Committee on Public Information for being too liberal. One of their favorite targets was the CPI's ties to the NPL. Creel's remarks were a major blunder.

Until this point, the president had given Creel his unconditional support, insisting that he took personal responsibility for the CPI and that Creel retained his total support. In the aftermath of this incident, Wilson began to reassess his position. During one of his informal discussions with his confidant Edward House, the president continued to defend Creel. House wrote in his diary that Wilson still believed that Creel's "work was well done and in a spirit quite in harmony with his, the president's views." Still, Wilson was worried that Creel had so antagonized influential figures in Congress that funding for the CPI would be jeopardized. He and House, therefore, discussed the possibility of replacing Creel with Frank Cobb, the editor of the *New York World* and a staunch supporter of the president.[189]

This was a discussion of possible options rather than a definitive decision on how to proceed. Wilson called Josephus Daniels, the Secretary of the Navy, and asked him to discuss the situation with Creel.[190] Daniels had been instrumental in persuading the president to appoint Creel as head of the CPI and the two worked well on its board of directors.

Daniels moved swiftly to quell the congressional calls for Creel to resign. Daniels talked with Creel and convinced him that an apology was in order. Creel then wrote a letter to Edward Pou, the chair of the House Rules Committee, stating that he had given a "thoughtless answer" and that he had come to "regret it deeply."[191]

Daniels and Pou were political allies in the North Carolina Democratic Party, so Pou bottled up a censure motion until Creel's apology could be drafted and sent to Congress. Creel continued to serve as the head of the CPI, and the president still included him as one of his more influential advisors. Still, Creel's credibility had been tarnished. Furthermore, with the war nearing its end, Creel made it increasingly clear that he disagreed with Wilson's decision to distance himself from the NPL and the progressive politics it embodied.

Creel and the Republican Primary

During the last months of the war, it was clear that the administration wanted to remain aloof from the bitter battle unfolding in Minnesota. Nevertheless, Creel and the CPI were drawn into the dispute. In June 1918, as the Republican primary for governor approached, the attacks on the Nonpartisan League became increasingly strident. Lindbergh was a popular political figure and a formidable challenger to Burnquist. As Burnquist and his supporters attacked the patriotic loyalty of the NPL and Lindbergh, the league countered by pointing to its working relationship with the Committee on Public Information.

Thus, Creel became an issue in the Minnesota elections. In May 1918, Creel wrote a private letter that was then publicly circulated in which he insisted that the league had given its "pledge of loyalty" to the war effort. Republican conservatives bitterly denounced Creel for becoming involved in partisan politics. He was, therefore, compelled to issue a statement distancing himself from the NPL. On the eve of the primary election, the government released a letter from Creel to Senator Knute Nelson to the public. In the letter, Creel insisted that he had no "connection, direct or indirect," with the league. In arranging a meeting between Townley and the president, Creel was merely trying to persuade Townley that this was a "war of self-defense" and that "the very life of the country depended upon understanding and support."[192] In other words, Creel had been cajoling Townley and the NPL into providing uncritical support for the war effort.

Creel followed up this statement with another one denying that he supported the NPL, and that the federal government had, in any way, recognized it as a spokesperson for the farmers of the Upper Midwest. In a letter to Tumulty released to the press, Creel insisted that "neither President Wilson nor any other official of government" had "recognized" the league. Wilson's meeting with Townley in November 1917 had been merely informational and did not represent an "endorsement." Of course, Creel did not believe this. In fact, he was eager to consolidate ties to the Nonpartisan League and to integrate it into the liberal wing of the Democratic Party. Still, Creel knew that the president had rejected this strategy and that his tenure as director of the Committee on Public Information would be swiftly terminated if he publicly backed the NPL.[193]

Creel and the President at Odds

Even after Lindbergh's defeat in the Republican primary, the Minnesota state government continued to batter the NPL, leaving the Wilson administration in the middle. By August 1918, the president had concluded that his administration should remain neutral in the bitter battle being fought between the league and the Minnesota Commission of Public Safety backed by Governor Burnquist. When a Minnesota business owner complained to the White House about the NPL, Wilson wrote to Tumulty that no response should be sent. The president concluded that there was "a very savage partisan fight on in the Northwest against the Non-Partisan League." Although there had been "repeated attempts to draw" the administration into the conflict, the "best plan" was to "ignore" any letters on the issue.[194]

Creel did not waver in his private view that Townley and the NPL were allies. In August 1918, he urged Bernard Baruch, the chair of the War Industries Board, to recommend Townley for a vacant position on the board. (Creel and Baruch had become friends when both worked on the president's 1916 reelection campaign.)[195] This appointment ignited a firestorm as Republicans condemned the administration for its links to the league. Under pressure from the mainstream media, the administration retreated, leading Baruch to request Lindbergh's resignation.[196]

Creel was furious. He wrote the president that there was "nothing more harmful" than "breaking down to the threat of a lot of reactionary politicians." After all, the NPL had been "absolutely and entirely loyal." Having given "time and sweat" to the effort to swing the NPL behind the war effort, it was "bitter to have all" of his "work undone by a single act of cowardice."[197] Wilson was not persuaded, so Lindbergh's resignation from the War Industries Board remained in effect.

Creel was caught in the middle. The president had determined that the federal government would not defend the Nonpartisan League from the relentless attacks of Governor Burnquist and the Minnesota Commission of Public Safety. As a result, Creel was compelled to distance himself from the league in his public pronouncements. At the same time, he continued to vouch for its total support for the war effort within the inner councils of the administration. In an effort to justify this contradictory policy to the NPL's leaders, Creel wrote to Thompson that he could not "afford to be put in the light of openly championing the Nonpartisan League" since this would "interfere" with his "advocacy of a square deal for the League" as a presidential advisor.[198]

The NPL's leadership was willing to accept this ambivalent stance, and the league remained an unwavering supporter of the administration's war policies until the conflict finally ended in November 1918. There were definite limits to what Creel could do. The league remained under intensive surveillance and the War Emergency Division was prepared to seek indictments for any of its organizers who indicated their opposition to the war. Still, the NPL's leaders were not prosecuted by the Department of Justice, and its newspapers were not banned from the mail. On balance, Townley continued to view the deal as worthwhile, and it continued in force despite its limitations.

The Nonpartisan League in Decline

In the immediate aftermath of the war, the National Nonpartisan League entered a downward spiral that soon led to its dissolution. Several factors contributed to this rapid decline, but one of the most critical was the lasting impact of the continuing attacks on the league during the wartime years.

Although Joe Gilbert had sharply criticized Townley's autocratic powers during the war and had been removed from any position of influence, he only officially left the NPL in the summer of 1919 to take a position with a Midwest cooperative organization.[199] Several other organizers who had also been active in the Socialist Party had joined Gilbert in criticizing Townley, and they, too, drifted out of the NPL after the war ended. Most of these resignations occurred quietly, but in April 1919, Arthur Le Sueur resigned from the league. Le Sueur had no intention of remaining quiet. He was soon engaged in public denunciations of Townley that undermined Townley's authority while demoralizing the league. After all, Le Sueur had been one of Townley's most influential advisors.[200]

Experienced members of the Socialist Party who had been recruited by Townley had provided the NPL with much of its strategic vision. Their resignations significantly contributed to the league's rapid decline. Another factor behind the decline was the economic downturn that followed at the end of the war. Prices of agricultural goods dropped sharply, and many small farmers were forced into bankruptcy. From the start, the NPL had accepted postdated checks as payment for membership dues. When crops were harvested and sold, bills accumulated during the year could be paid. This worked as long as farm prices remained high, but the system collapsed during an economic downturn. As a result, the league was stuck with two million dollars in postdated checks that could not be collected.[201]

To make a difficult situation even worse, Townley and Gilbert had to serve prison terms after appellate courts rejected their appeals. In February 1921, Gilbert began serving a one-year sentence for violating Minnesota's Sedition Act in a landmark case that had been appealed all the way to the U.S. Supreme Court. As soon as he completed that sentence in Red Wing, Minnesota, Gilbert was transferred to the jail in Jackson, Minnesota, to serve an additional three months for a conspiracy charge that had been levied against him and Townley.[202]

Townley began serving his three-month sentence for conspiracy in the Jackson jail in November 1921. He was released from prison just before Gilbert was sent to Jackson, so the two were not incarcerated at the same time. When Townley was set free in February 1922, he found that the league had moved on without him. He soon resigned as chair of the National Nonpartisan League. In October 1923, the North Dakota NPL disaffiliated from the regional organization, marking the effective end of the National Nonpartisan League.[203]

The North Dakota NPL remained a viable electoral force within that state's politics, but it was no longer the dynamic popular movement that it had been in its heyday during the wartime years.[204] The North Dakota NPL had some success in the 1930s during the Great Depression, when it pressured the state government into banning banks from foreclosing on small farmers. Nevertheless, the organization's momentum continued to dwindle and in 1956 it merged into the Democratic Party.[205]

Although the North Dakota NPL continued to function as a ginger group within the two major parties for three decades after the dissolution of the National Nonpartisan League, the situation in Minnesota was quite different. In 1922, a coalition of the remnants of the Minnesota NPL and progressive trade unions formed the Minnesota Farmer-Labor Party (FLP). Socialists who had been active in the league were instrumental in bringing farmers into the new party.[206]

From the start, the FLP eclipsed the Democratic Party and became the main opposition to the conservative politics of the Republican Party leadership. Nevertheless, it was only in the 1930s, with the advent of the Great Depression, that the Farmer-Labor Party could win statewide elections and control the state government. Floyd Olson campaigned on the FLP ticket and served as Minnesota's governor from 1931 until his death in 1936. Olson was closely aligned with President Franklin Roosevelt and the New Deal. As with the North Dakota NPL, the FLP lost momentum over time as factional disputes grew sharper. In 1944, the Farmer-Labor Party merged into Minnesota's Democratic Party, ending the most successful attempt to establish a broadly based alternative party.[207]

The National Nonpartisan League continued to influence

the politics of the northern Prairie states for decades after its dissolution. Still, its successors had lost their way as a vibrant, grassroots social movement.

The experience of the Nonpartisan League from the time it grew rapidly to when it became a target of repression remains highly relevant a century later. During the First World War, the NPL came under attack by a coalition of Minnesota's business leaders and the state government. Hoping to deflect this attack, the NPL dropped its initial doubts about the U.S. entry into the war for an enthusiastic support of the administration's policies. Still, President Woodrow Wilson had no intention of becoming involved in Minnesota's conflicts. Instead, the Justice Department continued to harass the league to ensure that it rigidly held to its pro-war policy. The attacks on the NPL during the war led to internal splits and a downward slide. In the midst of an unpopular war, and the trampling of civil liberties, there was very little scope for any form of dissent, even that advocated by progressive reformers who endorsed the war effort.

Conclusion: Civil Liberties during the First World War and Now

CIVIL LIBERTIES HAVE BEEN UNDER attack in the United States since the destruction of New York City's Twin Towers on September 11, 2001. Both federal and state governments have sought to suppress those viewed as extremists. In addition to these official actions, there have been vocal advocates from a wide range of ideological perspectives who have contended that certain opinions are so reprehensible that their expression should be banned from venues previously considered free speech forums.

For many Americans, the existing social system seems incapable of resolving major social problems. As a result, political viewpoints have become polarized. In this context, basic freedoms are often denied. Yet the right to dissent from government policies and to organize peaceful protests in opposition to those policies are fundamental rights essential to a truly democratic society. Although these rights are codified in the Constitution's Bill of Rights, they have been frequently curtailed in critical times in U.S. history.

The clash between a popular movement intent on reversing

the government's policy and an administration determined to suppress dissent was at its most acute during the First World War. By joining the war as a combatant nation, the United States was committed to the deployment of millions of soldiers to trench warfare at the Western Front in France and Belgium.[1] This deployment required the conscription of millions of soldiers, but it also necessitated the mobilization of the entire economy to produce the armaments and supplies the huge army would need.

The drastic switch to a war economy would have been difficult in any case, as the Second World War demonstrated. Still, there was a significant difference. A majority of the American populace supported the struggle to defeat the Nazis or, at least, acquiesced to it. The decision to enter the First World War in April 1917 was deeply unpopular, and President Woodrow Wilson knew it.

To silence the opposition to the war, an array of intelligence agencies covertly gathered information that was then used in the prosecutions of activists for allegedly violating the Espionage Act. In addition, front organizations were covertly funded to disrupt and demoralize the antiwar opposition.

Before the First World War, government intelligence agencies were small and sharply limited in their scope of activity. The enforcement of laws was the responsibility of state and local governments. To supplement the police, powerful corporations hired private detective agencies to counter union organizing drives.

The First World War dramatically altered this situation. The federal government's intelligence agencies grew rapidly, and the range of their targets was greatly expanded. Closely monitoring the activities of the antiwar opposition proved to be a lucrative field for the intelligence community. Even after the war ended, the left was perceived as a significant threat to those in power. The basis for J. Edgar Hoover's Federal Bureau of Investigation was set during the First World War.

In their drive to collect information on dissidents, intelligence agencies made use of a variety of surveillance methods, both legal and illegal. Even those methods that in themselves did not violate the Constitution were of doubtful legitimacy when directed at those organizing peaceful protests. Informants were placed in organizations such as the People's Council of America, and the information gathered was used to disrupt their activities. The Committee on Public Information implemented a program of psychological warfare against its own populace in an unsuccessful effort to manipulate public opinion, even going so far as to gain control of a newspaper so that it would promote the war among the Jewish population of the Lower East Side of New York.

The Justice Department obtained open-ended warrants to search IWW offices. Agents of the Bureau of Investigation trashed Wobbly offices as they executed these warrants. Actions such as these moved beyond the bounds of the legal, and yet they were viewed as inadequate. The U.S. Army's Military Intelligence Division broke into offices at night to carry out surreptitious raids on progressive organizations such as the People's Council and the National Civil Liberties Bureau, the predecessor of the American Civil Liberties Bureau. These night raids were flagrant violations of constitutional rights. The extensive program of intercepting letters for the thousands on the government's suspect list became blatantly illegal when it was extended to purely domestic mail. The Bureau of Investigation tapped telephones without obtaining warrants, highly questionable interceptions given the Fourth Amendment's provisions on search and seizure.

There seemed to be few limits on who could become the target of government repression. In the months immediately following the U.S. entry into the war, the Wilson administration was primarily concerned with the millions of immigrants from Germany and their families. Once internment camps were created to detain thousands of suspected "aliens," the government turned its attention to the radical left. The Industrial Workers of the World became a special focus for repression as it organized effective strikes in key industries.

Until this point, those who had come under intensive scrutiny had been either powerless or dissident outsiders. When the administration shifted its attention to antiwar progressives, it moved into a sensitive area. Progressives held positions of power and influence. Nevertheless, once the decision was made to silence them, the intelligence community undertook a coordinated campaign of repression utilizing the same methods that had previously been used to crush radicals.

There is a certain logic to this progression of events. In deciding to enter the war, the president committed the United States to continuing the conflict until Germany was totally defeated. He was convinced that anyone who dissented from this position had to be suppressed.

The coordinated assault on the antiwar opposition flagrantly violated fundamental constitutional norms. As president, Woodrow Wilson was ultimately responsible. Wilson viewed any criticism of his war policies as a personal insult. At the end of a lengthy patriotic speech on Flag Day in June 1917, he warned his audience that "woe be to the man or group of men that makes to stand in our way" to the total defeat of Germany in the war.[2] This was one promise the president kept.

In this context, the government moved swiftly from one set of potential enemies to another. Everyone was either wholeheartedly with the president's war policies or against them. Thus, the scope of repression continually expanded. Furthermore, Wilson was vindictive. Government repression continued, even after the target had been silenced.

Within the intelligence community, some agencies began to adopt a totalitarian perspective. Any opposition to the official wisdom, even a single individual talking to a friend, constituted a threat and had to be quashed. The Army's Military Intelligence Division created an elaborate network of informers who sent in reports on possible troublemakers. This network included attorneys, local union officials and even the YMCA. Wilson had no objections to the MID's creation of an extensive spy network. Indeed, he also believed that the government's repressive measures should be extended to individuals who opposed the war.

Nevertheless, when the MID's chief, Ralph Van Deman, joined with Charles Warren, an Assistant Attorney General in the Justice Department, in proposing that military tribunals be given jurisdiction to try civilians accused of opposing the war, the president blocked the move. The president was wary of delegating too much power to the military. Thus, there were limits to the intelligence community's actions, but they were very few indeed.

Within the administration, attorneys within the Justice Department were the most willing to set limits on government repression. John Lord O'Brian and Alfred Bettman of the War Emergency Division sought to limit prosecutions under the Espionage Act to those involved in organizations that posed a significant threat to the war effort. Still, they authorized the prosecution of those who merely suggested the war was being fought for profit and imperial gain. The government successfully argued in federal court that since the president claimed that the war was being fought to spread democracy, antiwar dissidents who proposed an alternative explanation were guilty of spreading "false reports."

Within months after the United States entered the war, progressives and social democrats became the primary targets of repression. Unfortunately, far too often, they relied on the good faith of the authorities. Progressives scrambled to formulate a policy that was critical of the war effort but remained within the parameters set by the federal government in its interpretation of the broadly phrased wording of the Espionage Act. This choice proved to be risky since the guidelines kept shifting as the scope for permitted dissent became increasingly narrower. The progressive challenge to the administration's war policies crumbled in the face of government repression.

There was an alternative to the hesitant stance taken by progressives. Eugene Victor Debs, the presidential candidate of the Socialist Party, demonstrated that through his actions. Debs and Senator Robert La Follette were highly respected and acted as the primary spokespersons for their respective political perspectives. In June 1918, Debs denounced the war in a speech delivered at a rally in Canton, Ohio, even though he knew he would likely be prosecuted. Debs was convicted of violating the Espionage Act and served two and a half years in a federal penitentiary. As a U.S. senator, La Follette was initially allowed a certain leeway. Nevertheless, he soon became the target of a coordinated attack involving much of the intelligence community. Under the impact of this assault, La Follette retreated into silence.

In no other period in U.S. history have fundamental constitutional rights been so drastically curtailed as they were during the First World War. Yet Woodrow Wilson was hardly a fervent ideologue. A pragmatic politician, his record before April 1917 was that of a mildly liberal Democratic Party centrist.

Nevertheless, once the United States entered the war, Wilson was prepared to authorize the ruthless suppression of the antiwar opposition, regardless of the flagrant violations of civil liberties that this entailed. Ideology is a less important explanation of dictatorial behavior than the threat posed by an organized opposition with a mass base of support. The case of the People's Council of America is an illuminating example. The PCA could be tolerated as long as it remained small and irrelevant, but once it began to gain momentum, the administration was determined to silence it.

As the conflict unfolded, power became concentrated in the White House. Woodrow Wilson was certain that he and he alone should make every important decision concerning the course of the war. Anyone who challenged this would become a target of government repression.

The Allies posed the essential issue underlying the conflict as autocracy versus democracy, that is, the rule of one person versus the rule of the entire populace. Yet it was Wilson who became the autocratic ruler of the United States. The irony of this situation did not go unnoticed.

Cecil Spring Rice had spent much of his life in the British diplomatic service before becoming ambassador to the United States. He was amazed by the power concentrated in the hands of one person, the president. In a letter to Edward Grey, the British foreign minister, sent in January 1917, Spring Rice wrote that he had been previously posted to Russia, Germany, the Ottoman Empire, and Persia. All four of these countries were ruled by "autocratic governments," and yet he had "never known any government as autocratic as this."[3]

The U.S. Constitution grants the president a great deal of power. Still, this was to be limited by the authority of Congress and the review of an independent judiciary. When the administration organized a venomous attack on Senator La Follette, it undermined the checks and balances that had been designed to prevent the kind of autocratic actions that the colonists had experienced within the British Empire. With Congress silenced, and the courts endorsing the entire range of repressive measures implemented by the government, the resulting power vacuum was filled by one person: the president.

The experience of the United States during the First World War provides an object lesson of what is likely to occur when power is concentrated in the hands of one person. With this power, the president, through his control of the federal government's agencies, can harass and suppress those who oppose his policies. He can do so openly and secretively. Even a century later, it is very difficult to determine exactly what Woodrow Wilson authorized, as well as the full extent of the covert operations undertaken by those within the intelligence community.

A truly democratic society requires a robust debate of public policy. Transparency in the operations of the government is an essential prerequisite to such a debate. A powerful presidency is bound to clash with the fundamental requirements of an open and transparent government.

No president has ever wielded the enormous power that Wilson commanded. Nevertheless, during the Cold War and its aftermath there has been a significant shift to a more powerful executive branch. Economic instability, the militarization of society, and the growing disaffection within the populace has created the context in which the president has become more powerful. This shift in power is likely to occur no matter what the ideology of the president might be. Still, when the White House is occupied by a right-wing authoritarian populist, this dynamic is intensified.

To counter this drift to a more repressive society, the secrets of the intelligence community need to be exposed. Everyone, including the president of the United States, must be held accountable for their actions.

During the First World War, the government suppressed those who criticized its war policies. This campaign undermined the fundamental protections guaranteed in the Bill of Rights. A genuinely democratic society requires free speech and a free press. Democracy is often raucous, and it can be time-consuming. Nevertheless, it is far better than any alternative. Democracy can only flourish when the debate on controversial issues of public policy is encouraged, and when any viewpoint, no matter how reprehensible it seems to some, is permitted within the public discourse.

CHRONOLOGY

August 4, 1914: The United Kingdom declares war on Germany.

February 1915: The Nonpartisan League is formed by Arthur Townley and Albert Bowen and begins organizing farmers in North Dakota.

March 2, 1917: A bill is introduced into Congress to enable merchant marine ships to be armed. Senator Robert La Follette leads a filibuster that prevents a vote on the measure before that session of Congress comes to an end on March 4.

March 15, 1917: Tsar Nicholas abdicates as mass demonstrations sweep through Russia. Power is shared by the Petrograd Soviet and a provisional, and more moderate, government.

April 6, 1917: Congress declares war on Germany. The United States enters World War I. La Follette speaks against the declaration of war.

April 7, 1917: An emergency convention of the Socialist Party convenes in St. Louis. After lengthy discussions, it overwhelmingly approves a resolution calling for militant resistance to the war effort. Eugene Debs is not present but enthusiastically supports the majority resolution.

April 13, 1917: The Committee on Public Information is created by a presidential resolution, and Woodrow Wilson then names George Creel to head it.

May 18, 1917: A bill establishing a system to conscript soldiers into the army is approved by Congress. La Follette speaks against the draft.

May 31, 1917: The People's Council for Democracy and the Terms of Peace is formed at a large rally held in Madison Square Garden in New York. It brings together a loose coalition of socialists, progressives and peace activists.

June 5, 1917: Registration Day. Millions of men aged between twenty-one and thirty-nine are required to register for the draft.

June 15, 1917: Congress passes the Espionage Act, and the president signs the bill. One provision holds that those obstructing the war effort or the draft can be sentenced to a prison term of up to twenty years. Hundreds of dissidents are jailed under this provision.

July 29, 1917: The American Alliance for Labor and Democracy is formed at a conference held in New York City. Covertly funded by the Committee on Public Information, the organization brings together leaders of the American Federation of Labor and pro-war social democrats. Its primary purpose is countering the People's Council.

September 1, 1917: The founding conference of the People's Council of America for Democracy and the Terms of Peace, scheduled to meet in Minneapolis, Minnesota, is banned by order of Governor Joseph Burnquist. A rump meeting is held in Chicago but is quickly dispersed by state militia.

September 20, 1917: La Follette delivers a speech in Minneapolis at a conference sponsored by the Nonpartisan League. He criticizes the decision to enter the war and suggests that the president had been warned beforehand that the Germans would attack the *Lusitania*, a British ocean liner sunk by a submarine's torpedo on May 7, 1915.

October 6, 1917: The Trading with the Enemy statute is approved by Congress and then signed by the president. A section of the bill establishes tight control over foreign language newspapers.

October 6, 1917: Threatened with expulsion from the Senate for the speech delivered at the conference sponsored by the Nonpartisan League, La Follette delivers a lengthy speech defending civil liberties.

October 1917: Attorney General Thomas Gregory creates the War Emergency Division to oversee the prosecution of cases arising from alleged violations of the Espionage Act. He names John Lord O'Brian to head the division.

November 7, 1917: Provisional government of Russia toppled by Bolsheviks. A new government led by Lenin committed to an immediate peace takes power.

November 23, 1917: The official newspapers of the Soviet Union, *Izvestia* and *Pravda*, publish the secret treaties signed by Czarist Russia and its allies, primarily the United Kingdom and France. The *Manchester Guardian* prints the treaties in full on November 26, 1917.

January 8, 1918: President Wilson speaks to Congress about U.S. war aims, providing his view of the 14 Points that were essential to a peace treaty.

March 3, 1918: Soviet Russia and Imperial Germany sign the Brest-Litovsk Treaty, a separate peace by which Russia cedes territory to Germany.

March 19, 1918: Irvine Lenroot wins hotly contested Republican primary for the U.S. Senate seat from Minnesota vacated by the accidental death of Paul Husting.

March 21, 1918: Scott Nearing is prosecuted under the Espionage Act for a pamphlet analyzing the war.

April 2, 1918: Lenroot elected to the U.S. Senate after a bitterly contested election defeating Victor Berger, the Socialist Party candidate, and John Davies, the Democrat.

June 5, 1918: Marlborough Churchill replaces Ralph Van Deman as director of the Army's Military Intelligence Division.

June 17, 1918: The incumbent governor, Joseph Burnquist, defeats Charles Lindbergh in the Republican Party's primary. Lindbergh had been endorsed by the Nonpartisan League. The primary had been bitterly contested. Burnquist would go on to win re-election in the November general election.

November 11, 1918: World War I ends as the German imperial government collapses. and the new government agrees to an unconditional surrender.

October 2, 1919: Woodrow Wilson suffers a massive stroke from which he never fully recovers. He is totally incapacitated for months.

May 1922: Townley resigns as leader of the National Nonpartisan League. The Nonpartisan League disintegrates soon after, remaining a significant force solely in North Dakota.

GLOSSARY

Biographical Profiles

Ames, Charles Wilberforce (1855–1921): Raised in Minnesota. After graduating from Cornell University, worked for his father on the staff of the *Christian Register* in Boston. In 1882, moved to St. Paul and bought shares in West Publishing Company, a leading publisher of law books. For many years served as president of West, where he succeeded in preventing the unionization of his workforce. Served as a member of the Minnesota Commission of Public Safety in 1917. In December 1917, Governor Joseph Burnquist appointed him as a special assistant with the primary responsibility for suppressing the Nonpartisan League.

Bettman, Alfred (1873–1945): Attended Harvard and Harvard Law School. Returned to hometown of Cincinnati, Ohio, where he practiced law. City solicitor from 1909 to 1911. Appointed deputy director of the War Emergency Division in October 1917. Primary authority within the Justice Department concerning the enforcement of the Espionage Act. Wrote prosecution briefs in cases that led to key Supreme Court decisions limiting free speech. After the war, he focused on the legal implications of city planning and zoning.

Bielaski, Alexander Bruce (1883–1964): Hired by the Department of Justice in 1904 as an examiner of expenditures made by U.S. attorneys around the country. Employed by the Bureau of Intelligence from its formation in 1908. Served as its chief from 1912 to 1919. From 1929 until his retirement, directed a private detective agency investigating arson cases.

Cahan, Abraham (1860–1951): Born in Lithuania into a devout Orthodox Jewish family. As a teenager active in the Socialist Revolutionary Party. Suspected by the czarist police, emigrated to the United States in 1882. Edited the newspaper of the Socialist Labor Party. In 1897, helped to found *Forverts* (*Jewish Daily Forward*), becoming its full-time editor in 1903. It soon became the dominant newspaper on New York's Lower East Side. Active in the social democratic wing of the Socialist Party. Originally opposed to the war, he muzzled *Forverts* under government pressure. Remained editor until 1946.

Creel, George Edward (1876–1953): Raised in Missouri. Became a reporter for the *Kansas City World* in 1894. Moved to Denver in 1910 and became an editorial writer for the *Denver Post* and then the *Rocky Mountain News*. Briefly served as police commissioner but was soon dismissed for cracking down on brothels. Worked for Woodrow Wilson's reelection in 1916 as a publicist. Appointed director of the Committee on Public Information in April 1917 until its dissolution in 1919. Was an unsuccessful candidate for the Democratic Party's nomination for governor of California in 1934, losing to Upton Sinclair. Wrote his memoirs and several other books in his later years.

Gilbert, Joseph (1865–1956): Born in London, England. Immigrated to the United States in 1884. Lived in Philadelphia where he became a lawyer. Moved to Seattle in 1900. Joined the Socialist Party and became state secretary. Edited socialist newspaper. Joined the staff of the Nonpartisan League in September 1915 and became organizing director. Prosecuted for a speech given in Kenyon, Minnesota, in August 1917. Conviction upheld by the U.S. Supreme Court with Justice Brandeis delivering a landmark defense of civil liberties. Active in the Cooperative Movement in the 1920s. From 1933 to his retirement in the 1950s edited the *Midland Cooperator*.

Gompers, Samuel (1850–1924): Born in London and immigrated with his family to New York City in 1863. Started working as a cigar maker while a teenager. Became an official of the Cigarmakers' Union in 1877. Helped to found the Federation of Organized Trade and Labor Unions in 1881, which became the American Federation of Labor in 1886. Served as president of the AFL from its founding until his death, with the exception of a single year out of office. An outspoken advocate of the war effort, he denounced those who opposed the war.

La Follette, Robert Marion, Sr. (1855–1925): Raised in Wisconsin. Became an attorney in Madison after graduating from the University of Wisconsin. Member of the U.S. House of Representatives from 1885 to 1891. Served as governor from 1900 until January 1906. U.S. Senator from then until his death. Opposed U.S. entry into the war and the conscription of soldiers. Defended free speech during wartime. After the war, continued to be a leading voice for progressive reform. Stood as an independent candidate for president in 1924 and received 16 percent of the popular vote. Died shortly afterward.

Lindbergh, Charles Augustus, Sr. (1859–1924): Shortly after his birth, his family left Sweden for Minnesota. Graduated from the University of Michigan Law School in 1883. Established a successful law practice in Little Falls, Minnesota. Served in the U.S. House of Representatives from 1907 to 1917. Unsuccessful candidate for U.S. Senate in 1916. Initially opposed the decision to enter the war but soon became a supporter of the war effort. Sought the Republican Party's nomination for governor in 1918 with the active support of the Nonpartisan League but was defeated. Died while seeking the nomination of the Farmer-Labor Party for governor in 1924.

Lochner, Louis Paul (1887–1975): Born in Illinois. Graduated from the University of Wisconsin in 1909. Became active in the Chicago peace movement prior to the advent of the First World War. Late in 1914 became executive director of the Emergency Peace Federation. Acted as secretary to Henry Ford's Peace Ship mission to Europe. From May 1917 to November 1919 served as secretary to the People's Council of America. After the war, worked as a journalist. Went to Berlin as a foreign correspondent in 1921 and joined the Berlin AP bureau in 1924. In 1941 was interned by the Nazis and freed five months latr in a prisoner exchange. After the Second World War, wrote books on recent German history and his memoirs.

Nearing, Scott (1883–1983): Raised in a coalmining town in Pennsylvania. Studied at the Wharton School of Business, receiving a PhD in economics in 1909. Taught at Wharton from 1908 to 1915 when he was fired for his radical views. Hired by the University of Toledo but was fired in 1917 for his antiwar views. Joined the Socialist Party in July 1917. Served as chair of the People's Council of America from September 1917 to its dissolution in October 1919. Indicted for allegedly violating the Espionage Act in March 1919, but acquitted in February 1919. Joined the Communist Party in 1927. Retreated to an isolated farm in Vermont in 1934, moving to another farm in Maine in 1952. Became famous after writing *The Good Life* (1937), a book promoting the simple, rural life.

O'Brian, John Lord (1874–1973): Graduated from Harvard in 1896. Received a law degree from the University of Buffalo in 1898. Joined one of the leading corporate law firms in upstate New York. Served as U.S. attorney for western New York from 1909 to 1914. In October 1917, named the director of the War Emergency Division, with overall authority for administering the laws designed to stifle antiwar dissent during the First World War. After his resignation in March 1919, resumed his activity as a corporate lawyer.

Spargo, John (1876–1966): Raised in Cornwall, England. Employed as a stonemason in Wales where he became active in the Social Democratic Federation. Immigrated to the United States in 1901. Became one of the leaders of the social democratic wing of the Socialist Party. Resigned in 1917 to become an outspoken advocate of the war effort. Led the American Alliance for Labor and Democracy, which was covertly funded by the federal government. In 1918, traveled to Italy as a representative of the Committee on Public Information, where he worked with pro-war socialists including Mussolini. Moved to Vermont and became an expert on its early history. Joined the Republican Party in the 1920s, moving toward its conservative wing.

Townley, Arthur Charles (1889–1959): Raised in Minnesota. Owned a large flax farm in North Dakota but went bankrupt in 1913 after snowstorms ruined his crop. Joined the Socialist Party, recruiting farmers on a minimal program of reforms. When the Party's leaders rejected this approach, he resigned. In February 1915, formed the Nonpartisan League and began touring North Dakota recruiting members. Served as its president from 1915 until May 1922. In 1923, tried to organize a network of cooperatives to stabilize the price of grains. Worked as a traveling salesperson in the 1930s. Became increasingly conservative and supported Senator Joseph McCarthy in the 1950s.

Wilson, Thomas Woodrow (1856–1924): Raised in the South. Graduated from Princeton University in 1879. Received a PhD in political science from Johns Hopkins in 1886. Appointed to the Princeton faculty in 1890. Served as president of Princeton from 1902 to 1910. Governor of New Jersey from 1911 to 1913. Nominated for president by the Democratic National Convention in June 1912. President of the United States from March 1913 to March 1921, winning reelection in November 1916. Disabled by a stroke in October 1919 and was incapacitated for the last months of his term in office. Continued to live in Washington, D.C., after leaving office.

Profiles of Organizations

American Alliance for Labor and Democracy (AALD): Formed in June 1917 as a counter to the People's Council of America. Led by Samuel Gompers and pro-war socialists. Covertly funded by the Committee on Public Information. Issued a large quantity of pro-war pamphlets. Organized a large rally in Minneapolis in September 1917. Dissolved in November 1919.

American Defense Society (ADS): Formed in August 1915 as a split from the National Security League to be more critical of the Wilson administration. Theodore Roosevelt served as honorary chair and publicly supported its activities. Once the United States entered the war, it pushed for a war to the finish and the harsh suppression of any dissent. Worked with the CPI and the intelligence community in covert operations aimed at discrediting the antiwar opposition. After the war ended, became a small far-right fringe group. In 1942, it disappeared from view.

Bureau of Intelligence of the Department of Justice (BI): Formed in 1908 as the intelligence agency for the Department of Justice. A small organization until April 1917 when the United States entered the war. Given the primary responsibility of investigating cases arising from the enforcement of the Espionage Act and other statutes designed to silence the antiwar opposition. Worked closely with the War Emergency Division. Bruce Bielaski served as its chief during the war. Renamed the Federal Bureau of Intelligence in July 1935.

Committee on Public Information (CPI): Created in April 1917 by an executive order signed by Woodrow Wilson. George Creel was chosen as chair. Funded primarily through the president's secret national security and defense fund. Produced huge quantities of pro-war propaganda. Seventy-five thousand volunteers gave short speeches promoting the war to a wide range of audiences. The CPI also engaged in covert operations, including the secret funding and direction of the American Alliance for Labor and Democracy. Also involved in overseas operations covertly aiding pro-war groups in Europe. Dissolved in June 1919.

Military Intelligence Division, U.S. Army (MID): Created in 1885. A small organization until the First World War, its primary purpose was the collection of information from military attachés at U.S. embassies. During the war, it grew rapidly as it sought to facilitate the war effort by silencing the antiwar opposition and breaking strikes. After the war, it returned to its original mission. Still exists as an agency within the Army's overall structure.

Minnesota Commission of Public Safety (MCPS): Created by the Minnesota legislature in April 1917 with sweeping powers to promote the war effort. Initially aimed at intimidating German-Americans, it then focused on the Industrial Workers of the World. After the federal government launched an assault on the IWW, the commission sought to suppress the Nonpartisan League. It was also instrumental in breaking a strike of tram workers in the Minneapolis area. Most of its members were corporate attorneys or business executives. Ceased to function in January 1919, although it was not officially dissolved until December 1920.

Nonpartisan League (NPL): Formed in February 1915 by Arthur Townley and Albert Bowen to gain reforms that would help small farmers. Grew rapidly and became the dominant force in North Dakota's politics by the 1916 election. Spread into the adjoining states. Under the pressure of repressive actions by state governments, as well as internal divisions and an economic downturn in the 1920s, it collapsed outside of North Dakota. In that state, it continued to function as a pressure group until it was absorbed by the Democratic Party in 1956.

People's Council of America for Democracy and the Terms of Peace (PCA): Initially organized at a meeting on May 31, 1917, in New York City. Brought together a wide range of peace organizations in coalition with the Socialist Party. Called for a speedy end to the war through a negotiated peace. Grew rapidly during the summer of 1917. Became a target of repression by the federal government. Its founding conference to be held in September 1917 in Minneapolis was banned by Minnesota's governor. Went into a decline and was largely inactive after the spring of 1918. Dissolved in October 1919.

Socialist Party of America (SP): Founded in the summer of 1901 at a conference held in Indianapolis, Indiana. Small at first, it grew rapidly. At its peak in 1912, 150,000 members were enrolled. Elected mayors, state legislators, and two members of the U.S. House of Representatives. Nominated Eugene Debs five times as its presidential candidate. From the start, deeply divided into moderate and radical wings. Opposed the war and became a target of repression by the federal government. This and the split of its leftwing into the Communist Party led to a sharp decline. Continues to exist today, but as a much smaller party.

War Emergency Division of the Department of Justice: Created by Attorney General Thomas Gregory in October 1917. Given overall authority by the Department of Justice to suppress antiwar activists. Advised the attorney general on relevant policy issues. Determined those aliens from enemy nations to be held in detention camps for the duration of the war. Directly supervised the prosecution of most cases involving the Espionage Act. Cases involving the IWW were handled by another section of the Justice Department, but the War Emergency Division established guidelines and set the overall direction of those cases as well. Headed by John Lord O'Brian with Alfred Bettman as his chief deputy. Dissolved on May 31, 1919.

BIBLIOGRAPHY

Books and Pamphlets

Adler, Cyrus. *Jacob H. Schiff: His Life and Letters.* Two Volumes. Garden City, NY: Doubleday, Doran, 1929.

American Defense Society. *Handbook of the American Defense Society.* New York, NY: 1918.

Ascoli, Peter. *Julius Rosenwald: The Man Who Built Sears, Roebuck and Advanced the Cause of Black Education in the American South.* Bloomington, IN: University of Indiana Press, 2006.

Axelrod, Alan. *Selling the Great War: The Making of American Propaganda.* New York, NY: Palgrave Macmillan, 2009.

Bailey, Thomas A., and Paul B. Ryan. *The* Lusitania *Disaster: An Episode in Modern Warfare and Diplomacy.* New York, NY: Free Press, 1975.

Baker, Ray Stannard, ed. *Woodrow Wilson: Life and Letters.* Eight Volumes. Garden City, NY: Doubleday, Page, 1928–1939.

Bell, Lauren Cohen. *Filibustering in the U. S. Senate.* Amherst, NY: Cambria, 2011.

Bidwell, Bruce W. *History of the Military Intelligence Division, Department of the Army General Staff, 1775–1941.* Frederick, MD: University Publications, 1986.

Blackorby, Edward C. *Prairie Rebel: The Public Life of William Lemke.* Lincoln, NE: University of Nebraska Press, 1963.

Boylan, James R. *Revolutionary Lives: Anna Strunsky and William English Walling.* Amherst, MA: University of Massachusetts Press, 2011.

H.W. Brands. *TR: The Last Romantic.* New York, NY: Basic Books, 1997.

Brown, Curt. *Minnesota, 1918.* St. Paul, MN: Minnesota Historical Society, 2018.

Buckingham, Peter H. *Rebel Against Injustice: The Life of Frank P. O'Hare.* Columbia, MO: University of Missouri Press, 1996.

Buenker, John D. *The Progressive Era, 1893–1914.* Madison, WI: Wisconsin Historical Society, 1998.

Capozzola, Christopher. *Uncle Sam Wants You: World War I and the Making of the Modern America.* Oxford, England: Oxford University Press, 2008.

Chambers, John Whiteclay, II. *To Raise an Army: The Draft Comes to a Modern America.* New York, NY: Free Press, 1987.

Chernow, Ronald. *The House of Morgan: An American Banking Dynasty and the Rise of Modern Finance.* New York, NY: Atlantic Monthly Press, 1990.

Chester, Eric Thomas. *The Wobblies in Their Heyday: The Rise and Destruction of the Industrial Workers of the World during the World War I Era.* Santa Barbara, CA: Praeger, 2014.

_______. *Free Speech and the Suppression of Dissent during World War I.* New York, NY: Monthly Review Press, 2020.

Chrislock, Carl Henry. *The Upper Midwest Norwegian-American Experience in World War I.* Northfield, MN: Norwegian American Historical Society, 1981.

_______. *The Minnesota Public Safety Commission.* St. Paul, MN: Minnesota Historical Society Press, 1991.

Cocks, F. Seymour. *The Secret Treaties and Understandings.* London, England: Union of Democratic Control, 1918.

Coffman, Edward M. *The Hilt of the Sword: The Career of Peyton C. March.* Madison, WI: University of Wisconsin Press, 1966.

Cohen, Naomi Wiener. *Jacob H. Schiff: A Study in Jewish Leadership.* Hanover, NH: University Press of New England, 1999.

Commons, John Rogers. *Why Workingmen Support the War.* New York, NY: American Alliance for Labor and Democracy, 1918.

Cook, Fred J., *The FBI Nobody Knows.* New York, NY: Macmillan, 1964.

Craig. Douglas B. *Progressives at War: William G. McAdoo and Newton D. Baker, 1863–1941.* Baltimore, MD: Johns Hopkins University Press, 2013.

Creel, George. *Wilson and the Issues.* New York, NY: Century, 1916.

_______. *How We Advertised America.* New York, NY: Harpers and Sons, 1920.

_______. *Rebel at Large: Recollections of Fifty Crowded Years.* New York, NY: G. P. Putnam's, 1947.

Cuff, Robert D. *The War Industries Board: Business-Government Relations during World War I.* Baltimore, MD: Johns Hopkins Press, 1973.

Daniels, Josephus. *The Wilson Era.* Two Volumes. Chapel Hill, NC: University of North Carolina Press, 1944–46.

Davison, Charles Stewart. *"Treason": Popular Misapprehension of the Scope of the Law.* [New York]: 1917.

Doan, Edward N. *The La Follettes and the Wisconsin Idea.* New York, NY: Rinehart, 1947.

Doorley, Michael. *Irish-American Diaspora Nationalism: The Friends of Irish Freedom, 1916–1935.* Dublin, Ireland: Four Courts Press, 2005.

Douthit, Davis. *Nobody Owns Us: The Story of Joe Gilbert, Midwestern Rebel.* Chicago, IL: Cooperative League of the USA, [1948].

Foner, Eric. *A Short History of Reconstruction, 1863–1877.* New York, NY: Harper and Row, 1990.

Foner, Philip Sheldon. *The History of the Labor Movement in the United States.* Eleven Volumes. New York, NY: International Publishers, 1947–1987.

Gal, Allon. *Brandeis of Boston.* Cambridge, MA: Harvard University Press, 1980.

Gieske, Millard L. *Minnesota Farmer Laborism: The Third Party Alternative.* Minneapolis, MN: University of Minnesota Press, 1979.

Gieske, Millard L. and Stephen J. Keillor. *Norwegian Yankee: Knute Nelson and the Failure of American Politics, 1860–1923.* Northfield, MN: Norwegian American Historical Association, 1995.

Gilbert, James L. *World War I and the Origins of U. S. Military Intelligence.* Lanham, MD: Scarecrow Press, 2012.

Goren, Arthur A. *New York Jews and the Quest for Community: The Kehillah Experiment, 1908–1922.* New York, NY: Columbia University Press, 1970.

Gregory, Thomas Watt. *Annual Report of the Attorney General of the United States.* Washington, D.C.: GPO, 1918.

Grubbs, Frank Leslie. *The Struggle for Labor Loyalty: Gompers, the A.F. Of L. and Pacifists, 1917–1920.* Durham, NC: Duke University, Press, 1968.

Gwynn, Stephen, ed. *The Letters and Friendships of Sir Cecil Spring Rice: A Record.* Boston, MA: Houghton Mifflin, 1929.

Haines, Lynn, and Dora Haines. *The Lindberghs.* New York: Vanguard, 1931.

Hamilton, John Maxwell. *Manipulating the Masses: Woodrow Wilson and the Birth of American Propaganda.* Baton Rouge, LA: Louisiana State University Press, 2020.

Hartshorn, Peter. *I Have Seen the Future: A Life of Lincoln Steffens.* Berkeley, CA: 2011.

Hillquit, Morris. *Loose Leaves from a Busy Life.* New York, NY: Macmillan, 1934.

Hochschild, Adam. *Rebel Cinderella: From Rags to Riches to Radical, the Epic Journey of Rose Pastor Stokes.* New York, NY: Houghton, Mifflin Harcourt, 2020.

Hodgson, Godfrey. *Woodrow Wilson's Right Hand: The Life of Colonel House.* New Haven, CT: Yale University Press, 2006.

Hornaday, William T. *Awake! America: Object Lessons and Warnings.* New York, NY: Moffett, Yard, 1918.

Hudelson, Richard, and Carl Ross. *By the Ore Docks.* Minneapolis, MN: University of Minnesota Press, 2006.

Jeffrey-Jones, Rhodri. *The FBI: A History.* New Haven, CT: Yale University Press, 2007.

Jensen, Joan M. *The Price of Vigilance.* New York, NY: Rand McNally, 1968.

Jenson, Carol E. *Agrarian Pioneer in Civil Liberties: The Nonpartisan League in Minnesota during World War I.* New York, NY: Garland, 1986.

Johnston, Robert D. *The Radical Middle Class: Populist Democracy and the Question of Capitalism in Progressive Era Portland, Oregon.* Princeton, NJ: Princeton University Press, 2003.

Daniel Katz. *All Together Different: Yiddish Socialists, Garment Workers and the Labor Roots of Multiculturalism.* New York, NY: New York University Press, 2011.

Kaufman, Stuart B., Peter J. Albert and Grace Palladino. *The Samuel Gompers Papers.* Thirteen Volumes. Urbana, IL: University of Illinois Press, 1991–2010.

Kennedy, Samuel V., III. *Samuel Hopkins Adams and the Business of Writing.* Syracuse, NY: Syracuse University Press, 1999.

Kraft, Barbara S. *The Peace Ship: Henry Ford's Pacifist Adventure in the First World War.* New York, NY: Macmillan, 1978.

La Follette, Belle Case, and Lola La Follette. *Robert M. La Follette.* Two Volumes. New York, NY: Macmillan, 1953.

Lansing, Michael J. *Insurgent Democracy: The Nonpartisan League in North American Politics.* Chicago, IL: University of Chicago Press, 2015.

Larson, Bruce Llewelyn. *Lindbergh of Minnesota: A Political Biography.* New York, NY: Harcourt, Brace, Jovanovich, 1973.

Larson, Simeon. *Labor and Foreign Policy: Gompers, the AFL and the First World War, 1914–1918.* Rutherford, NJ: Fairleigh Dickinson Press, 1974.

Levine, Lawrence W. *Defender of the Faith: William Jennings Bryan, The Last Decade, 1915–1925.* New York, NY: Oxford University Press, 1965.

Levine, Louis. *The Women's Garment Workers' Union: A History.* New York, NY: B. W. Huebsch, 1924.

Lindbergh, Charles Augustus, Sr. *Your Country at War and What Happens to You After a War.* Washington, D.C.: National Capital Press, 1917.

Link, Arthur Stanley. *Wilson: Confusions and Crises: 1915–1916.* Princeton, NJ: Princeton University Press, 1964.

_______. *Wilson: Campaigns for Progressivism and Peace, 1916–1917.* Princeton, NJ: Princeton University Press, 1965.

_______, ed. *Papers of Woodrow Wilson.* 69 Volumes. Princeton, NJ: Princeton University Press, 1966–1992.

Lipsky, Seth. *The Rise of Abraham Cahan.* New York, NY: Schocken, 2013.

Lochner, Louis Paul. *Always the Unexpected.* New York, NY: Macmillan, 1956.

Madison, Charles Allen. *Jewish Publishing in America: The Impact of Jewish Writing on American Culture.* New York, NY: Sanhedrin Press, 1976.

Manahan, James. *Trials of a Lawyer.* Minneapolis, MN: Farnham, 1933.

Mandel, Bernard. *Samuel Gompers: A Biography.* Yellow Springs, OH: 1963.

Maney, Patrick J. *"Young Bob" La Follette: A Biography of Robert M. La Follette, Jr., 1895–1953.* Columbia, MO: University of Missouri Press, 1978.

Manor, Ehud. *Louis Miller and Di Wahrheit: Yiddishism, Zionism and Socialism in New York, 1905–1915*. Portland, OR: Sussex, 2012.

March, Peyton Conway. *The Nation at War.* Garden City, NY: Doubleday, Doran, 1932.

Marchand, C. Roland. *The American Peace Movement and Social Reform, 1889–1918.* Princeton, NJ: Princeton University Press, 1972.

Margulies, Herbert F. *Senator Lenroot of Wisconsin: A Political Biography, 1900–1929.* Columbia, MO: University of Missouri Press, 1977.

Mason, Alpheus Thomas. *Brandeis: A Free Man's Life.* New York, NY: Viking, 1946.

Maxwell, Robert S. *Emanuel L. Philipp: Wisconsin Stalwart.* Madison, WI: State Historical Society of Wisconsin, 1959.

McMeekin, Sean. *The Russian Revolution: A New History.* London, England: Profile, 1917.

McCoy, Alfred W. *Policing America's Empire: the United States, the Philippines and the Rise of the Surveillance State.* Madison, WI: University of Wisconsin Press, 2009.

Melanson, Philip H. *The Secret Service, The Hidden History of an Enigmatic Agency.* New York, NY: Carroll and Graf, 2002.

Miller, Sally M. *Victor Berger and the Promise of Constructive Socialism, 1910–1920.* Westport, CT: Greenwood, 1973.

_______. *From Prairie to Prison: The Life of Social Activist Kate Richards O'Hare.* Columbia, MO: University of Missouri Press, 1993.

Millikan, William. *A Union Against Unions: The Minneapolis Citizens Alliance Fight Against Organized Labor, 1903–1947.* St. Paul, MN: Minnesota Historical Society Press, 2001.

Miraldi, Robert. *The Pen Is Mightier: The Muckraking Life of Charles Edward Russell.* New York, NY: Palgrave, Macmillan, 2003.

Mock, James Robert, and Cedric Larson. *Words that Won the War: The Story of the Committee on Public Information, 1917–1919.* Princeton, NJ: Princeton University Press, 1939.

Mock, James Robert. *Censorship.* Princeton, NJ: Princeton University Press, 1941.

Mollenhoff, David V. *Madison: The Formative Years.* Dubuque: IA: Kendall/Hunt, 1982.

Morison, Elting E. *Letters of Theodore Roosevelt.* Eight Volumes. Cambridge, MA: Harvard University Press, 1951–54.

Morlan, Robert L. *Political Prairie Fire: The Nonpartisan League, 1915–1922.* Minneapolis, MN: University of Minnesota Press, 1955.

Mougel, Nadege, trans. by Julie Gratz. *World War I Casualties.* Szy-Chazelles, France: Centre Européen Robert Schuman, 2011.

National Civil Liberties Bureau. *War-Time Prosecutions and Mob Violence*

Involving the Right of Free Speech, Free Press, and Peaceful Assemblage. New York, NY: NCLB, 1919.

National Nonpartisan League. *Memorial to the Congress of the United States Concerning Conditions in Minnesota, 1918.* St. Paul, MN: NPL, 1918.

______. *Origins, Purposes and Methods of Operation, War Program and Statement of Principles* ([St. Paul, MN]: NPL, 1917.

Nearing, Scott. *The Great Madness.* New York, NY: Rand School, 1917.

______. *The Trial of Scott Nearing and the American Socialist Society.* New York, N. Y.: Rand School, 1919.

Nelson, Arthur M, ed. *Martin County in the World war, 1917–1919.* Fairmont, MN: Sentinel, 1920.

Neubeck, Deborah K. *Guide to the Microfilm Edition of the National Nonpartisan League Papers.* St. Paul, MN: Minnesota Historical Society, 1970.

O'Brian, John Lord. *Civil Liberty in War Time.* Washington, D.C.: GPO, 1919.

Peterson, H. C., and Gilbert C. Fite. *Opponents of War, 1917–1918.* Madison, WI: University of Wisconsin Press, 1957.

Pratt, Norma Fain. *Morris Hillquit: A Political History of an American Jewish Socialist.* Westport, CT: Greenwood Press, 1979.

Read, Anthony, and David Fisher. *Colonel Z: The Life and Times of a Master of Spies.* London, England: Hodder and Stoughton, 1984.

Robinson, Elwyn B. *History of North Dakota.* Lincoln, NE: University of Nebraska Press, 1966.

Rosenthal, Morton. *Louis Marshall: Defender of Jewish Rights.* Detroit, MI: Wayne State University, 1965.

Ruotsila, Markku. *John Spargo and American Socialism.* New York, NY: Palgrave Macmillan, 2006.

Russell, Charles Edward. *The Story of the Nonpartisan League.* New York, NY: Harper and Brothers, 1920.

______. *Bare Hands and Stone Walls: Some Recollections of a Side-Line Reformer.* New York, NY: Charles Scribner's Sons, 1933.

Saltmarsh, John A. *Scott Nearing: The Making of a Homesteader.* White River Junction, VT: Chelsea Green, 1998.

Sanders, Ronald. *The Lower East Side Jews: An Immigrant Generation.* New York, NY: Harper and Row, 1969.

Saul, Norman E. *The Life and Times of Charles R. Crane, 1858–1939; American Businessman, Philanthropist and a Founder of Russian Studies in America.* Lanham, MD: Lexington Books, 2013.

Schaffer, Ronald. *America in the Great War. The Rise of the War Welfare State.* New York, NY: Oxford University Press, 1991.

Schmahl, Julius, ed. *Minnesota Legislative Manual, 1919.* St. Paul, MN: 1919.

Seymour, Charles. *The Intimate Papers of Colonel House.* Four Volumes. New York, NY: Houghton Mifflin, 1926–28.

Shannon, David. *Socialist Party of America: A History.* New York, NY: Macmillan, 1955.

Spargo, John. *Report on the Non-Partisan League of North Dakota and Various Other States.* St. Louis, MO: Socialist Party, [1917].

Steffens, Lincoln. *The Autobiography of Lincoln Steffens.* Two Volumes. New York, NY: Harcourt Brace, 1931.

Stephenson, George M. *John Lind of Minnesota.* Minneapolis, MN: University of Minnesota Press, 1935.

Stevenson, Archibald, ed. *Revolutionary Radicalism: Its History, Purpose and Tactics.* Two Volumes. Albany, NY: J. B. Lyon, 1920.

Talbert, Roy, Jr. *Negative Intelligence: The Army and the American Left, 1917–1941.* Jackson, MI: University of Mississippi Press, 1991.

Theoharis, Athan, Susan Rosenfeld, and Richard Gid Powers, eds. *The FBI: A Comprehensive Reference Guide.* Phoenix, AZ: Oryx, 1998.

Thompson, Clarence Smedley. *Report on the Formation of the American Defense Society.* New York, NY: ADS, [1916].

Timberlake, James H. *Prohibition and the Progressive Movement, 1900–1920.* Cambridge, MA: Harvard University Press, 1963.

Trachtenberg, Alexander, ed. *The American Labor Yearbook, 1917–18.* New York, NY: Rand School of Social Science, 1918.

Tribe, Laurence H. *American Constitutional Law.* Minneola, NY: Foundation Press, 1978.

Unger, Nancy. *Fighting Bob La Follette: the Righteous Reformer.* Chapel Hill, NC: University of North Carolina Press, 2000.

U. S. Senate Historical Office, *U. S. Senate Elections, Expulsions* (Washington D.C.: GPO, 1995).

Urofsky, Melvin, and David M. Levy, eds. *Letters of Louis Brandeis.* Four Volumes. Albany, NY: State University of New York Press, 1971–78.

Wade, Rex Arvin. *The Russian Search for Peace, February–October 1917.* Palo Alto, CA: Stanford University Press, 1969.

Weber, Ralph E., ed. *The Final Memoranda: Major General Ralph H. Van Deman, USA ret.; 1865–1952; Father of U.S. Military Intelligence.* Wilmington, DE: Scholarly Resources, 1988.

Who Was Who in American History—The Military. Chicago, IL: Marquis Who's Who, 1975.

Wingerd, Mary Lethert. *Claiming the City: Politics, Faith, and the Power of Place in St. Paul.* Ithaca, NY: Cornell University Press, 2001.

Winter, Ella, and Granville Hicks, eds. *The Letters of Lincoln Steffens.* Two Volumes. New York, NY: Harcourt Brace, 1938.

Yockelson, Mitchell. *The War Department: Keeper of the Nation's Enemy Aliens During World War I.* Society for Military History, 1998.

Zeuch, W. E. *The Truth About the O'Hare Case.* St. Louis, MO: Frank P. O'Hare, [1919].

Articles and Unpublished Documents

Alexander, Charles C. "Prophet of American Racism: Madison Grant and the Nordic Myth." *Phylon* 23 (1962): 73–90.

Blythe, Wilson C. "Arthur L. Wagner, Military Educator and Modernizer." *Army History* (Winter 2013): 22–31.

Cary, Lorin Lee. "The Wisconsin Loyalty Legion, 1917–1919." *Wisconsin Magazine of History* 53 (Autumn 1969): 33–50.

Cooke, Gilbert W. "The North Dakota State Mill and Elevator." *Journal of Political Economy* 46 (February 1938): 23–51.

Dawidowicz, Lucy S. "Louis Marshall and the *Jewish Daily Forward*: An Experiment in Wartime Censorship, 1917–1918." In Moishe Altbauer, et al., *For Max Weinreich on His Seventieth Birthday: Studies in Jewish Languages, Literature, and Society.* The Hague, Holland: Mouton, 1964

Epperson, Ivan H. "Missourians Abroad No.3-George Creel." *Missouri Historical Review* 12 (January 1918): 100–110.

Giffin, Frederick C. "Morris Hillquit and the War Issue in the New York Mayoralty Campaign of 1917." *International Social Science Review* 74 (1999): 115–28.

Guekens, Laurence. "Bettman of Cincinnati". In Donald A. Krueckenberg, ed., *The American Planners: Biographies and Recollections.* New York, NY: Methuen, 1983.

Haines, Austin P. "An Adjournment of Common Sense." *New Republic* 16 (September 7, 1918): 158–59.

_______. "Borrowing with a Club." *New Republic* 18 (March 29, 1919): 273–74.

Hendrickson, Kenneth E., Jr. "The Pro-War Socialists, the Social Democratic League and the Ill-Fated Drive for Industrial Democracy." *Labor History* 11 (Winter 1970): 304–22.

Jenson, Carol E. "Loyalty as a Political Weapon." *Minnesota History* 43 (Summer 1972): 42–57.

La Follette, Robert Marion. "The Armed Ship Bill Meant War." *La Follette's Magazine* 9 (March 1917):1–4.

Millikan, William. "Defenders of Business: The Minneapolis Civic and Commerce Association Versus Labor during World War I." *Minnesota History* 50 (Spring 1986): 2–17.

Morlan, Robert L. "The Nonpartisan League and the Minnesota Campaign of 1918." *Minnesota History* 34 (Summer 1955): 221–252.

Neuberger, Richard L. "The Hero Had a Father." *Esquire* 3 (March 1937): 206–209.

O'Brian, John Lord. "Reminiscences of John Lord O'Brian." Transcript. New York, NY: Columbia University Oral History Project, 1952.

Soucek, Jonathan. "Under Pressure: The Nonpartisan League in South Central Minnesota." *Journal of Undergraduate Research at Mankato State University* 17 (2017): 1–20.

Spargo, John. "Second Minority Report of the Committee on War and Militarism." *Milwaukee Leader,* April 12, 1917.

Starr, Karen. "Fighting for a Future: Farm Women of the Nonpartisan League." *Minnesota History* (Summer 1983), 48: 255–62.

Sweeney, Arthur. "Charles Wilberforce Ames." *Minnesota Historical Bulletin* 4 (August 1921): 124–29.

Vladeck, Stephen D. "Enemy Aliens, Enemy Property and Access to the Courts." *Lewis and Clark Law Review* 11 (December 2007): 964–89.

Ward, Robert D. "The Origins and Activities of the National Security League, 1914–1919," *Mississippi Valley Historical Review* 47 (June 1956): 51–65.

Newspapers and Journals

Capital Times
La Follette's Magazine
Milwaukee Journal
Minneapolis Morning Tribune
New Ulm Review
New York Times
Nonpartisan Leader
Wisconsin State Journal

Microfilm Archives

Albert, Peter J., and Harold L. Miller, eds. *American Federation of Labor Records: The Samuel Gompers Era.* Microfilm. 135 Reels. Sanford, NC: Microfilming Corporation of America, 1979.

Socialist Party of America Papers, Duke University, Durham, North Carolina in *Socialist Party of America Papers,* Microfilm (Glen Rock, NJ: Microfilming Corporation of America),

Wilson, Thomas Woodrow. *Woodrow Wilson Papers.* Microfilm. 542 Reels. Washington, D.C.: Library of Congress, 1973.

Archives

National Archives, College Park, Maryland

Record Group 28, Post Office
Record Group 38, Chief of Naval Operations
Record Group 59, State Department
Record Group 60, Justice Department
Record Group 63, Committee on Public Information
Record Group 65, Bureau of Investigation
Record Group 165, Military Intelligence Division

Hoover Institution on War, Revolution and Peace
Stanford University, Palo Alto, California
David Starr Jordan Papers
John Lord O'Brian

Minnesota Historical Society, St. Paul, Minnesota
Charles Ames
John Lind
Minnesota Public Safety Commission
Nonpartisan League

University of Buffalo, Buffalo, New York
Charles B. Sears Law Library
John Lord O'Brian

Columbia University, New York City, New York
Rare Book and Manuscript Library
Lincoln Steffens
James Graham Phelps Stokes

New York Historical Society, New York City, New York
American Defense Society

Hebrew Union College, Cincinnati, Ohio
American Jewish Archives
Louis Marshall

Library of Congress, Washington, D.C.
Manuscript Division
Gilbert Roe
Robert Marion La Follette Sr.
John Purroy Mitchel
Law Library
Transcript of Record, *Gilbert v. Minnesota*

Notes

Introduction

1. Nadege Mougel, trans. Julie Gratz, *World War I Casualties* (Szy-Chazelles, France: Centre Européen Robert Schuman, 2011); Philip J. Haythornwaite, *The World War One Source Book* (London, England: Arms and Armour, 1992), 309.

Chapter 1: Targeting the Jewish Community of New York City

1. The 1920 Census recorded a total population in the United States of one hundred and six million. At the same time, the total population of New York City was 5,400,000. The Census determined that there were 1,600,000 Jews residing within the city limits in 1920, nearly 30 percent of the total population.
2. Meyer London was elected to the U. S. House of Representatives on the Socialist Party ticket in 1914, 1916, and 1920. *New York Times*, June 9, 1926.
3. Ivan H. Epperson, "Missourians Abroad No. 3—George Creel," *Missouri Historical Review* 12 (January 1918): 102–8; Woodrow Wilson to George Creel, October 27, 1914, Correspondence of George Creel, Record Group 63, Box 3, National Archives, College Park, MD.
4. *New York Times*, May 31, 1917; Frank Leslie Grubbs, *The Struggle for Labor Loyalty: Gompers, the A.F. of L. and Pacifists, 1917–1920* (Durham, NC: Duke University, Press, 1968), 30–32.
5. Eric Thomas Chester, *The Wobblies in Their Heyday: The Rise and Destruction of the Industrial Workers of the World during the World War I Era* (Santa Barbara, CA: Praeger, 2014), 29,65.
6. *New York Times*, June 24, 1917; American Alliance for Labor and

Democracy, Circular Letter, August 15, 1917, Microfilm, Reel 86, Peter J. Albert and Harold L. Miller, eds., *American Federation of Labor Records: The Samuel Gompers Era* (Sanford, NC: Microfilming Corporation of America, 1979).

7. Memorandum, "Unofficial War Activities," December 12, 1922, James Graham Phelps Stokes Papers, Box 112, Rare Book and Manuscript Library, Columbia University, New York.
8. Chester Wright to Samuel Gompers, July 23, 1917, *American Federation of Labor Records*, Microfilm, Reel 86.
9. *New York Times*, September 21, 1945.
10. *New York Times*, August 6, 1917; Chester M. Wright, "An Appeal for Peace," *The* Western Comrade (April 1915): 2:23.
11. George Creel to Samuel Gompers, July 26, 1917, Microfilm, Reel 86, *American Federation of Labor Records*. Creel sent this letter to confirm the decisions made at the discussion the two had held the previous day.
12. Creel to Gompers, July 26, 1917, Microfilm, Reel 86, *American Federation of Labor Records*. The quote from the next paragraph comes from the same source.
13. Samuel Gompers to Robert Maisel, July 31, 1917, Microfilm, Reel 86, *American Federation of Labor Records*; Samuel Gompers to Robert Maisel, August 2, 1917, Microfilm, Reel 86, *American Federation of Labor Records*; "Unofficial War Activities," Stokes Papers, Box 112, Columbia University.
14. American Alliance for Labor and Democracy, August 13, 1917, *American Federation of Labor Records*, Microfilm, Reel 87.
15. *New York Times*, December 27, 1951.
16. Henry Slobodin, Memorandum, August 10, 1017, File 862.20211/521, State Department Decimal Files, 1910–1929, Records of the State Department, Record Group 59, National Archives, College Park, MD. The next paragraphs are from the same source.
17. Leland Harrison to Robert Lansing, August 20, 1917, File 862.20211/521.
18. Robert Lansing to Woodrow Wilson, August 27, 1917, File 862.20211/521.
19. *New York Times*, October 6, 1917.
20. *New York Times*, October 8, 1917.
21. Eric Thomas Chester, *Free Speech and the Suppression of Dissent During World War I* (New York, NY: Monthly Review Press, 2020), 327–29.
22. *New York Times*, October 8, 1917.
23. Louis Marshall to Abraham Cahan, October 8, 1917, Case 47751, Case Files, Box 79, Records Relating to the Espionage Act, Office of the Solicitor, Entry 40, Records of the Post Office, Record Group 28, National Archives, Washington, D.C.

24. Abraham Cahan to Louis Marshall, October 8, 1917, Case 47751, Record Group 28, National Archives.
25. Louis Marshall to William Lamar, September 8, 1918, Case 47751, Record Group 28, National Archives.
26. Morton Rosenthal, *Louis Marshall: Defender of Jewish Rights* (Detroit, MI: Wayne State University, 1965), 104.
27. Louis Marshall to Julian Mack, October 31, 1917, Box 158, Louis Marshall Papers, American Jewish Archives, Hebrew Union College, Cincinnati, Ohio.
28. Marshall to Mack, October 31, 1917, Box 158, Marshall Papers, American Jewish Archives.
29. Abraham Cahan to Louis Marshall, October 19, 1917, Marshall Papers, American Jewish Archives.
30. Louis Marshall to William Lamar, September 8, 1918, Case 47751, Case Files, Record Group 28, National Archives.
31. Cahan to Marshall, October 19, 1917, Box 51, Louis Marshall Papers, American Jewish Archives, Hebrew Union College.
32. Robert Maisel to Samuel Gompers, [August 1917], Reel 87, Gompers Papers.
33. J. V. Foster, Report, September 26, 1917, File 9-12-338, Box 56, Classified Subject Files, Records of the Department of Justice, Record Group 60, National Archives, College Park, MD.
34. Bernard Mandel, *Samuel Gompers: A Biography* (Yellow Springs, OH: 1963), 404. Gompers visited Britain, France, Belgium and France. His visit boosted the morale of the pro-war social democrats, but it is not clear that he swayed those social democratic leaders who were growing increasingly weary of the war. He returned to New York on November 3, 1918. *New York Times*, November 4, 1918.
35. *New York Sun*, August 26, 1918.
36. *New York Evening World*, August 28, 1918.
37. Robert Maisel to Harry Haas, September 9, 1918, File N-4-39, Box 25, Correspondence Relating to Press Censorship, Records of the Military Intelligence Division, Record Group 165, National Archives, College Park, MD.
38. Maisel to Haas, September 9, 1918, File N-4-39, RG 165, National Archives.
39. George Creel to William Lamar, September 6, 1918, Box 14, Papers of George Creel, Entry 1, Records of the Committee on Public Information, Record Group 63, National Archives, College Park, MD.
40. C. Roland Marchand, *The American Peace Movement and Social Reform, 1889–1918* (Princeton, N.J.: Princeton University Press, 1972), 318.

Chapter 2: Quashing the People's Council of America

1. Barbara S. Kraft, *The Peace Ship: Henry Ford's Pacifist Adventure in the First World War* (New York, NY: Macmillan, 1978), 16, 271; Frank Leslie Grubbs, *The Struggle for Labor Loyalty: Gompers, the A.F. Of L. and Pacifists, 1917–1920* (Durham, NC: Duke University, Press, 1968), 14, 22.
2. Memorandum, Bruce Bielaski to Thomas Gregory, March 12, 1918, File OG 24713, Records of the Bureau of Investigation, Record Group 65, National Archives, College Park, MD.
3. Grubbs, *Struggle for Labor Loyalty*, 22. After graduating from the University of Wisconsin, where he became involved in peace activities, Lochner was hired by the Chicago Peace Society in the spring of 1914. He then became actively involved in organizing the Emergency Peace Federation. After coming to Europe on Henry Ford's *Peace Ship* in December 1915, Lochner stayed as a member of the Neutral Conference for Continuous Mediation. He returned from Europe in early 1917 to join the EPF in its futile efforts to forestall a declaration of war. Lochner was close to the Socialist Party and taught at the Rand School. Kraft, *The Peace Ship*, 15, 271.
4. C. Roland Marchand, *The American Peace Movement and Social Reform, 1889–1918* (Princeton, NJ: Princeton University Press, 1972), 295; Grubbs, *Struggle for Labor Loyalty*, 28; Circular Letter, "First American Conference for Democracy and Terms of Peace," [May 1917], David Starr Jordan Papers, Box 65, Hoover Institution on War, Revolution and Peace, Stanford University, Palo Alto, CA.
5. Emily Greene Balch worked as a social worker at a settlement house. In 1896, she started teaching at Wellesley College and was made a professor in 1913. Balch became active in the peace movement during the war and took a leave of absence from Wellesley. In 1918, when she tried to return to academia, the college administration refused to let her resume her position. Balch then began working in the peace movement on a full-time basis. She was awarded the Nobel Peace Prize in 1946. *New York Times*, January 11, 1966.

   Judah Magnes was a prominent Jewish theologian. From 1909 to 1910. he served as the rabbi of the Temple Emanuel in Manhattan, the synagogue of the most influential members of the Jewish community in New York City. Starting in 1909, Magnes headed the Kebillah, an effort to unite New York's Jewish community. In the fall of 1916, Magnes began to voice his opposition to the drift to war. His decision to become one of the leaders of the People's Council caused his estrangement from the bankers and corporate lawyers who held power within the Jewish community. In 1922, Magnes moved to Palestine.

Arthur A. Goren, *New York Jews and the Quest for Community: The Kehillah Experiment, 1908–1922* (New York, NY: Columbia University Press, 1970), 231–34; Arthur A. Goren, *American National Biography* (New York, NY: Oxford University Press, 1999), 14: 322.

6. Circular Letter, "First American Conference," Jordan Papers, Box 65, Hoover Institution, Stanford University, Palo Alto, CA.
7. *New York Times*, May 31, 1917.
8. *New York Times*, June 1, 1917; Circular Letter, "First American Conference," Box 65, Jordan Papers, Hoover Institution; Grubbs, *Struggle for Labor Loyalty*, 34.
9. *New York Times*, June 1, 1917.
10. *New York Times*, June 1, 1917.
11. Markku Ruotsila, *John Spargo and American Socialism* (New York, NY: Palgrave Macmillan, 2006), 46, 77; Eric Thomas Chester, *True Mission: Socialists and the Labor Party Question* (New York, NY: Pluto, 2004).
12. *New York Times*, June 2, 1917; "The Socialist Party and the War," in Alexander Trachtenberg, ed., *The American Labor Yearbook, 1917–18* (New York, NY: Rand School of Social Science, 1918), 50; David Shannon, *Socialist Party of America: A History* (New York, NY: Macmillan, 1955) 94, 97, 288. The referendum allowed Socialist Party members to vote on two different resolutions on the war, section by section. Thus, an exact count of the support of each resolution is difficult to ascertain, but every section of the majority resolution pledging militant opposition to the war received at least 21,000 votes, while no section of the pro-war resolution received more than 8,000 votes.
13. John Spargo to Chester Wright, July 11, 1917, Microfilm, Reel 85, *American Federation of Labor Records: The Samuel Gompers Era* (Sanford, NC: Microfilming Corporation of America, 1979). Spargo mentions in this letter that he is responding to a query from Wright dated July 8, 1917. This letter is not contained in the Gompers Papers microfilm. Spargo informed Wright that he was concentrating his efforts on creating a new third party. This would become the National Party, a short-lived organization of progressives who supported the war.
14. John Spargo, Transcript, "Reminiscences of John Spargo", Columbia University Oral History, 1950, Microfilm (Glen Rock, NJ: Microfilming Corp. of America, 1972).
15. *New York Times,* July 29, 1917.
16. Samuel Gompers to Robert Maisel, July 31, 1917, Microfilm, Reel 86, *American Federation of Labor Records: The Samuel Gompers Era,* (Sanford, NC: Microfilming Corporation of America, 1979).
17. *New York Times,* July 29, 1917.

18. American Alliance for Labor and Democracy, Press Release, August 22, 1917, Microfilm, Reel 87, *American Federation of Labor Records.*
19. John Spargo to Samuel Gompers, July 30, 1917, Microfilm, Reel 86, *American Federation of Labor Records.*
20. Sinclair resigned from the Socialist Party on July 16, 1917. Parts of his letter of resignation appeared in the *New York Times*, July 18, 1917.
21. Spargo to Gompers, July 30, 1917, Microfilm, Reel 86, *American Federation of Labor Records.*
22. F. Seymour Cocks, *The Secret Treaties and Understandings* (London, England: Union of Democratic Control, 1918).
23. Executive Committee of the Petrograd Soviet, Public Statement, May 2, 1917, in Barbara C. Allen, ed., *Leaflets of the Russian Revolution* (Chicago, IL: Haymarket, 2018), 59.
24. People's Council of America, Press Release, June 28, 1917, Socialist Party of America Papers, Duke University, Durham, NC, in *Socialist Party of America Papers*, Microfilm, Reel 6 (Glen Rock, NJ: Microfilming Corporation of America, 1975–77).
25. During the first months after the United States entered the war, Wilson stuck to vague generalities in discussing a possible end to the conflict. Yet in a confidential cable to Elihu Root, who was in Russia as part of a commission urging the new provisional government to remain in the war, the president warned the members of the commission to not "speak of the terms of peace or of settlement which will be insisted on by the United States." The president was "reserving" his views on these issues "until very different circumstances arise." Woodrow Wilson to Elihu Root, June 26, 1917, in Arthur Link, ed., *Papers of Woodrow Wilson* (Princeton, NJ: Princeton University Press, 1983), 43:15.
26. Minutes of the 16th Meeting of the Organizing Committee of the People's Council, August 7, 1917, File OG 8000-13332, Records of the Bureau of Investigation, Record Group 65, National Archives, College Park, MD.
27. Robert D. Johnston, *The Radical Middle Class: Populist Democracy and the Question of Capitalism in Progressive Era Portland, Oregon* (Princeton, NJ: Princeton University Press, 2003), 33–34.
28. *Washington Evening Star*, August 9, 1917. The next paragraph relies on the same source.
29. Robert La Follette, "Peace Proposal," August 11, 1917, File #47607, Case Files, Records Relating to the Espionage Act, Office of the Solicitor, Entry 40, Records of the Post Office, Record Group 28, National Archives, Washington, D.C.
30. George Creel, *How We Advertised America* (New York, NY: Harper and Sons, 1920), 458. Creel wrote this lengthy volume to give an official gloss to the activities of the Committee on Public Information. He

failed to mention the American Alliance for Labor and Democracy even once in describing the CPI's efforts during the war. Instead, in an appendix listing the committee's literature there is a list of pamphlets produced by the AALD, stating that it acted as a division of the CPI.

31. John Rogers Commons, *Why Workingmen Support the War* (New York, NY: American Alliance for Labor and Democracy), 191.
32. Robert Maisel to Samuel Gompers, August 10, 1917, Samuel Gompers Papers, Files of the Office of the President, State Historical Society of Wisconsin, Microfilm, Reel 87, *American Federation of Labor Records: The Samuel Gompers Era* (Sanford, NC: Microfilming Corporation of America, 1979); Samuel Gompers to Robert Maisel, July 31, 1917, Microfilm, Reel 86, *American Federation of Labor Records.* Fifty dollars in 1917 would have roughly the same purchasing power as $1,000 now.
33. Maisel to Gompers, August 10, 1917, Microfilm, Reel 87, *American Federation of Labor Records.*
34. Robert Maisel to Samuel Gompers, [August 1917], Files of the Office of the President, State Historical Society of Wisconsin, Microfilm, Reel 87, *American Federation of Labor Records: The Samuel Gompers Era* (Sanford, NC: Microfilming Corporation of America, 1979). Cochran was wealthy, having inherited a fortune derived from a large carpet factory that his maternal grandfather had started in Yonkers, New York. He was also a successful real estate developer in Baltimore. Cochran was a Christian socialist and a philanthropist. *New York Times,* July 28, 1902*; New York Times,* March 7, 1915.
35. Grubbs, *Struggle for Labor Loyalty*, 55–56.
36. Chester Wright to Samuel Gompers, [August 1917], Microfilm, Reel 87, *American Federation of Labor Records.*
37. Grubbs, *Struggle for Labor Loyalty*, 59. Although Van Lear upheld the right of the People's Council to hold its conference in Minneapolis, he generally avoided any discussion of the war. Van Lear did state that once war was declared "all of us must do our duty" and comply with the government's orders. Iric Nathanson, "Thomas Van Lear: City Hall's Working-Class Champion," *Minnesota History* (Summer 2015): 64: 230.
38. James Graham Phelps Stokes, Memorandum, "Unofficial War Activities of Captain J. G. Phelps Stokes," December 12, 1923, J. G. Phelps Stokes Papers, Box 112, Rare Book and Manuscript Library, Columbia University, New York.
39. Stokes, Memorandum, "Unofficial War Activities," December 12, 1923, Box 112, Stokes Papers, Rare Book and Manuscript Library, Columbia University, New York.
40. Woodrow Wilson to Richard Heath Dabney, August 13, 1917, in Arthur Link, ed., *The Papers of Woodrow Wilson* (Princeton, N.J.:

Princeton University Press, 1983), 43:437. Dabney and Wilson had become friends while students at the University of Virginia. Dabney taught history at his alma mater. His letter was printed in the *New York Times* on August 1, 1917. It attacked the "peace-prattle" of the People's Council and stressed the need to "crush Prussian power."

41. Josephus Daniels Diary, August 17, 1917, in Link, ed., *The Papers of Woodrow Wilson,* 43:512. In April 1917, Attorney General Thomas Gregory commissioned an advisory opinion on the question of a declaration of martial law. James Proctor was in private practice, but he had previously served as a staff attorney within the Justice Department. Proctor wrote a memorandum holding that martial law could not be declared by either the president or Congress unless there was a genuine possibility of an imminent invasion or a "real rebellion" with the civil courts unable to function. Neither condition existed in the United States during the First World War, so a declaration of martial law would be in violation of the Constitution. Eric Thomas Chester, *Free Speech and the Suppression of Dissent during World War I* (New York, NY: Monthly Review Press, 2020), 253, 256–58, 445.
42. Chester Wright to Samuel Gompers, August 20, 1917, Microfilm, Reel 87, *American Federation of Labor Records.*
43. Thomas E. Campbell, Report, August 27, 1917, File 10110-219, Correspondence of the Military Intelligence Department, Record Group 165, National Archives, College Park, Maryland.
44. Thomas E. Campbell, Report, [September 1917], File 10110-219, Correspondence of the Military Intelligence Department, Record Group 165, National Archives.
45. *New York Times*, August 30, 1917.
46. Joseph Burnquist, Proclamation, August 28, 1917, enclosed with Louis Lochner to Woodrow Wilson, August 28, 1917, in Link ed., *Papers of Woodrow Wilson*. 44:78.
47. *New York Times*, August 31, 1917.
48. Grubbs, *Struggle for Labor Loyalty*, 62–64; Arthur A. Goren, *New York Jews and the Quest for Community: The Kehillah Experiment, 1908–1922* (New York, NY: Columbia University Press, 1970), 232.
49. *New York Times*, September 6, 1917.
50. *New York Times*, September 8, 1917.
51. *New York Times*, September 18, 1917; Scott Nearing, *The Trial of Scott Nearing and the American Socialist Society* (New York, N. Y.: Rand School, 1919), 107.
52. John A. Saltmarsh, *Scott Nearing: The Making of a Homesteader* (White River Junction, VT: Chelsea Green, 1998), 95, 111, 122.
53. Saltmarsh, *Scott Nearing,*108.

54. Saltmarsh, *Scott Nearing,*139, 158.
55. Report, Charles Jenkins, September 18, 1917, File OG 8000-10849, Records of the Bureau of Investigation, 190822, Record Group 65, National Archives, College Park, MD.
56. Report, Charles Jenkins, September 18, 1917, File OG 8000-10849, Records of the Bureau of Investigation, 190822, Record Group 65, National Archives, College Park, Maryland; Bruce Bielaski to Roger Baldwin, November 23, 1917, File OG 8000-10849, Records of the Bureau of Investigation, 1908-22, Record Group 65, National Archives.
57. William Campbell, Report, December 6, 1917, File OG 8000-10849, Records of the Bureau of Investigation, 1908–22, Record Group 65, National Archives. On December 2, 1917, Nearing delivered a speech in Louisville, Kentucky, that was transcribed by BI agents. The transcript is included in this report by a BI agent.
58. Scott Nearing, *The Great Madness* (New York, NY: Rand School, 1917), 5–6.
59. Nearing, *The Great Madness,* 36.
60. Bruce Bielaski to John Lord O'Brian, November 5, 1917, File OG 8000-10849, Records of the Bureau of Investigation, 1908-22, Record Group 65, National Archives.
61. Brandeis inserted the entire pamphlet into his dissent in the case that arose from the circulation of Tucker's pamphlet. *Pierce v. US*, 252 US 239 (1920). On Tucker, see J. Robert Constantine, *Letters of Eugene V. Debs* (Urbana: University of Illinois Press, 1990), 2:441.
62. *New York Times,* August 27, 1917; *New York Times,* September 27, 1917; *Albany Times Union*, March 8, 1920.
63. The director of the War Emergency Division, John Lord O'Brian, acted as the liaison with the broader intelligence community. Once a week, he convened a meeting of representatives from all of government's intelligence agencies to review major investigations. He was in contact with the attorney general and other high officials in the Wilson administration. O'Brian also personally reviewed every order authorizing the detention of an alien enemy, that is, recent immigrants who had not yet become U.S. citizens and who had voiced their opposition to the war. John Lord O'Brian, "Reminiscences of John Lord O'Brian" (Columbia University Oral History Project), 1952, 241, 248, 252.

    Given these responsibilities, O'Brian delegated the decision as to who would be prosecuted under the Espionage Act to his deputy, Alfred Bettman. Bruce Bielaski as chief of the Bureau of Investigation sent frequent reports to Bettman, who reviewed them to determine whether there was sufficient evidence to warrant the Justice Department going to a grand jury to request an indictment

64. The Espionage Act, June 5, 1917, *Congressional Record*, 65th Congress, Sess. 1, 219; Eric Thomas Chester, *Free Speech and the Suppression of Dissent during World War I* (New York, NY: Monthly Review Press, 2020), 27.
65. Alfred Bettman to John Lord O'Brian, November 8, 1917, Class 9-19, Central Classified Files, Record Group 60, Box 758, Records of the State Department, National Archives, College Park, MD.
66. *Pierce v. US*, 252 US 251 (1920). For the president's speech of April 2, 1917, see Link, ed., *The Papers of Woodrow Wilson*, 41:519–27.
67. *Pierce v. US*, 252 US 267, 269 (1920).
68. Thomas Gregory to John Lord O'Brian, December 26, 1917, O'Brian Papers, Box 17, Charles B. Sears Law Library, University of Buffalo, New York.
69. Thomas Gregory to Charles Clyne, January 29, 1918, Box 963, Class 9-19-102, Central Classified Files, Record Group 60, Records of the State Department, National Archives.
70. Sally M. Miller, *Victor Berger and the Promise of Constructive Socialism, 1910–1920* (Westport, CT: Greenwood Press, [1973]), 189, 203; *New York Times*, March 10, 1918; *New York Times*, February 1, 1921.
71. Saltmarsh, *Scott Nearing*, 141.
72. William Offley to Bruce Bielaski, February 11, 1918, File OG 8000-10849, Records of the Bureau of Investigation, 1908–22, Record Group 65, National Archives.
73. Bruce Bielaski to Frank Garbarino, February 18, 1918, File OG 8000-10849, Records of the Bureau of Investigation, 1908-22, Record Group 65, National Archives; Frank Garbarino to Bruce Bielaski, March 5, 1918, File OG 8000-10849, Records of the Bureau of Investigation, 190822, Record Group 65, National Archives.
74. Bruce Bielaski to Frank Garbarino, 1918, File OG 8000-10849, Records of the Bureau of Investigation, 1908-22, Record Group 65, National Archives; Report, J. F. McDevitt, April 11, 1918, File OG 8000-10849, Records of the Bureau of Investigation, 1908-22, Record Group 65, National Archives.
75. Saltmarsh, *Scott Nearing*, 246–47, 316. Nearing and Helen Knothe were married in 1948.
76. *New York Tribune*, February 11, 1918.
77. *New York Tribune*, February 12, 1918.
78. Alfred Bettman to Bruce Bielaski, February 18, 1918, File OG 8000-10849, Records of the Bureau of Investigation, 1908–22, Record Group 65, National Archives; John Lord O'Brian to Bruce Bielaski, File OG 8000-10849, Records of the Bureau of Investigation, 1908–22, Record Group 65, National Archives.

79. *Cincinnati Enquirer*, March 22, 1918; Scott Nearing, *The Trial of Scott Nearing and the American Socialist Society* (New York, NY: Rand School, 1919).
80. Financial Statement of the People's Council, September 14, 1917, File OG 30749, Records of the Bureau of Investigation, 1908–22, Record Group 65, National Archives; Report, J. W. Kemp, April 29, 1918, File OG 8000-10849, Records of the Bureau of Investigation, 1908–22, Record Group 65, National Archives. Kemp excerpted notes from a Bureau of Investigation file on the People's Council. Unfortunately, the original file seems to have been destroyed.
81. *New York Times*, February 20, 1919.
82. Memorandum, Bruce Bielaski to Thomas Gregory, January 16, 1918, File OG 8000-10849, Records of the Bureau of Investigation, 1908–22, Record Group 65, National Archives.
83. Don Rathbun, Report, March 7, 1918, File OG 18789, Records of the Bureau of Investigation, 1908–22, Record Group 65, National Archives.
84. H. H. Dooley, Report, July 15, 1918, File OG 30749, Records of the Bureau of Investigation, 1908–22, Record Group 65, National Archives.
85. Thomas G. Patten to William Lamar, October 11, 1917, File 50206, Case Files, Records Relating to the Espionage Act, Office of the Solicitor, Entry 40, Records of the Post Office, Record Group 28, National Archives, Washington, D.C.; J. B. Smith to John A. Nash, December 12, 1917, File 50206, Case Files, Records Relating to the Espionage Act, Office of the Solicitor, Entry 40, Record Group 28, National Archives. Patten held the position of New York City Postmaster. Smith served as a chief assistant to Lamar. Nash was an attorney on Lamar's staff.
86. Grubbs, *Struggle for Labor Loyalty*, 127.
87. Grubbs, *Struggle for Labor Loyalty*, 143–44.
88. Grubbs, *Struggle for Labor Loyalty*., 145.

Chapter 3: Intimidating Senator Robert La Follette

1. Nancy Unger, *Fighting Bob La Follette: The Righteous Reformer* (Chapel Hill, NC: University of North Carolina Press, 2000), 129–34; John D. Buenker, *The Progressive Era, 1893–1914* (Madison, WI: Wisconsin Historical Society, 1998), 485–88.
2. Unger, *La Follette*, 129.
3. Woodrow Wilson, Campaign Speech in New Haven, Connecticut, September 25, 1912, in Arthur Link ed., *Papers of Woodrow Wilson* (Princeton, NJ: Princeton University Press, 1978), 25:247.
4. *New York Times,* March 15, 1913; *New York Times*, March 14, 1913.
5. Melvin I. Urofsky and David Levy, eds., *Letters of Louis D. Brandeis* (Albany, NY: State University of New York Press, 1972), 2: 330; Allon

Gal, *Brandeis of Boston* (Cambridge, MA: Harvard University Press, 1980), 121.

6. Alfred Lief, *Brandeis: The Personal History of an American Ideal* (New York, NY: Stackpole, 1936), 347.
7. Belle Case La Follette and Lola La Follette, *Robert M. La Follette* (New York, NY: Macmillan, 1953), 1:568.
8. Unger, *Fighting Bob La Follette*, 183.
9. *New York Times*, February 13, 1917; Ronald Chernow, *The House of Morgan: An American Banking Dynasty and the Rise of Modern Finance* (New York, NY: Atlantic Monthly Press, 1990), 101–2.
10. *New York Times*, February 13, 1917.
11. Woodrow Wilson, Speech to a Joint Session of Congress, February 26, 1917, in Arthur Link ed., *Papers of Woodrow Wilson* (Princeton, NJ: Princeton University Press, 1983), 41:286; Woodrow Wilson to William McAdoo, February 24, 1917, Link ed., *Papers of Woodrow Wilson,* 41: 279–80.
12. *New York Times*, March 4, 1917.
13. *New York Times*, March 5, 1917.
14. Robert La Follette, "The Armed Ship Bill Meant War," *La Follette's Magazine* 9 (March 1917): 1; La Follette and La Follette, *Robert M. La Follette,* 1: 604–6.
15. *New York Times*, March 5, 1917.
16. La Follette and La Follette, *Robert M. La Follette,* 1: 619–20.
17. Arthur Wilson Link, *Campaigns for Progressivism and Peace, 1916–1917* (Princeton, NJ: Princeton University Press, 1965), 370.

    The first filibuster took place during the first session of Congress in September 1789. Various states were interested in having the new nation's capital located in their state, so they stalled the debate. In general, filibusters were infrequent in the nearly one hundred and twenty years during which there were no rules forcing an end to debate. (Lauren Cohen Bell, *Filibustering in the U.S. Senate* (Amherst, NY: Cambria, 2011), 30, 70–73.
18. Woodrow Wilson, Speech to a Joint Session of Congress, April 2, 1917, in Link ed., *Papers of Woodrow Wilson,* 41: 519–521.
19. Robert La Follette, Speech, April 4, 1917, *Congressional Record,* 65th Congress, 1st Session, 224, 228.
20. La Follette, Speech, April 4, 1917, *Congressional Record,* 65th Congress, 1st Session, 230–1.
21. La Follette, Speech, April 4, 1917, *Congressional Record,* 65th Congress, 1st Session, 228.
22. *New York Times*, April 4, 1917; *New York Times*, April 6, 1917.
23. *New York Times*, April 5, 1917; *New York Times*, April 18, 1917; *New York Times*, April 20, 1917.

24. Robert La Follette, Speech, April 27, 1917, *Congressional Record,* 65th Congress, 1st Session,1357–58.
25. La Follette, Speech, April 27, 1917, *Congressional Record,* 65th Congress, 1st Session, 1356–57.
26. La Follette, Speech, April 27, 1917, *Congressional Record,* 65th Congress, 1st Session, 1364.
27. *New York Times,* May 16, 1917; *New York Times,* May 18, 1917.
28. Lucius Nieman to Joseph Tumulty, July 27, 1917, in Link ed., *Papers of Woodrow Wilson,* 43: 319.
29. La Follette and La Follette, *Robert M. La Follette,* 1: 608.
30. Woodrow Wilson to Thomas Gregory, July 7, 1917, in Link ed., *Papers of Woodrow Wilson,* 43: 117. Nieman's memorandum is not included in the presidential papers.
31. Woodrow Wilson to Thomas Gregory, July 20, 1917, Microfilm, Series Two, *Woodrow Wilson Papers* (Washington, D.C.: Library of Congress, 1973).
32. Thomas Gregory to Woodrow Wilson, July 22, 1917, in Link ed., *Papers of Woodrow Wilson,* 43: 243.
33. Newton Baker to Woodrow Wilson, July 23, 1917, Microfilm, Series Two, *Woodrow Wilson Papers.*
34. Lucius Nieman to Joseph Tumulty, July 27, 1917, in Link ed., *Papers of Woodrow Wilson,* 43: 319.
35. *Milwaukee Journal,* July 27, 1917.
36. Woodrow Wilson to Newton Baker, September 1, 1917, Microfilm, Series Three, Reel 152, *Woodrow Wilson Papers* (Washington, D.C.: Library of Congress, 1973).
37. Woodrow Wilson to Joseph Tumulty, [July 1917], Microfilm, Series Four, Case 3735, Reel 353, *Woodrow Wilson Papers* (Washington, D.C.: Library of Congress, 1973).
38. The president generally avoided the issue of the terms of peace in his public statements, although members of Congress understood his position. He made his position explicitly clear in a confidential communication to the Root Commission that visited Russia in the summer of 1917. On June 26, 1917, Wilson wrote a note to Robert Lansing, the secretary of state, to be transmitted to the members of the U.S. mission to Russia warning that it was "not advisable" for them "to speak of the terms of peace" when meeting with officials in the provisional government. Indeed, the president was "himself reserving all such utterances until very different circumstances arise." The following day, Lansing sent a cable to Root that contained this message. (Robert Lansing to Elihu Root, June 27, 1917, in Arthur Link, ed., *Papers of Woodrow Wilson* (Princeton, NJ: Princeton University Press, 1983), 43:15.)

39. Robert La Follette to Gilbert Roe, June 2, 1917, Box 117, Gilbert Roe Papers in La Follette Family Papers, Manuscripts, Library of Congress, Washington, D.C.
40. Robert La Follette to the Family, June 23, 1917, Box A-20, La Follette Family Papers, Library of Congress.
41. Frank Leslie Grubbs, *The Struggle for Labor Loyalty: Gompers, the A.F. Of L. and Pacifists, 1917–1920* (Durham, NC: Duke University, Press, 1968), 28, 34.
42. *New York Times,* August 1, 1917.
43. La Follette and La Follette, *Robert M. La Follette,* 2:739–40.
44. Robert La Follette to the Family, [July 1917], Box A-20, La Follette Family Papers, Library of Congress.
45. Rex Arvin Wade, *The Russian Search for Peace, February–October 1917* (Palo Alto, CA: Stanford University Press, 1969), 29.
46. Robert La Follette, Jr. to Philip La Follette, June 22, 1917, Box 86, Series E, La Follette Papers, Library of Congress, Washington, D.C.; La Follette and La Follette, *Robert M. La Follette,* 2:753; Lincoln Steffens to Edward House, June 20, 1917, in Ella Winter and Granville Hicks, eds, *The Letters of Lincoln Steffens* (New York, NY: Harcourt Brace, 1938), 1: 399.
47. F. Seymour Cocks, *The Secret Treaties and Understandings* (London, England: Union of Democratic Control, 1918).
48. La Follette and La Follette, *Robert M. La Follette,* 2:753; Lincoln Steffens, *The Autobiography of Lincoln Steffens* (New York, NY: Harcourt Brace, 1931), 2: 770–71.
49. Robert La Follette to the Family, [July 1917], Box A-20, La Follette Family Papers, Library of Congress.
50. Rex Arvin Wade, *The Russian Search for Peace, February–October 1917* (Palo Alto, CA: Stanford University Press, 1969), 91.
51. *New York Times*, April 21, 1917; La Follette and La Follette, *Robert M. La Follette,* 2:753.
52. La Follette and La Follette, *Robert M. La Follette,* 2:752-54; Charles Seymour, ed., *The Intimate Papers of Colonel House* (New York, NY: Houghton Mifflin, 1928), 3:51; Steffens, *Autobiography*, 770.
53. La Follette and La Follette, *Robert M. La Follette,* 2:754, 756.
54. Robert La Follette, "Peace Proposal," August 11, 1917, File #47607, Case Files, Records Relating to the Espionage Act, Office of the Solicitor, Entry 40, Records of the Post Office, Record Group 28, National Archives, Washington, D. C.; La Follette and La Follette, *Robert M. La Follette,* 2:754, 756; *New York Times*, August 12, 1917.

    The peace program of the Russian soviets evolved over time. In a final version issued on October 21, 1917, less than three weeks before the Bolshevik seizure of power, the Central Executive Committee of the Soviet Council of Workers and Soldiers presented a detailed set of proposals that were published in full in the *New York Times*. One point in this proposed peace program called for an "international fund" to finance the rebuilding of an independent Belgium. (*New York Times*, October 22, 1917).

55. *New York Times*, August 12, 1917. La Follette's proposal was not a new one. Allen Benson sought and won the Socialist Party's presidential nomination in 1916 based on this proposal. Once the United States entered the war, Benson became an uncritical booster of the war effort.
56. Sean McMeekin, *The Russian Revolution: A New History* (London, England: Profile, 2021), 28–29. On November 10, 1917, a few days after the Bolsheviks had gained power, Leon Trotsky, as foreign minister of the new regime, announced the publication of the secret treaties. A few days later, *Izvestiya*, the official newspaper of the Soviet government, began publishing the secret treaties. The *Manchester Guardian* then printed an English translation of the secret treaties on February 7, 1918.
57. La Follette and La Follette, *La Follette,* 2: 758; *Springfield Republican,* August 16, 1917; *New York Times,* August 7, 1917.
58. *New York Times,* August 16, 1917.
59. H. W. Brands, *T. R.: The Last Romantic* (New York, NY: Basic Books, 1997), 718, 774.
60. Eric Thomas Chester, *True Mission: Socialists and the Labor Party Question* (New York, NY: Pluto, 2004), 126, 139.
61. *New York Times,* August 16, 1917.
62. La Follette and La Follette, *La Follette,* 2: 762–63.
63. Alfred Jaques to Thomas Gregory, October 11, 1917, Straight Numerical Series, Entry 112-B, Records of the Department of Justice, Record Group 60, National Archives, College Park, Maryland.
64. Gilbert Roe, Brief, Appendix 3, January 1, 1918, in *Report,* Senate Committee on Privileges, January 1, 1918, Congressional Committee Reports, P93/6: L13; Robert La Follette, Speech, September 20, 1917, Nonpartisan League Papers, Microfilm, Reel 14, Minnesota Historical Society, St. Paul Minnesota. The transcript of the speech submitted by Roe to the subcommittee is the version La Follette believed to be correct, except that it did not include two interjections made by hecklers. The transcript submitted by Roe was taken by a NPL stenographer. The next paragraphs are from the same sources.
65. *New York Times*, October 6, 1917; *New York Times*, October 10, 1917.
66. La Follette and La Follette, *Robert M. La Follette,* 2:883. The Associated Press's admission that its original report of the St. Paul speech had been erroneous came in a letter from Frederick Roy Martin, the assistant

manager of the AP, to Senator Atlee Pomerene, dated May 23, 1918. Martin claimed the AP had only been recently notified that the accuracy of its report was in doubt. (Frederick Martin to Atlee Pomerene, May 23, 1918, in United States Senate, 65th Congress, 2nd Session, Senate Committee on Privileges and Elections, *Report Relative to the Resolution from the Minnesota Commission on Public Safety Petitioning for Proceedings Looking to the Expulsion of Senator Robert M. La Follette* (Washington, D.C.: GPO, 1918), 2:160.

67. Robert La Follette to Atlee Pomerene, October 11, 1917, in Senate Committee on Privileges and Elections, *Report*; *New York Times*, September 24, 1917.
68. La Follette and La Follette, *La Follette*, 2:772.
69. *New York Times*, September 24, 1917.
70. John Lord O'Brian to Albert Burleson, January 3, 1918, File 47436, Box 46, Case Files, Records Relating to the Espionage Act, Entry 40, Office of the Solicitor, Records of the Post Office, Record Group 28, National Archives, Washington, D.C.; William Lamar to John Lord O'Brian, February 4, 1918, File 47436, Box 46, Case Files, Records of the Post Office, Record Group 28, National Archives, Washington, D.C.
71. O'Brian to Burleson, January 3, 1918, File 47436, Box 46, Case Files, Records Relating to the Espionage Act, Entry 40, Office of the Solicitor, Records of the Post Office, Record Group 28, National Archives, Washington, D. C.
72. The prevailing U.S. Supreme Court decision as of the First World War was Kilbourn v. Thompson (103 US 168 (1880)). Justice Samuel Miller in a unanimous decision declared that the constitutional provision on congressional immunity "exempts" any member of Congress from prosecution "for any vote, or report or action in their respective House, as well as oral debate." (103 US 169).

    This case did not directly involve questions of free speech, but Miller referred to an earlier case as "authoritative." That case came from Massachusetts Supreme Court. Massachusetts had a clause in its constitution similar to that in the U.S. Constitution concerning legislative immunity. In *Coffin v. Coffin* (4 Mass 1), Chief Justice Theophilus Parsons ruled that the article "ought not to be construed strictly, but liberally," Cited in *Kilbourn v. Thompson* (103 US 203)).

    This left the issue of whether a speech delivered in a public forum by a member of Congress on an issue of public policy then before Congress was protected speech. One could plausibly argue that, under a liberal interpretation of the congressional immunity clause, such a speech was in furtherance of "the execution of the office" as provided in *Coffin v. Coffin*.

The issue was not specifically addressed until 1972. Chief Justice Warren Burger in a majority opinion in *U.S. v. Brewster* (408 US 501 (1972)) held that members of Congress engage in a variety of "legitimate" activities that had "never been seriously contended" to be covered by the immunity clause. Burger listed as one of those "speeches delivered outside of Congress." (408 US 512).

Contrary to Burger, the issue was in doubt as of the First World War. The possibility that the courts might rule in La Follette's favor was one factor in the Justice Department's decision to not prosecute him for the speech delivered before the NPL conference in September 1917.

The constitutional issues involved with congressional immunity are summarized in Louis Fisher and Katy J. Harrigar, *American Constitutional Law*, Eighth Edition (Durham, NC: Carolina Academic Press, 2007), 241.

73. Robert La Follette to the Family, September 27, 1917, Box A-20, La Follette Family Papers, Library of Congress.
74. Robert La Follette to the Family, September 27, 1917, Box A-20, La Follette Family Papers, Library of Congress.
75. Of the fifteen senators expelled from the U.S. Senate, fourteen had aligned themselves with the Confederate States during the Civil War. Prior to that, a senator had been expelled for his involvement in an abortive paramilitary expedition to seize Florida from Spain and then to transfer it to the British Empire. (U.S. Senate Historical Office, *U. S. Senate Elections, Expulsions* (Washington D.C.: GPO, 1995)).
La Follette's case was unique in that he was threatened with expulsion from the Senate for giving a speech in opposition to the First World War. Still, Victor Berger was actually expelled from the U.S. House of Representatives for his opposition to the First World War. (Zechariah Chafee, Jr., *Free Speech in the United States* (Cambridge, MA: Harvard University Press, 1941), 248–51.)
76. *New York Times*, October 6, 1917.
77. La Follette and La Follette, *Robert M. La Follette,* 2:817.
78. Robert La Follette, Speech, October 6, 1917, *Congressional Record*, 65th Congress, 1st Session, p. 7878.
79. La Follette and La Follette, *Robert M. La Follette,* 2:754, 756.
80. La Follette, Speech, October 6, 1917, *Congressional Record*, 65th Congress, 1st Session, 7882.
81. La Follette, Speech, October 6, 1917, *Congressional Record*, 65th Congress, 1st Session, p. 7882.
82. *Arver v. United States*, 245U.S.366(1918). The unanimous decision upholding the Selective Service Act was written by Edward White, chief justice.

83. La Follette, Speech, October 6, 1917, *Congressional Record*, 65th Congress, 1st Session, 7885.
84. In October 1917, Wilson wrote to Creel to underscore "how entirely the work being done by the Committee meets with my approval." He also confirmed that he had "kept in touch" with the activities of the Committee on Public Information by holding frequent meetings with Creel. (Woodrow Wilson to George Creel, October 27, 1914, Box 3, Correspondence of George Creel, Record Group 63, National Archives, College Park, Maryland.)
85. American Defense Society Executive Committee to Joseph Burnquist, September 30, 1917, File 103.8.4F, Papers of the Minnesota Commission on Public Safety, Minnesota Historical Society, St. Paul, Minnesota.
86. American Defense Society, Circular Letter, October 13, 1917, Box 9, Papers of the American Defense Society, New York Historical Society, New York, New York. The next two paragraphs are based on this source.
87. Public Statement, Minnesota Commission on Public Safety, September 25, 1917, File 103. L. 8. 4F, Papers of the Minnesota Commission on Public Safety, Minnesota Historical Society, St. Paul, Minnesota.
88. *New York Times*, November 3, 1917.
89. *New York Times*, November 3, 1917.
90. La Follette and La Follette, *La Follette,* 2:771; *Kansas City Star*, September 24, 1917.
91. Theodore Roosevelt to Theodore Roosevelt, Jr., November 29, 1917, Elting E. Morison, ed., *Letters of Theodore Roosevelt, The Days of Armageddon, 1914–1919* (Cambridge, MA: Harvard University Press, 1954), 8: 1257.
92. La Follette and La Follette, *La Follette* 1:299; Robert Miraldi, *The Pen Is Mightier: The Muckraking Life of Charles Edward Russell* (New York, NY: Palgrave Macmillan, 2003), 131, 232, 238–39.
93. *New York Times,* August 15, 1917; Robert Miraldi, *The Pen Is Mightier: The Muckraking Life of Charles Edward Russell* (New York, NY: Palgrave Macmillan, 2003), 253.
94. *New York Times*, August 15, 1917.
95. La Follette and La Follette, *La Follette,* 2:760, from the *Minneapolis Tribune*, September 7, 1917.
96. *New York Times,* October 9, 1917.
97. Samuel V. Kennedy, III, *Samuel Hopkins Adams and the Business of Writing* (Syracuse, NY: Syracuse University Press, 1999), 112–16.
98. *New York Tribune*, November 11, 1917; *New York Tribune,* November 25, 1917. The *Wisconsin State Journal* reprinted the second article, December 6, 1917.

99. La Follette and La Follette, *La Follette* 1: 196–97; 2:887–8.
100. La Follette and La Follette, *La Follette,* 2:887.
101. Norman E. Saul, *The Life and Times of Charles R. Crane, 1858–1939; American Businessman, Philanthropist and a Founder of Russian Studies in America* (Lanham, MD: Lexington Books, 2013), 98.
102. *New York Times*, October 10, 1917.
103. *New York Times*, October 10, 1917.
104. United States Senate, 65th Congress, 2nd Session, Senate Committee on Privileges and Elections, *Report Relative to the Resolution from the Minnesota Commission on Public Safety Petitioning for Proceedings Looking to the Expulsion of Senator Robert M. La Follette* (Washington, D.C.: GPO, 1918).
105. La Follette and La Follette, *La Follette* 2:805.
106. *New York Times*, October 17, 1917. This article carries the entire statement conveyed to the sub-committee by La Follette.
107. Atlee Pomerene to Robert La Follette, November 5, 1917, Box B81, La Follette Papers, Library of Congress.
108. Pomerene to La Follette, December 1, 1917, Box B81, La Follette Papers, Library of Congress.
109. La Follette and La Follette, *La Follette,* 2:802.
110. *New York Times*, December 5, 1917.
111. Report, Senate Committee on Privileges, 44 P93/6: L13, January 1, 1918.
112. Gilbert Roe, Brief, January 1, 1918, in Senate Committee on Privileges, Report, 44 P93/6: L13.
113. David V. Mollenhoff, *Madison: The Formative Years* (Dubuque: IA: Kendall/Hunt, 1982), 284; Saul, *The Life and Times of Charles R. Crane,* 98. Jones had been an editor at *Collier's*, a leading muckraking journal.
114. Mollenhoff, *Madison,* 284, 287.
115. Wisconsin State Journal, August 23, 1917.
116. Mollenhoff, *Madison,* 285.
117. Bruce Bielaski to George Mayo, November 2, 1917, File OG 85502, Records of the Bureau of Investigation, 1908–22, Record Group 65, National Archives, College Park, Maryland.
118. *Capital Times*, December 12, 1918.
119. Report, George Mayo, December 2, 1917, File OG 85502, Records of the Bureau of Investigation, 1908-22, Record Group 65, National Archives, College Park, Maryland; Memorandum, George Mayo, "Capital City Times," February 9, 1918, File OG 85502, Records of the Bureau of Investigation, Record Group 65, National Archives; W.N. Parker to Bruce Bielaski, December 2, 1918, File OG 85502, Records of the Bureau of Investigation, Record Group 65, National Archives.

Parker was the agent in charge of the Madison office of the Bureau of Investigation.

120. Parker to Bielaski, December 2, 1918, File OG 85502, Records of the Bureau of Investigation, Record Group 65, National Archives; Report, George Mayo, March 4, 1918, File OG 85502, Records of the Bureau of Investigation, Record Group 65, National Archives.
121. La Follette and La Follette, *La Follette* 2:824; *Capital Times*, February 7, 1925.
122. Report, George Mayo to Bruce Bielaski, March 4, 1918, File OG 85502, Records of the Bureau of Investigation, Record Group 65, National Archives.
123. Bruce Bielaski to William Lamar, March 3, 1918, Parker to Bruce Bielaski, December 2, 1918, File OG 85502, Records of the Bureau of Investigation, Record Group 65, National Archives.
124. La Follette and La Follette, *La Follette,* 2: 807; *New York Times,* November 26, 1917.
125. Emerson Ela to Thomas Gregory, March 4, 1918, File OG 24713, Records of the Bureau of Investigation, Record Group 65, National Archives.
126. Ela to Gregory, March 4, 1918, File OG 24713, Records of the Bureau of Investigation, National Archives.
127. Bruce Bielaski to Thomas Gregory, Memorandum, March 12, 1918, File OG 24713, Records of the Bureau of Investigation, Record Group 65, National Archives.
128. Memorandum, George Mayo, "Final Report," April 9, 1918, File OG 85502, Records of the Bureau of Investigation, Record Group 65, National Archives.
129. *New York Times*, October 22, 1917; Herbert F. Margulies, *Senator Lenroot of Wisconsin: A Political Biography, 1900–1929* (Columbia, MO: University of Missouri Press, 1977), 230.
130. La Follette and La Follette, *La Follette,* 2:858-9.
131. [Robert La Follette], Editorial, *La Follette's Magazine,* December 1917.
132. Gilbert Roe to Charles Crowhart, December 29, 1917, Section I, B 82, Gilbert Roe Papers, in La Follette Papers, Library of Congress.
133. Margulies, *Senator Lenroot,* 237, 241.
134. Margulies, *Senator Lenroot,*19, 39, 77; Unger, *Fighting Bob La Follette,* 134.
135. *Milwaukee Journal,* March 9, 1918; *Milwaukee Journal,* March 15, 1918; "Loyalty," Speech, March 8, 1918, Box 5, Irvine Lenroot Papers, Manuscripts, Library of Congress, Washington, D.C. Davies, a Democratic Party stalwart, had served as the first chair of the Federal Trade Commission.

136. *Milwaukee Journal,* March 13, 1918; La Follette and La Follette, *La Follette,* 2:868.
137. Woodrow Wilson to Thomas Marshall, March 15, 1918, in Arthur Link, ed., *The Papers of Woodrow Wilson* (Princeton, NJ: Princeton University Press, 1984), 47:40.
138. Wilson to Marshall, March 15, 1918, in Link, ed., *The Papers of Woodrow Wilson,* 47:40–1.
139. La Follette and La Follette, *La Follette,* 2:871; *New York Times,* March 27, 1918.
140. *Milwaukee Journal,* March 30, 1918.
141. *Milwaukee Journal,* March 16, 1918; *Milwaukee Journal,* March 16, 1918.
142. *Milwaukee Journal,* March 29, 1918.
143. [Robert La Follette], Editorial, *La Follette's Magazine,* March 1918. The next paragraph is drawn from the same editorial.
144. Woodrow Wilson to Thomas Marshall, April 12, 1918, Arthur Link, ed., *The Papers of Woodrow Wilson* (Princeton, NJ: Princeton University Press, 1984), 47:326.
145. La Follette and La Follette, *La Follette,* 2: 873; Sally M. Miller, *Victor Berger and the Promise of Constructive Socialism, 1910–1920* (Westport, CT: Greenwood Press, [1973]), 189.
146. La Follette and La Follette, *Robert M. La Follette, 2*: 897.
147. [Robert La Follette], Editorial, *La Follette's Magazine,* January 1918. The next paragraphs are drawn from the same editorial.
148. [Robert La Follette], "The War," *La Follette's Magazine,* June 1918.
149. *La Follette's Magazine,* September 1918.

Chapter 4: The Nonpartisan League: Cooptation and Repression

1. Charles Edward Russell, *Bare Hands and Stone Walls: Some Recollections of a Side-Line Reformer* (New York: Charles Scribner's Sons, 1933), 344.
2. Robert Morlan, *Political Prairie Fire: The Nonpartisan League, 1915–1922* (Minneapolis: University of Minnesota Press, 1955), 23.
3. Michael J. Lansing, *Insurgent Democracy: The Nonpartisan League in North American Politics* (Chicago, IL: University of Chicago Press, 2015),15.
4. Lansing, *Insurgent Democracy,* 15; Morlan, *Political Prairie Fire,* 25–26; Russell, *Bare Hands,* 338.
5. Lansing, *Insurgent Democracy,* 12–13.
6. Morlan, *Political Prairie Fire,* 24.
7. Lansing, *Insurgent Democracy,* 15; Morlan, *Political Prairie Fire,* 25–26; Russell, *Bare Hands,* 330.
8. Morlan, *Political Prairie Fire,* 50.
9. Morlan, *Political Prairie Fire,* 47–50.

10. Morlan, *Political Prairie Fire*, 89.
11. Morlan, *Political Prairie Fire*, 89.
12. Lansing, *Insurgent Democracy*, 29.
13. Eric Chester, *True Mission: The Labor Party Question in the U.S.* (Sterling, VA: Pluto, 2004), 52–68.
14. Millard L. Gieske, *Minnesota Farmer Laborism: The Third Party Alternative* (Minneapolis, MN: University of Minnesota Press, 1979), 11.
15. *New York Times*, March 18, 1917.
16. Antoinette Funk to Woodrow Wilson, June 17, 1918, in Arthur Link, ed., *Papers of Woodrow Wilson* (Princeton, NJ: Princeton University Press, 1985), 48:345. The quote in the next paragraph is from the same source.
17. Eric Thomas Chester, *The Wobblies in Their Heyday: The Rise and Destruction of the Industrial Workers of the World during the World War I Era* (Santa Barbara, CA: Praeger, 2014), 118–19.
18. Lansing, *Insurgent Democracy*,13.
19. Extract from the Minutes of the 5th Conference of the Agricultural Workers' Industrial Union, Kansas City, Missouri, June 3, 1917, File 9140–4541, Box 2105, Record Group 165, Correspondence of the Military Intelligence Division, National Archives, College Park, MD.
20. *Nonpartisan Leader*, June 7, 1917.
21. Eric Thomas Chester, *Yours for Industrial Freedom: The Industrial Workers of the World from the Inside* (Amherst, MA: Levellers Press, 2017), 14–15.
22. Morlan, *Political Prairie Fire*, 110.
23. *Nonpartisan Leader*, April 26, 1917.
24. Lansing, *Insurgent Democracy*, 249; Henry Teigan to Carl Thompson, June 8, 1917, Microfilm, Roll 2, *Nonpartisan League Papers*, Minnesota Historical Society, St. Paul, Minnesota.
25. Davis Douthit, *Nobody Owns Us: The Story of Joe Gilbert, Midwestern Rebel* (Chicago, IL: Cooperative League of the USA, [1948]), 48, 61–67, 101–2.
26. Resolution of the North Dakota Nonpartisan League, June 7, 1917, *Nonpartisan League Papers*, Microfilm, Roll 4. The quote in the next paragraph is from the same source.
27. *Nonpartisan Leader*, June 7, 1917.
28. *Nonpartisan Leader*, August 14, 1917.
29. Robert Lansing to Elihu Root, June 27, 1917, in Link, ed., *Papers of Woodrow Wilson*, 43:15.
30. *Nonpartisan Leader*, August 30, 1917.
31. Robert Lansing to Elihu Root, June 27, 1917, in Link, ed., *Papers of Woodrow Wilson*, 43:15.

32. *Nonpartisan Leader,* September 6, 1917.
33. Henry Teigan to Daniel O'Connell, August 9, 1917, *Nonpartisan League Papers,* Microfilm, Reel 3. O'Connell had proposed that the NPL enter into an electoral alliance that would include the People's Council of America. Teigan agreed with the idea in principle, but he ruled out an explicit alliance.
34. George Creel, Note, [n.d.], Papers of George Creel, Box 2, Manuscript Division, Library of Congress., Washington, D.C.
35. *New York Times,* March 19, 1922.
36. George Creel to John A. Simpson, May 13, 1918, Correspondence of George Creel, Box 3, Records of the Committee on Public Information, Record Group 63, National Archives.
37. Lansing, *Insurgent Democracy*, 103.
38. Arthur Townley to Woodrow Wilson, September 10, 1917, in Link ed., *Papers of Woodrow Wilson*, 44:183; Woodrow Wilson to Joseph Tumulty, September 17, 1917, Link, ed., *Papers of Woodrow Wilson*, 44:206.
39. *Nonpartisan Leader*, September 7, 1917; Charles Edward Russell, *The Story of the Nonpartisan League* (New York: Harper and Brothers, 1920), 24.
40. Morlan, *Political Prairie Fire*, 143.
41. Robert La Follette, Speech, September 20, 1917, Nonpartisan League Papers, Microfilm, Reel 14, Minnesota Historical Society, St. Paul.
42. *Nonpartisan Leader,* October 4, 1917.
43. John Thompson to George Creel, October 29, 1917, Correspondence of George Creel, Box 23, Records of the Committee on Public Information, Record Group 63, National Archives.
44. Woodrow Wilson, "An Address to the American Federation of Labor," November 12, 1917, in Link, ed., *Papers of Woodrow Wilson*, 45:13.
45. George Creel to Samuel Gompers, November 9, 1917, Correspondence of George Creel, Box 10, Records of the Committee on Public Information, Record Group 63, National Archives.
46. *Nonpartisan Leader,* December 10, 1917.
47. George Creel to John Thompson, July 12, 1917, Correspondence of George Creel, Box 24, Records of the Committee on Public Information, Record Group 63, National Archives.
48. Russell, *The Nonpartisan League,* 245; George Creel to John Thompson, May 26, 1917, Correspondence of George Creel, Box 23, Records of the Committee on Public Information, Record Group 63, National Archives.
49. Russell, *The Story of the Nonpartisan League,* 245.
50. Morlan, *Political Prairie Fire*, 44.

51. Lansing, *Insurgent Democracy*, 84–87.
52. Carol E. Jenson, "Loyalty as a Political Weapon," *Minnesota History* 43 (Summer 1972): 44.
53. William Millikan, *A Union Against Unions: The Minneapolis Citizens Alliance Fight Against Organized Labor, 1903–1947* (St. Paul: Minnesota Historical Society Press, 2001), 104; *Biographical Dictionary of the Federal Judiciary* (Lanham, MD: Bernan, 2001).
54. *New York Times*, July 10, 1917; Jenson, "Loyalty," *Minnesota History* 43:46.
55. Bruce Larson, "Lind, John," *American National Biography*, 13:683–84.
56. Chester, *The Wobblies in Their Heyday*, 118–32.
57. John Lind to William B. Wilson, July 31, 1917, Lind Papers, File 143.5.12.5B, Minnesota Historical Society, St. Paul; John Lind to Thomas Gregory, July 26, 1917, Lind Papers, File 143.5.12.5B, Minnesota Historical Society, St. Paul. Gregory was the U.S. Attorney General.
58. Millikan, *A Union Against Unions*, 103, 105–6.
59. Most IWW activists considered themselves to be industrial union socialists. They believed that electoral politics was secondary to organizing at the workplace, but they were willing to support socialist candidates such as Eugene Debs. William D. Haywood and Frank Bohn, *Industrial Socialism* (Chicago, IL: Charles Kerr, 1911).

    The French syndicalists were anarchists and therefore opposed in principle to engaging in the electoral arena. Nevertheless, the IWW and the French syndicalists shared a commitment to building militant, grassroots industrial unions. Melvyn Dubofsky, *We Shall Be All* (Champaign, IL: University of Illinois Press, 1969), 167–69.
60. Millikan, *A Union Against Unions*, 106.
61. On Woodrow Wilson's decision to make the IWW a priority target for repression at the federal level, see Chester, *The Wobblies in Their Heyday*, 154–56.
62. Morlan, *Political Prairie*, 221.
63. Jenson, "Loyalty," *Minnesota History* 43 (Summer 1972):49; Henry Libby to Gustav Lindquist, February 14, 1918, File 103.L.8.4F, Main Files, Minnesota Commission of Public Safety, Minnesota Historical Society, St. Paul. Lindquist served as Burnquist's private secretary; National Nonpartisan League, *Memorial to the Congress of the United States Concerning Conditions in Minnesota, 1918* (St. Paul, MN: NPL, 1918), 28–29.
64. Jenson, "Loyalty," 50.
65. Jenson, "Loyalty," 50.
66. *Nonpartisan Leader*, March 4, 1918.

67. National Nonpartisan League, *Memorial*, 40–44.
68. National Nonpartisan League, *Memorial*, 45–48.
69. National Nonpartisan League, *Memorial*, 20–28. The following paragraphs are drawn from the same source.
70. Arthur Sweeney, "Charles Wilberforce Ames," *Minnesota Historical Bulletin* 4 (August 1921): 124–29.
71. Jenson, "Loyalty," 47; John Lind to Thomas Gregory, April 25, 1918, File 190470, Entry A1-112B, Straight Numerical Series, Records of the Department of Justice, Record Group 60, National Archives.
72. Memorandum, "Chronology," [October 1918], Charles Ames Papers, File 143.C.1.5B, Minnesota Historical Society, St. Paul.
73. The director of the War Emergency Division, John Lord O'Brian, delegated the decision as to who would be prosecuted under the Espionage Act to his deputy, Alfred Bettman. Bruce Bielaski as chief of the Bureau of Investigation sent frequent reports to Bettman, who reviewed them to determine whether there was sufficient evidence to warrant the Justice Department going to a grand jury to request an indictment. John Lord O'Brian, "Reminiscences of John Lord O'Brian," Columbia University Oral History Project, 1952, 241, 248, 252.
74. Memorandum, "Chronology," [October 1918], Charles Ames Papers, File 143.C.1.5B.
75. Millikan, *A Union Against Unions*, 125–26.
76. Millikan, *A Union Against Unions.*, 128.
77. Millikan, *A Union Against Unions*, 129–31.
78. Mary Lethert Wingerd, *Claiming the City: Politics, Faith, and the Power of Place in St. Paul* (Ithaca, NY: Cornell University Press, 2001), 201; Millikan, *A Union Against Unions*, 133.
79. Wingerd, *Claiming the City*, 201.
80. George M. Stephenson, *John Lind of Minnesota* (Minneapolis, MN: University of Minnesota Press, 1935), 335; Wingerd, *Claiming the City*, 201.
81. Millikan, *A Union Against Unions*, 132–33.
82. Ames, "Chronology," [October 1918], Charles Ames Papers, File 143.C.1.5B., Minnesota Historical Society, St. Paul, Minnesota.
83. Gieske, *Minnesota Farmer Laborism*, 11.
84. Memorandum, "Chronology," [October 1918], Charles Ames Papers, File 143.C.1.5B.
85. Charles Ames to Marlborough Churchill, June 24, 1918, Charles Ames Papers, File 143.C.1.5B; Bidwell, *History of the Military Intelligence Division*, 191; *New York Times, November 8,* 1911; *New York Times,* November 5, 1913.
86. Memorandum, "Chronology," [October 1918], Charles Ames Papers,

File 143.C.1.5B; Charles Ames to A. R. Allen, March 29, 1918, Charles Ames Papers.

87. Charles Ames to Joseph Burnquist, February 19, 1918, Papers of the Minnesota Commission of Public Safety, File F135, 130.L. 84F, Minnesota Historical Society, St. Paul. The next paragraph is drawn from the same source.
88. Charles Ames to Charles Coffin, July 1, 1920, Charles Ames Papers, File 143.C1.4F, Box 4. Coffin was the president of General Electric. Ames sent him a copy of the *Protocols* with his favorable comments.
89. *Nonpartisan Leader*, December 27, 1920.
90. Ames, "Chronology," [October 1918], Charles Ames Papers, File 143.C.1.5B; Charles Ames to Joseph Burnquist, February 19, 1918, Papers of the Minnesota Public Safety Commission, F135, 130.L.84F, Minnesota Historical Society, St. Paul.
91. Alfred Bettman to A. Bruce Bielaski, January 30, 1918, File OG 46899, Records of the Bureau of Investigation, 1908–22, Record Group 65, National Archives, College Park, MD.
92. Alfred Bettman to A. Bruce Bielaski, February 18, 1918, File OG 46899, Records of the Bureau of Investigation, 1908–22, National Archives.
93. Bruce Bielaski to Hinton Clabaugh, February 18, 1918, File OG 46899, Records of the Bureau of Investigation, 1908–22, National Archives.
94. Report, Julius Rosin, March 18, 1918, File OG 46899, Records of the Bureau of Investigation, 1908–22, Record Group 65, National Archives.
95. *Nonpartisan Leader*, June 9, 1918.
96. *Spokane Daily Chronicle*, February 14, 1951; Millikan, *A Union Against Unions*, 119, 388.
97. Michael P. Malone, *James J. Hill: Empire Builder of the Northwest* (Norman, OK: University of Oklahoma Press, 1996), 177, 265.
98. Report, Julius Rosin, March 18, 1918, File OG 46899, Records of the Bureau of Investigation, 1908–22, Record Group 65, National Archives. The next paragraph is drawn from the same source.
99. Report, Thomas Campbell, [June 1918], File OG 196837, Records of the Bureau of Investigation, 1908–22, Record Group 65, National Archives.
100. Report, March 18, 1918, File OG 46899, Records of the Bureau of Investigation, 1908–22, Record Group 65, National Archives. The next paragraph is drawn from the same source.
101. Bruce Bielaski to Alfred Bettman, May 1, 1918, File OG 46899, Records of the Bureau of Investigation, 1908–22, Record Group 65, National Archives.
102. Report, Julius Rosin, March 18, 1918, File OG 46899, Records of the Bureau of Investigation, National Archives.

103. George Creel to Woodrow Wilson, January 28, 1918, in Link, ed., *Papers of Woodrow Wilson,* 46:160.
104. Louis Seibold to Joseph Tumulty, February 14, 1918, in Link, ed., *Papers of Woodrow Wilson,* 46:248.
105. Woodrow Wilson to George Creel, February 18, 1918, in Link; ed., *Papers of Woodrow Wilson,* 46:369.
106. Bruce Llewelyn Larson, *Lindbergh of Minnesota: A Political Biography* (New York, NY: Harcourt, Brace, Jovanovich, 1973), 54–56, 176–78, 191–96.
107. Charles August Lindbergh, Sr., *Your Country at War and What Happens to You After a War* (Washington, D.C.: National Capital Press, 1917), 210–13.
108. Lindbergh, *Your Country at War,* 209–10.
109. Robert L. Morlan, "The Nonpartisan League and the Minnesota Campaign of 1918," *Minnesota History* 34 (Summer 1955): 224; National Nonpartisan League, *Origins, Purposes and Methods of Operation, War Program and Statement of Principles* ([St. Paul, MN]: NPL, 1917).
110. National Nonpartisan League, *War Program.*
111. Morlan, "The Nonpartisan League," *Minnesota History* 34:230.
112. Morlan, "The Nonpartisan League," *Minnesota History*, 34:228–29.
113. Morlan, "The Nonpartisan League," *Minnesota History*, 34:229.
114. Richard Hudelson and Carl Ross, *By the Ore Docks (*Minneapolis, MN: University of Minnesota Press, 2006), 85.
115. Larson, *Lindbergh of Minnesota*, 235; Carol E. Jenson, "Loyalty," 55; Lynn Haines and Dora Haines, *The Lindberghs* (New York: Vanguard, 1931), 219. Lynn Haines was a journalist and a friend of Lindbergh's. Haines does not provide a location or a date for the rally that ended with shots being fired at Lindbergh's car.
116. National Nonpartisan League, *Memorial to the Congress of the United States Concerning Conditions in Minnesota, 1918* (St. Paul, MN: NPL, 1918), 56.
117. Lansing, *Insurgent Democracy,* 121.
118. Jenson, "Loyalty," 55.
119. Alfred Bettman to Bruce Bielaski, May 11, 1918, File OG 196937, Files of the Bureau of Investigation, Record Group 65, National Archives; Bruce Bielaski to Alfred Bettman, May 16, 1918, File OG 196937, Files of the Bureau of Investigation, Record Group 65, National Archives.
120. Bettman to Bielaski, May 11, 1918; Bruce Bielaski to Alfred Bettman, May 16, 1918, File OG 196937, Files of the Bureau of Investigation, Record Group 65, National Archives.
121. Alfred Bettman to Bruce Bielaski, May 29, 1918, File OG 196937, Files of the Bureau of Investigation, National Archives.

122. Alfred Bettman to Bruce Bielaski, June 3, 1918, File OG 196937, Files of the Bureau of Investigation, National Archives.
123. Bruce Bielaski to Thomas Campbell, June 5, 1918, File OG 196937, Files of the Bureau of Investigation, National Archives.
124. Report, Thomas Campbell, [June 17, 1918], File OG 196937, Files of the Bureau of Investigation, Record Group 65, National Archives, College Park, Maryland. The information on Lindbergh's book had been provided by an unnamed NPL official, probably Le Sueur, to Alfred Jaques, the U.S. attorney for Minnesota. The date on the report has faded and has become unreadable. The report was received at the headquarters of the Bureau of Investigation on June 17, 1918.
125. Report, M. J. Murray, June 12, 1918, File OG 196937, Files of the Bureau of Investigation, Record Group 65, National Archives, College Park, Maryland. The next paragraph is from the same source.
126. Alfred Bettman to Bruce Bielaski, August 21, 1918, File OG 196937, Files of the Bureau of Investigation, National Archives.
127. Report, Thomas Campbell, October 5, 1918, File OG 196937, Files of the Bureau of Investigation, National Archives.
128. Alfred Bettman to Bruce Bielaski, October 27, 1918, File OG 196937, Files of the Bureau of Investigation, National Archives.
129. The official result gave Burnquist nearly 200,000 votes to 150,000 for Lindbergh in the 1918 Republican primary. All of the election statistics in the next paragraphs come from the state's official handbook. Those for 1916 are derived from the *Minnesota Legislative Manual* (St. Paul, MN: 1919). Those for the 1916 election come from *Minnesota Legislative Manual* (St. Paul, MN: 1917).
130. The 1916 vote total for the Republican primary was 213,000. The total vote in the 1918 Republican primary came to 350,000.
131. In Hennepin County, Minneapolis, and environs, more than 74,000 votes were cast in the 1918 primary. The total number of votes coming from soldiers normally residing in Hennepin for the 1918 primary was 231.
132. In 1916, 390,000 votes were cast in the general election, while the vote total only reached 369,000 in the 1918 general election.
133. *Minneapolis Morning Tribune*, June 19, 1918; Larson, *Lindbergh of Minnesota*, 244.
134. The total vote in the Republican primary in Pipestone County rose from 525 in the 1916 election to 1,977 in 1918.
135. In 1916, Burnquist received 71 percent of the total vote in the Republican primary. In defeating Lindbergh in the 1918 primary, Burnquist won 54 percent of the total vote. Burnquist gained 63 percent of the total vote for governor in the 1916 general election. In the 1918 general

election, Burnquist received only 45 percent of the total vote. The two candidates opposing him, Fred Wheaton, the Democratic Party candidate, and David Evans, the Farmer-Labor Party candidate, split the opposition vote, enabling Burnquist to be reelected.

136. National Nonpartisan League, *Origins, Purposes and Methods of Operation, War Program and Statement of Principles*, St. Paul, MN, 1917.
137. Bruce Bielaski to Thomas Campbell, April 19, 1918, File OG 46889, Records of the Bureau of Investigation, Record Group 65, National Archives.
138. Arthur Le Sueur to Thomas Campbell, April 26, 1918, File OG 46889, Records of the Bureau of Investigation, National Archives.
139. Alfred Bettman to Bruce Bielaski, May 16, 1918, File OG 46889, Records of the Bureau of Investigation, National Archives. The next paragraph relies on the same source.
140. Bruce Bielaski to Thomas Campbell, May 28, 1918, File OG 46889, Records of the Bureau of Investigation, National Archives.
141. Melvin Hildreth to John Lord O'Brian, May 9, 1918, File 9–5–409, Classified Case Files, Records of the Department of Justice, Record Group 60, National Archives, College Park, MD.
142. Memorandum to Melvin Hildreth, [May 1918], File 9–5–409, Classified Case Files, Records of the Department of Justice, National Archives.
143. Hildreth to O'Brian, May 9, 1918, File 9–5–409, Classified Case Files, Record Group 60, National Archives; John Lord O'Brian to Melvin Hildreth, May 21, 1918, File 9–5–409, Classified Case Files, Records of the Department of Justice, Record Group 60, National Archives, College Park, Maryland.
144. Hildreth to O'Brian, [May 1918}, File 9–5–409, Classified Case Files, Records of the Department of Justice, National Archives.
145. John Lord O'Brian to Melvin Hildreth, June 1, 1918, File 9–5–409, Classified Case Files, Records of the Department of Justice, National Archives; John Lord O'Brian to Melvin Hildreth, June 24, 1918, File 9–5–409, Classified Case Files, Records of the Department of Justice, National Archives.
146. Melvin Hildreth to John Lord O'Brian, June 13, 1918, File 9–5–409, Classified Case Files, Records of the Department of Justice, National Archives.
147. John Lord O'Brian to Joseph Burnquist, July 10, 1918, File 9–5–409, Classified Case Files, Records of the Department of Justice, National Archives.
148. Thomas Gregory to C. E. Brenchain, April 20, 1918, File 9–5–409, Classified Case Files, Records of the Department of Justice, National Archives.

149. Eric Foner, *A Short History of Reconstruction, 1863–1877* (New York, NY: Harper and Row, 1990), 196–97. The U. S. Supreme Court consolidated several cases in deciding the Civil Rights Cases. Opinions in the case can be found at 109 U.S. 3 (1883). Only Justice John Marshall Harlan dissented from the majority ruling that greatly limited the scope of the Fourteenth Amendment.
150. *United States vs. Harris,* 106 US 629 (1883).
151. John Lord O'Brian, *Civil Liberty in War Time* (Washington, D.C.: GPO, 1919), 14. The quote in the next paragraph is from the same source.
152. *Nonpartisan Leader*, December 27, 1920.
153. The constitution adopted by Minnesota in 1859 shortly after it became a state did not provide for an appellate court of appeals between the district court and the state's Supreme Court. Furthermore, the 1859 constitution set the number of Supreme Court justices at three. As a result, the Minnesota Supreme Court was overwhelmed by the number of appeals. In 1913, the state legislature enacted an interim solution. It authorized the members of the state's Supreme Court to appoint two commissioners who would have all of the powers of those elected as justices. Commissioners served a six-year term but could be reappointed. Even after the bill was enacted, the Minnesota Supreme Court still found its docket to be overloaded and could only choose a few cases for review. Russel O. Gunderson, *A History of the Minnesota Supreme Court* ([St. Paul, MN]: 1937), 143.
154. Report, Julius Rosin, March 18, 1918, File OG 46899, Records of the Bureau of Investigation, National Archives, College Park, MD.
155. Douthit, *Nobody Owns Us*, 138, 141.
156. Douthit, *Nobody Owns Us*, 143.
157. *State v. Gilbert*, December 20, 1918, *Northwestern Reporter* 169 (1919); 791. No dissent was noted to Taylor's ruling. Taylor was one of the two commissioners appointed to the Minnesota Supreme Court in 1913. He served in this position until he retired in 1930, having been reappointed twice. Gunderson, *Minnesota Supreme Court*, 144.
158. *State v. Gilbert,* December 20, 1918, *Northwestern Reporter* 169 (1919): 791.
159. Joseph McKenna, *Gilbert v. Minnesota* (1920), 254 U.S. 328.
160. Louis Brandeis, *Gilbert v. Minnesota* (1920), 254 U.S. 335. In fact, the Minnesota Sedition Act was not enforced after the First World War had come to an end.
161. John Marshall, *Barron v. Mayor and City Council of Baltimore*, 32 U.S. 243 (1833).
162. Rufus Peckham, *Lochner v. New York*, 198 U.S. 45 (1905).
163. Louis Brandeis, *Gilbert v. Minnesota,* 254 U.S. 343.

164. Edward Sanford, *Gitlow v. New York*, 268 U.S. 666; Oliver Wendell Holmes, Jr., *Gitlow v. New York*, 268 U.S. 672.
165. *State v. Townley* et al., April 21, 1921, *Northwestern Reporter* 182 (1921): 775–77.
166. *Northwestern Reporter* 182 (1921): 778.
167. *New York Times*, July 13, 1919; *New York Times*, April 30, 1921; *Northwestern Reporter* 182 (1921) 773; Morlan, *Political Prairie Fire*, 336.
168. *Biographical Directory of the United States Congress, 1774–1789* (Washington, D.C.: GPO, 1989). Wade was nominated for a post as federal judge by Woodrow Wilson and approved by Congress in March 1915. A Democrat, he had previously served a term in the U. S. House of Representatives. In 1918, Wade sentenced Daniel Wallace to the maximum term of twenty years for giving a speech in Davenport, Iowa, that criticized the war.
169. Charles Ames to Martin Wade, October 3, 1918, File 9–5–409, Classified Case Files, Records of the Department of Justice, Record Group 60, National Archives, College Park, MD.
170. *New York Times*, August 18, 1946.
171. Claude Porter to R. T. Scott, June 27, 1919, File 9–5–409, Classified Case Files, Records of the Department of Justice, Record Group 60, National Archives. Scott was acting as the private secretary of Palmer. Having recently been named attorney general, Palmer wanted a report on the NPL.
172. S. M. Canby to Ralph Van Deman, December 31, 1917, File 9140–4541, Record Group 165, Correspondence of the Military Intelligence Division, National Archives. This was an interchange at the highest levels of the intelligence community. Canby enclosed a memorandum on the Nonpartisan League drawn up by the staff of the ONI.
173. Marlborough Churchill to Intelligence Officers, July 1, 1918, File 9140–4541, Correspondence of the Military Intelligence Division, National Archives; Marlborough Churchill to George Creel, June 8, 1918, File 9140–4541, Correspondence of the Military Intelligence Division, National Archives.

    Churchill wrote to Ames asking him to provide the Military Intelligence Division with information he collected on the League and Ames agreed to do this. Marlborough Churchill to Charles Ames, June 7, 1918, File 9140–4541, Correspondence of the Military Intelligence Division, National Archives; Charles Ames to Marlborough Churchill, June 24, 1918, File 9140–454, Correspondence of the Military Intelligence Division, National Archives.
174. Frederick G. Knabenshue to Marlborough Churchill, August 15, 1918,

File 9140–4541, Record Group 165, Correspondence of the Military Intelligence Division, National Archives.

175. Marlborough Churchill to Robert Maddox, July 29, 1918, File 9140–4541, Record Group 165, Correspondence of the Military Intelligence Division, National Archives; E. R. White to Marlborough Churchill, August 1, 1918, File 9140–7116, Record Group 165, Correspondence of the Military Intelligence Division, National Archives.
176. George Creel to Woodrow Wilson, February 19, 1918, in Link, ed., *Papers of Woodrow Wilson,* 46: 386–87.
177. Arthur Bestor to John Thompson, February 8, 1918, Correspondence of George Creel, Box 2, Records of the Committee on Public Information, Record Group 63, National Archives.
178. Arthur Townley to Woodrow Wilson, March 20, 1918, in Link, ed., *Papers of Woodrow Wilson,* 47:87; Woodrow Wilson to Joseph Tumulty, March 20, 1918, Link, ed., *Papers of Woodrow Wilson* 47: 88; David Houston to Woodrow Wilson, March 28, 1918, in Link, ed., *Papers of Woodrow Wilson*, 47:178.
179. James Caldwell and Christian Wendt, March 31, 1918, Link, ed., *Papers of Woodrow Wilson,* 47:216–17.
180. Woodrow Wilson to George Creel, April 1, 1918, Link, ed., *Papers of Woodrow Wilson*, 47:218.
181. Josiah Seymour Currey, *Chicago: Its History and Builders* (Chicago, IL: S. J. Clarke, 1912), 279.
182. Dixon Williams to Woodrow Wilson, April 3, 1918, Link, ed., *Papers of Woodrow Wilson*, 47: 235.
183. Williams to Wilson, April 3, 1918, Link, ed., *Papers of Woodrow Wilson*, 47: 236–37. The following paragraphs are from the same source. Mills became president of the Midland Bank in 1919. *Commercial West,* August 16, 1919, 36:32. Libby, a machinist, had previously been vice president of the Minnesota Federation of Labor. He also served a term in the state legislature as a Republican.
184. William Colver to Joseph Tumulty, March 18, 1917, Link, ed., *Papers of Woodrow Wilson*, 47:54. The next two paragraphs are from the same source.
185. Woodrow Wilson to Vance McCormick, March 18, 1918, Link, ed., *Papers of Woodrow Wilson*, 47:53–54; Stephenson, *Lind*, 339.
186. Stephenson, *Lind*, 339; Millard L. Gieske, *Minnesota Farmer Laborism: The Third Party Alternative* (Minneapolis, MN: University of Minnesota Press, 1979), 39, 47. The National Party was initiated in 1917 by pro-war socialists and attracted supporters of Prohibition and progressives. It dissolved in 1919. Kenneth E. Hendrickson, Jr., "The Pro-War Socialists, the Social Democratic League and the Ill-Fated Drive for

Industrial Democracy in America," *Labor History* 11 (Summer 1970): 304–22.

187. George Creel to Woodrow Wilson, April 2, 1918, Link, ed., *Papers of Woodrow Wilson*, 47:226.
188. *New York Times,* May 14, 1918.
189. Edward House, Diary, May 7, 1918, in Link, ed., *Papers of Woodrow Wilson,* 48:51.
190. Josephus Daniels, Diary, May 16, 1918, in Link ed., *Papers of Woodrow Wilson*, 48:45.
191. *New York Times*, May 18, 1918.
192. George Creel to John A. Simpson, May 13, 1918, Correspondence of George Creel, Box 3, Records of the Committee on Public Information, Record Group 63, National Archives; *New York Times*, June 26, 1918. The article is dated June 25, 1918, and the election took place the next day.
193. George Creel to Joseph Tumulty, July 12, 1918, Woodrow Wilson Papers, Series 4, Case 4556, Library of Congress, Washington, in Microfilm, Reel 369, *Woodrow Wilson Papers* (Washington D.C.: Library of Congress, 1973).
194. Woodrow Wilson to Joseph Tumulty, August 3, 1918, in Link, ed., *Papers of Woodrow Wilson*, 49:172.
195. George Creel, *Rebel at Large: Recollections of Fifty Crowded Years* (New York: G. P. Putnam's, 1977), 154.
196. George Creel to Woodrow Wilson, September 12, 1918, in Link, ed., *Papers of Woodrow Wilson,* 49: 536; Larson, *Lindbergh of Minnesota,* 251.
197. George Creel to Woodrow Wilson, September 18, 1918, in Link, ed., *Papers of Woodrow Wilson,* 50:64–65.
198. George Creel to John Thompson, October 17, 1918, Correspondence of George Creel, Box 23, Records of the Committee on Public Information, Record Group 63, National Archives.
199. Douthit, *Nobody Owns Us,* 161, 167.
200. Lansing, *Insurgent Democracy,* 197; Morlan, *Political Prairie Fire*, 304.
201. Morlan, *Political Prairie Fire*, 346.
202. Douthit, *Nobody Owns Us,* 178, 188–89.
203. Morlan, *Political Prairie Fire*, 337–38, 341, 346.
204. Elwyn B. Robinson, *History of North Dakota* (Lincoln, NE: University of Nebraska Press, 1966), 389–93.
205. Robinson, *History of North Dakota*, 431.
206. Gieske, *Minnesota Farmer Laborism*, 11.
207. John Earl Haynes, *Dubious Alliance: The Making of Minnesota's DFL Party* (Minneapolis, MN: University of Minnesota Press, 1984), 14, 18, 23.

Conclusion

1. By the end of the war in November 1918, the United States had sent two million soldiers overseas. At that time, there were more than 1,300,000 U.S. soldiers holding the trenches of the Western Front. Fifty thousand U. S. soldiers died in combat, another 25,000 died from the flu and nearly 200,000 had been seriously wounded. Philip J. Haythornwaite, *The World War One Source Book* (London, England: Arms and Armour, 1992), 309.
2. Woodrow Wilson, Speech, June 14, 1917, in Arthur Link ed., *Papers of Woodrow Wilson* (Princeton, NJ: Princeton University Press, 1983), 42:504.
3. Stephen Gwynn, ed., *The Letters and Friendships of Sir Cecil Spring Rice* (New York, NY: Houghton Mifflin, 1929), 2: 372.

Index

www.ingramcontent.com/pod-product-compliance
Lightning Source LLC
Jackson TN
JSHW070052121225
94826JS00001B/1
* 9 7 8 1 6 8 5 9 0 1 2 6 4 *